A Woman's Guide to Sleep Disorders

Meir H. Kryger, M.D.

Past President, American Academy of Sleep Medicine

Foreword by Barbara Phillips, M.D., M.S.P.H.

Introduction by Richard Gelula, M.S.W.,
CEO, National Sleep Foundation

McGraw·Hill

New York   Chicago   San Francisco   Lisbon   London   Madrid   Mexico City
Milan   New Delhi   San Juan   Seoul   Singapore   Sydney   Toronto

Library of Congress Cataloging-in-Publication Data

Kryger, Meir H.
    A woman's guide to sleep disorders / Meir Kryger ; foreword by Barbara
Phillips.
        p.   cm.
    ISBN 0-07-142527-6 (alk. paper)
    1. Sleep disorders—Treatment.   2. Women—Health and hygiene.
3. Insomnia.   I. Title.

    RC548.K79   2004
    616.8'498'0082—dc22   2003022474

2 3 4 5 6 7 8 9 0   FGR/FGR   0 9 8 7 6 5

ISBN 0-07-142527-6

Photos in Chapter 18 are courtesy of Bill Peters, Winnipeg, Manitoba.

McGraw-Hill books are available at special quantity discounts to use as premiums and
sales promotions, or for use in corporate training programs. For more information, please
write to the Director of Special Sales, Professional Publishing, McGraw-Hill, Two Penn
Plaza, New York, NY 10121-2298. Or contact your local bookstore.

DISCLAIMER
The book describes diagnoses, tests, and treatments for many sleep disorders. If you have
a sleep problem, I strongly recommend that you not attempt to diagnose or treat yourself,
and that you always deal with your family doctor. Self-diagnosis and treatment can be
dangerous. Some of the medications mentioned in this book used to treat sleep disorders
were originally released to treat other conditions. Thus, some of the treatments are "off-
label." Speak to your doctor about any medications you may be prescribed. Brand names
of drugs are capitalized in this text and are the property of the manufacturer. Chemical
names of these drugs will be lowercased. Under no circumstances use prescription drugs
that were prescribed to someone else.

This book is printed on acid-free paper.

*This book is dedicated to my wife, Barbara,
and my children, Shelley, Michael, and Steven.*

Contents

Foreword

by Barbara Phillips

Meir Kryger literally wrote the book about sleep medicine. He is the first editor and driving force behind the standard medical textbook, *Principles and Practice of Sleep Medicine. Principles and Practice* was a long overdue accomplishment; it pulled together the available knowledge about sleep and its disorders into one source, and is now widely acknowledged as the text of sleep medicine. Every sleep medicine clinician has a copy of that book readily available.

A Woman's Guide to Sleep Disorders is the same sort of accomplishment. Dr. Kryger has crafted this book in response to women's largely unaddressed needs regarding sleep. In addition to chapters about medically recognized sleep disorders such as narcolepsy and sleep apnea, he has included chapters on pregnancy, menopause, and family life. Although these are vital issues for most women at some time or another, most clinicians, even sleep clinicians, are not very good at addressing them.

The truth is, women sleep differently than men. A consistent finding in the medical literature has been that women report a greater need for sleep than do men. In surveys, women report spending more time in bed than do men, but also report more sleep problems, including inadequate sleep time and insomnia. However, studies of sleep quality by objective measurement tend to find very few objective differences between sleep quality in young men and women. With aging, it appears that women may actually fare better than men. Some (but not all) research indicates that older women who do not experience specific problems with sleep actually sleep more soundly than their male counterparts.

Among the reasons that women sleep "differently" from men are the facts that insomnia is clearly more prevalent in women than in men, and pregnancy and menopause appear to affect sleep. Nocturnal trips to the bathroom are a significant problem for both genders with aging, but younger women tend to find this less disruptive than do younger men.

Several chapters in this book are particularly noteworthy. Chapter 4 addresses the effects of pregnancy on sleep. This issue is like the elephant in the room that nobody wants to talk about! Sleep problems in pregnant women are nearly universal. Shockingly little is known or written about this. Dr. Kryger has done women a favor by bringing the issue out in the open. The disruption in sleep that accompanies menopause receives careful discussion in Chapter 5. Chapters 7 and 9 address the truism that "a woman's work is never done." Working women come home to their second (and maybe third) job: caretaking. The very real sleep problems resulting from the tendency of women to take care of everyone else's needs before taking care of their own are covered in these chapters. Chapter 12 is entitled "Sleep Breathing Disorders: Snoring and Sleep Apnea." Although sleep apnea can be deadly, surveys of medical schools have repeatedly demonstrated that sleep disorders receive short shrift in the curriculums of doctors-to-be; the average medical student receives about one hour of education about sleep and sleep disorders. If the student learns about sleep apnea at all, he or she is likely to hear that sleep apnea is much more prevalent in men than in women. As a result, clinicians may overlook or discount symptoms related to sleep and breathing problems in women. However, recent work demonstrates that postmenopausal women have a risk of sleep apnea similar to that of men. Dr. Kryger's chapter helps women to recognize signs and symptoms of this condition, and provides advice about when to seek help for herself or for a family member.

When I asked him why he wrote the book, Dr. Kryger said, "Sleep disorders are very common at all stages of a woman's life. Women have sleep problems men never have (pregnancy, menopause, as caregivers, etc.), and sleep problems frequently are seen as men's diseases, and women get missed or undiagnosed. Also the twenty-four/seven world has resulted in even more sleep deprivation in women since they are still usually the main caregiver in the family."

As a sleep clinician who is also a woman, I read this book with both professional and personal interest. And I learned a lot! You will, too.

Barbara Phillips, M.D., M.S.P.H., is currently Professor of Pulmonary and Critical Care Medicine in the Departments of Internal Medicine and Preventive Medicine at the University of Kentucky College of Medicine. Dr. Phillips is board certified in Internal Medicine, Pulmonary Medicine, Critical Care Medicine, and Sleep Medicine. She directs the Sleep Clinic and Sleep Fellowship at the University of Kentucky College of Medicine, and is Medical Director of the Sleep Disorders Center at Samaritan Hospital in Lexington. She is a past member and President of the American Board of Sleep Medicine, and currently serves on the boards of the American Academy of Sleep Medicine and the National Sleep Foundation.

Preface

Although sleep disorders are very common and there has been an enormous upsurge of interest in sleep and its disorders in the past few years, millions of people are still sleepy and in distress because of undiagnosed sleep problems. The National Sleep Foundation estimates that up to forty-seven million American adults may be putting themselves at risk for injury and health and behavior problems because they aren't getting enough sleep to ensure alertness the next day. In 2003 the National Institutes of Health estimated that between fifty and seventy million Americans of all ages have sleep-related problems. Unfortunately, too often it is women whose sleep disorders are undiagnosed or misdiagnosed.

Unlike men, women have sleep problems related to hormonal and bodily changes from menstruation, pregnancy, and menopause; this situation is compounded by the likelihood that their sleep disorders will be missed by doctors and even by the women themselves. Women lose sleep because of their role in the family and the demands of today's twenty-four/seven world. Disorders often are missed because though women have the same sleep disorders as men, the way these disorders manifest can be very different. For example, women with sleep apnea have symptoms of depression more often than men with apnea. Misdiagnosis occurs because of lack of education of doctors about women's sleep problems.

In the mid 1970s when I reported one of the first cases in North America of what eventually became known as sleep apnea, I thought I was describing an exquisitely rare condition. In the next two decades it became apparent that sleep apnea was a very common disorder, as common as asthma, affecting millions of people all over the world. This condition was not new, but people who had it were being misdiagnosed and treated for the wrong condition. Sleep apnea and other sleep breathing disorders were seen as problems of overweight men who snore and were thought to be very uncommon or even nonexistent in women. Until 1993 few doctors even looked for sleep apnea in females in the general population. It has since become clear that about 2 percent of all adult women have sleep apnea. Just as males who had sleep apnea went undiagnosed for many years, until recently women with sleep apnea were also misdiagnosed and treated for other conditions such as depression. It was assumed by the medical community that women just don't snore!

It is imperative that more attention be given to the sleep disorders that can cause misery and even death in women. Women often face lengthy delays in getting the right treatment due to the general lack of recognition of their sleep problems. For instance, shockingly, women with narcolepsy on average end up waiting *fifteen years* for correct diagnosis—often after consulting many doctors. This incurable condition creates real dilemmas for women. For example, how do you take care of children and/or have a career when you can't stay awake? I encountered one patient who was referred to me only after she had fallen asleep driving and crashed. Her two-year-old daughter was killed.

Another widespread problem is caused by the potentially fatal link between sleep apnea and heart disease. Sleep apnea involves episodes of stopping breathing that reduces blood oxygen, causes high blood pressure and stresses the cardiovascular system, which causes heart disease. Before menopause women are usually protected from cardiovascular disease by their hormones; however, sleep breathing disorders may counteract that protection. Additionally, untreated patients have an increased risk of death from the effects of the condition on other organs. Most people do not appreciate how deadly a sleep disorder can be; thus it is vitally important to a woman's health and well-being to get a correct diagnosis and treatment.

In the past twenty-five years, I have treated more than two thousand female patients with sleep problems and have seen firsthand the disastrous consequences of years of misdiagnosis and lack of treatment. I want this book to help women by raising awareness of the effects of sleep disorders on their daily (and nightly) lives. I expose how undiagnosed sleep problems can affect women's lives. I describe conditions including insomnia, restless legs syndrome, narcolepsy, sleep apnea, side effects of medications, and more, which affect women. I provide tips on how readers can recognize their sleep disorders, and educate them on what treatment or strategy will help.

As sleep problems can occur at any stage of a woman's life, my sincere hope is that this book will provide women the tools they need to recognize and understand their sleep disorders and those of family members, help them get treatment, and serve as an invaluable lifetime reference. Millions of women are concerned about how to deal with sleep disorders in themselves and in family members. My goal throughout this book is to educate and empower women, helping them to be wide awake and alert and able to enjoy life to the fullest.

Acknowledgments

In the summer of 2002, a woman with narcolepsy and I were being interviewed on the radio about the impact of sleep disorders on someone's life. A couple of hours later, when I was back in my office, I received a phone call from Jackie Joiner, a literary agent from Toronto who asked me about the impact of sleep disorders in women and as we were chatting, it became obvious to both of us that the general public did not appreciate that there are many sleep problems that women have that men do not, and that because of the special role that women play in society that sleep disorders were going to impact them differently. Thus the book was born. As an aside, when I asked Jackie for references (after all she was a total stranger calling me from Toronto) she gave me the name of Mr. David Roosevelt, who indeed was the grandson of Franklin and Eleanor Roosevelt, which lead to my contacting Mr. Roosevelt. He raved about Jackie as an editor and then we had a nice chat about his grandparents.

This book is being published in both the United States and Canada. This required a great deal of cross-border cooperation (between two companies that normally compete) and a great deal of text flying back and forth via the Internet. I want to thank Lynne Missen, my editor at HarperCollins Canada. Lynne was able to see the book from both sea level and 30,000 feet and guided me when I strayed off course. I would also like to thank Michele Pezzuti, my editor at McGraw-Hill Trade, USA. She and her team did a splendid job in copyediting the text. Kathy Dennis, the project editor at McGraw Hill, and Noelle Zizter, the managing editor at HarperCollins patiently took hundreds of pages of text and turned out a volume that hopefully will help thousands of women. In precisely the time it takes for human gestation, nine months, the teams at HarperCollins and McGraw-Hill gave birth to a bouncing baby book.

A special thanks to Dr. Norah Vincent, a colleague and clinical psychologist, who provided the content on the behavioral treatment of insomnia. Swen

Salgadoe, a Northwest flight attendant I am proud to say happens to be my niece, loves her job, has mastered overcoming jetlag, and supplied an insider's view about how she did it.

Dr. David Kristo, Lieutenant Colonel, Medical Corps, U.S. Army, at the Walter Reed Medical Center provided information about how people in the military are evaluated for sleep disorders in the United States.

I also want to thank the following friends and colleagues who reviewed parts of the book and made excellent suggestions and corrected errors: Dr. C. K. Yuen, Dr. Marcia Fleisher, Dr. Mark Mahowald, Dr. Barbara Phillips, Dr. Jodi Mindell, and Dr. Richard Ferber.

I am grateful to the American Academy of Sleep Medicine and the National Sleep Foundation for giving me permission to use information from and provide links to their websites.

Giant bouquets go to Pat Britz, Marcia Stein, Richard Gelula, Zoe Pouliot, and Joy Lertzman who reviewed the manuscript and turned my sometimes jargon-heavy writing style into something more appropriate.

Finally a huge hug, kiss, and so forth to my wife, Barbara, who reviewed and edited the text and put up with my laptop often on the corner of the kitchen table while I was writing this.

Introduction

by Richard Gelula

Sleep is a fundamental aspect of all animal life. For humans, sleep comprises approximately one-third of our lives. The alternating pattern of waking in the daytime and sleeping during the darkness of night is so ingrained in human experience that we barely have a perspective on it at all. When we start thinking about sleep, many questions occur to us. What is sleep? Why do people and animals sleep at all? What occurs during sleep? What does it do for us? What happens if we don't sleep or sleep too little? What causes the feelings of sleepiness and fatigue, and why do we feel this way when we have stayed awake too long? Does the sleep of women differ from that of men? What about the sleep of children, adolescents, and the elderly?

People who pick up a book about sleep often do so because they or a family member or friend is having some difficulty with sleep. Sometimes, they have simply become curious about this essential part of our nature and want to learn more. Whichever the case, *A Woman's Guide to Sleep Disorders* is a great starting point. It's written by an excellent guide who is not only informed and authoritative, but who has a sensitive manner and whose approach to human health is holistic. Dr. Kryger's methods combine an understanding of how lifestyle, outlook, and the physical and mental aspects of life combine. This is essential for understanding, diagnosing, and treating sleep problems because many of them derive from or are related to other physical, psychological, or lifestyle causes or patterns.

In fact, sleep specialists—whether they are physicians, psychologists, other clinicians, or technologists—frequently have this trait. As a group, they share an unusual warmth and sensitivity to people and their circumstances. Perhaps it is because they have spent many nights observing people sleep. That means that they themselves are familiar with the ill effects of staying awake overnight and have experienced the effects of sleep deprivation. Then, too, they have seen thousands of people whose physical or mental health and circumstances have declined as their sleep problems have progressed. They have come to learn just how important sleep is to human functioning, a fact that our culture and society frequently deny or put at a very low priority.

Thus, the health-care professional trained in sleep science and sleep medicine has an extremely valuable perspective, one that can make an enormous contribution to public and individual-patient health. It is a perspective born out of research, which shows that many if not all key aspects of human function and performance depend on sufficient high-quality sleep.

Increasingly we live in a world that operates twenty-four hours a day, seven days a week. This means that there are activity options at all hours of the night—something that, other than stargazing, was not true in the past. It also means that someone has to work to keep all of those things happening—whether it is in stores, factories, utilities, or transportation. Even though we pride ourselves on living in the information age, these practices that discount the natural sleep-wake rhythms only expand because we choose to remain ignorant or to reject the facts about the consequences of sleep deprivation. Our society generally functions with the belief that these effects are minor or acceptable. Sleep investigations conducted by Dr. Kryger and many sleep research colleagues demonstrate the opposite.

Many institutions ignore the importance of sleep, including our schools. In North America, most high schools start between 7:00 and 7:30 in the morning. To arrive at school for these early start times, students usually "awaken" one to two hours earlier. I use the word "awaken" advisedly because observations of classes in early-starting high schools show that most students put their heads down for at least a few minutes in their classes. In a society now consumed by the challenge of increasing educational achievement, we seem to have forgotten a basic concept: students must be awake to learn in class! Research by Dr. Mary Carskadon of Brown University has shown that teens need great amounts of sleep, about nine and one-quarter hours per night and they have a sleep-phase delay, meaning teens have a natural tendency to be awake and alert until late into the night. As a result, many of our children are unlikely to feel sleepy until 11:00 p.m. or midnight. If that is the case, it is entirely unreasonable for them to awaken by 6:00 a.m., and doing so leaves them sleep deprived and mentally and physically unprepared for what they have to do during the day. Does this circumstance—and other failures to acknowledge the need for sleep—cause the high rate of drowsy-driving car crashes among teen and young adult drivers—55 percent of all such crashes in two studies. All of the sleep researchers and clinicians I know would say, "Undoubtedly, yes!"

Many people, particularly women, wish they could sleep and stay asleep when they have the opportunity to do so. Every year the National Sleep Foundation conducts its Sleep in America poll and has found consistently high rates of insomnia, particularly among women. In 2002, we found that 63 percent of adult women respondents (eighteen years and older) reported symptoms of insomnia a few nights per week or more—compared to 54 percent for men. Many attributed this to stress, which afflicted 26 percent of polled women and 16 percent of males. Women also complain of being awakened frequently by others, including children (21 percent of all women respondents reported this, but only 12 percent of male adults) and snoring spouses (22 percent of women reported this, but only 7 percent of men). Such awakenings disrupt and shorten sleep and can adversely affect health, mood, performance, and safety. Clearly, they lead to daytime sleepiness, which 20 percent of women (and 13 percent of men) reported experiencing a few days each week or more.

This book addresses all of these problems and may motivate you to take action to change sleeping arrangements or family behavior patterns—or to seek help. It will also guide you on how to address insomnia and other sleep problems.

People like Dr. Kryger, who has devoted his professional life to teaching others about sleep, have also contributed to organizations like the National Sleep Foundation. Together, we are making inroads into society's disregard for sleep. We are working to change people's perceptions about it. As long as our work is incomplete, however, individuals will have to mobilize themselves to recognize the important role of sleep in their lives and they will have to prepare themselves to take action. They will have to learn about sleep, seek help for sleep-related problems, and make getting proper amounts of sleep a priority. Additionally, they can work with others to see that institutions that affect our lives—schools, the workplace, community activities, or health-care organizations—also adopt sleep-supportive practices. Such advocacy will reduce accidents, improve health, and even add to the bottom line of institutions. And when you and your family members have sufficient high-quality sleep, you will hear more laughter and discover that there are more opportunities for fun.

Finally, as you read and learn from Dr. Kryger, you will also find valuable resources and a partner in your quest for sleep at www.sleepfoundation.org.

Richard Gelula, M.S.W.
CEO, National Sleep Foundation

Part I

A Good Night's Sleep: What Is Normal? What Is Abnormal?

1

What Is Sleep?

Y ou wake in the middle of the night worried about personal or work issues. You know you have to get up early to drop the kids off at day care, then rush to work for an early meeting. You eventually fall back to sleep, only to be dragged awake again by the alarm clock. You are cranky and yell at the kids, trying to rush everyone out of the house so you can get to work for that meeting. By the time you get to the meeting, it's difficult to pay attention; you can neither concentrate nor listen to others.

You're driving down the highway. You feel an uncontrollable urge to shut your eyes. You turn on the radio, pop a candy into your mouth, and start to sing along with the radio. You roll down the window. Maybe you slap your face to give yourself a lift. These are all attempts to stay awake. But they are short-lived. Nothing seems to be working. You cannot overcome the urge to fall asleep.

How often have you been affected by such severe sleepiness? Every year, sleepy drivers cause an estimated 20 percent of car accidents, as high as 1.2 million crashes, resulting in huge numbers of deaths and injuries and billions in property damage. Furthermore, an estimated $18 billion is lost each year in productivity and injuries due to daytime sleepiness. Why does this happen, and what can you do about it?

Why do some people fall asleep within minutes and others take more than an hour to drop off? Why do our bodies need sleep? What's normal? Why do babies need more sleep than adults? How do the biological changes that occur during menstruation, pregnancy, and menopause affect women's sleep? Why do we dream? Why don't we move in response to what we are dreaming?

What happens to our bodies when we are sleep-deprived? How do you know when you are sleep-deprived and what are the consequences? Is your snoring bed partner actually in danger? What signs of sleep problems should be discussed with your doctor?

This book addresses all of these questions and more so that you can reach a better understanding of the signs of your own sleep deprivation and the importance of sleep to your life and good health. Symptoms of sleep problems you or your family or friends may be suffering from, as well what can be done to manage these problems and ensure healthy, sufficient high-quality sleep, are covered. In particular, this book comprehensively examines the unique world of women's sleep and recent studies relevant to its effect on women's health.

Sleep medicine is such a new field that even sleep specialists are still learning about it. As you will learn, there are many mysteries remaining about the nature of sleep.

What Is Sleep?

Before the nineteenth century, people believed that sleep was a form of reversible death. It was assumed that when you slept, you died, and suffering and pain ceased. And when you woke up, you came back from the dead. Even medical textbooks in the 1800s promoted this notion of sleep as a form of reversible death. Dr. Robert MacNish wrote in *Philosophy of Sleep* in 1830: "Sleep is the intermediate state between wakefulness and death: wakefulness is regarded as the active state of all the animal and intellectual functions and death as that of their total suspension."

A turning point occurred in the twentieth century, when it became apparent that the brain was indeed active during sleep. In 1928, a German doctor, Hans Berger, successfully measured and recorded electrical activity from the sleeping brain through electrodes placed on the scalp. This was the first EEG (electroencephalogram). Soon techniques were devised to measure the millionths of volts of electrical energy put out by the human brain during sleep to provide a more accurate picture of the brain's activity. In 1953 at the University of Chicago, Nathaniel Kleitman and his student, Eugene Aserinsky, measured the EEG and eye movements in babies. They described what became known as rapid eye movement (REM) sleep. Scientists then realized that there were three states of being: non-REM sleep, REM sleep, and wakefulness. It was soon discovered that REM sleep is the time when one is most likely to experience vivid dream imagery.

Further studies then ascertained that there were actually several types or stages of sleep. Using brainwaves and other measures, non-REM sleep was divided into four stages. Typically, as one goes from stage one to four, brainwaves become progressively slower and the size of the brainwaves become increasingly bigger and sleep is deeper and deeper. Stages three and four are frequently combined and called slow-wave sleep, deep sleep, or even delta sleep. Consequently, a more detailed picture of the brain's electrical activity during sleep emerged—one that represented the states and stages of sleep during the sleep cycle.

Figure 1-1 States and Stages of Sleep

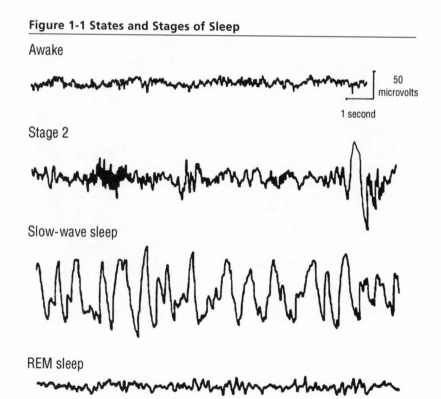

Awake

50 microvolts

1 second

Stage 2

Slow-wave sleep

REM sleep

Rapid eye movement (REM) sleep continues to be a mysterious state. We do not yet know why we have REM and why the brain behaves the way it does in this state. What has been shown is that the brain in REM seems to be as active as it is during wakefulness, and it seems to be doing a lot of work as the brain cells use a great deal of energy. As shown on the previous page, even the EEG in REM is similar to that seen in wakefulness.

There are two important manifestations of REM sleep. First, except for the major breathing muscle, the diaphragm and some sphincters at the top and the bottom of our gastrointestinal tract, most of our muscles are, in fact, paralyzed during REM sleep. Second, in spite of this outer paralysis, some cells in the pons, a primitive part of the brain, suddenly become active and

Figure 1-2 REM Sleep and the Brain

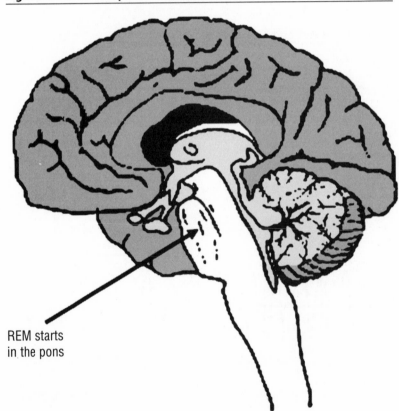

REM starts
in the pons

create electrical storms. The electrical activity created by these storms works its way through the central nervous system. When these electrical impulses work their way through the part of the brain that controls eye movements, the rapid eye movements characteristic of this state of sleep occur. When these impulses pass through the parts of the nervous system that control breathing and the cardiovascular system, there are often irregularities in the pattern of breathing as well as in heart rate and blood pressure. Another curious and not yet understood event that occurs during REM sleep is that males have erections of their penis, and females have engorgement of the blood vessels of the vagina. This happens every single time a person dreams, as often as three to five times each night. Curiously, sexual thoughts or dreams are not believed to cause these events.

Paradoxically, a normal feature of sleep is that we have brief awakenings (also called arousals) during a normal night of sleep. These arousals are brief, usually only seconds long, and we don't remember them. A normal person might experience about five of these awakenings an hour in response to a sensation or as a protection from danger. These responses are something we are born with: a newborn must be able to arouse if its breathing passage is blocked by bedding, in order to move into a position where breathing can start again. People with some of the diseases we will describe in this book wake up ten times more often than normal. An adult who stops breathing during sleep must arouse to start breathing again. These many awakenings reduce the amount of time the person spends in sleep stages so that he or she is unable to experience the amount of continuous high-quality sleep necessary for daytime alertness. The result is often daytime sleepiness and difficulty performing daily activities.

Why Do We Sleep?

All animals, including humans, sleep. When animals are prevented from sleeping they eventually die. Despite the thousands of experiments that have been done to study sleep, none has been able to declare with assurance the reason why all animals sleep. It is possible that in different species sleep serves a different function. For instance, most animals spend their time looking for food when they are awake and then find a safe place to sleep and hide from predators. Animals near the top of their food chain, such as lions, seem to sleep when and where they want.

We do not know why we sleep, just as we don't know why we are awake. Reasons typically given for why we sleep include conservation of energy, the restoration of important bodily functions, and the repair of damaged tissues. For example, some hormones are secreted mainly during sleep. Such theories are attractive, but all of these functions could be met by simply resting and having whatever hormones are secreted during sleep secreted during rest, not necessarily having the brain go into an unconscious state. We do know this for sure: if people do not sleep the right amount, they feel rotten the next day, their brains do not work properly, and they might be quite mentally impaired and unable to perform complex tasks. You certainly do not want a sleep-deprived pilot to be flying you across the Pacific. Even the medical profession now admits that sleep-deprived doctors might be a hazard to their patients.

We can conclude that sleep serves many important functions, and that the different types of sleep fulfill different needs. For instance, stages three and four, "slow-wave sleep," are believed to be the type required to feel refreshed upon awakening. Many scientists believe that REM sleep is the time when memories are saved in our nervous system. The right amount of sleep really does contribute to making you feel vigorous and in a great mood. Shakespeare was probably correct when he wrote in Macbeth that sleep was "Chief nourisher in life's feast."

How Much Sleep Do We Need?

How much we sleep, when we sleep, and how much deep sleep and dreaming sleep we need varies with age. Thus, seven to nine hours of sleep, which is adequate for most adults, would leave the average nine-year-old extremely sleepy during the daytime. Figure 1.3 shows sleep requirements for different ages. As you can see, there are ranges for each age group. The amount of sleep a woman needs is an individual characteristic just like her height. Each person needs his or her own unique amount of sleep. The amount of sleep needed is that which makes you wide awake and alert. Research has also shown a link between sleep time and health: women who sleep much more or much less

Figure 1-3 Hours of Sleep Needed Changes with Age

Age	Hours asleep in a 24-hour period	Hours spent napping
Birth to 2 months	10½ to 18	5 to 10*
2 months to 12 months	14 to 15	2½ to 5
12 months to 18 months	13 to 15	2 to 3
18 months to 3 years	12 to 14	1½ to 2½
3 years to 5 years	11 to 13	0 to 2½
5 years to 12 years	9 to 11	**
Teenage years	8 to 10	**
Adult years	7 to 9	**

Data obtained from several sources, including www.sleepfoundation.org/
publications/J&Jbrochure.pdf

*A newborn will sleep any time, day or night.
**Excessive napping at these ages may indicate a sleep problem.

than the average are at increased risk of disease. For example, a study of 71,000 nurses published in 2003 showed that those sleeping five hours or less had a 45 percent greater risk of developing heart disease than those sleeping eight hours. Those sleeping nine to eleven hours increased their risk by 38 percent.

In general, the amount of sleep decreases with age. Babies spend an enormous amount of time sleeping (although it may not feel that way to their sleep-deprived parents); for the first few months of life, most infants sleep at any time during the twenty-four-hour day. Finally and mercifully for the parents, they start to have long periods of sleep mostly at night. Infants and toddlers nap. By the time children go to school, most will no longer nap.

The amount of REM sleep also decreases with age. Newborns spend roughly half their sleep time in REM sleep. In adults the amount of REM experienced during sleep goes down to between 20 to 25 percent The amount of slow-wave sleep is also much higher in children; the time most people spend in slow-wave sleep decreases with aging. Some elderly people may have no slow-wave sleep. This is the sleep state during which most of the human growth hormone is secreted.

Exasperatingly for their parents, some children start to have a characteristic sleep pattern in their teenage years. Rather than go to bed at the most common times, between 10:30 and midnight in North America, teenagers do not feel sleepy at bedtime, but instead begin to sleep later and awaken later than they did during childhood years. On school nights, it may take them several hours to fall asleep, leaving a teen unable to get the approximate eight to ten hours of sleep he or she needs to wake on time and be alert throughout the day. A mother may find herself dragging an unwilling and unresponsive teenager out of bed. Thus, for the first few hours of the schoolday, a teenager may seem to be in a daze or may actually be asleep and consequently might perform very poorly. On weekends, these teenagers generally sleep until noon or even much later. For them to try to be alert at 9:00 a.m. would be like the average person trying to be alert at 2:00 or 3:00 in the morning. It simply does not work. In the afternoon and evening, these adolescents frequently get a second wind.

Older persons, especially after retirement, may start to nap again. Whether reduced nighttime sleep in the elderly is a consequence of the daytime naps is not clear. Many elderly people sleep poorly not just because of their age, but also as a consequence of a medical condition, medications, pain, sensitivity to their environment, or disruptions and changes in their sleep pattern. A survey of sleep in the older population, released in 2003, showed that older people without medical problems usually have normal sleep.

The Body Clock

How does your body know when it is time to go to sleep and to wake up? In your brain, in a place called the suprachiasmatic nucleus (SCN), there is a collection of cells that have the ability to keep time and function as a pacemaker for your sleep-wake cycle. It turns out that this pacemaker controls not only the times when you are sleepy or alert, but it also controls the function of many systems in the body. The word *many*, in fact, may be an understatement. *Most* of the systems in the body have a pattern that varies over a twenty-four-hour period. This is true for the secretion of many hormones, blood pressure, heart rate, and other functions in the body. This natural, internal rhythm in function has been called the *circadian rhythm*. The word comes from *circa* meaning "about" and *diem* meaning "day." In other words, the circadian rhythm changes the way many systems in the body work over the twenty-four-hour day so that the function of the systems matches what the body needs. As a result, we usually don't have to go to the bathroom and we don't have hunger at night. If you have traveled across time zones you know how discombobulated or out of sync you can feel because of a disconnect between your own body clock and the time where you happen to be.

One of the great mysteries of science, which has only recently been solved, is how the brain knows what time it is. Is it morning yet and time to wake up? Suppose we were living on a planet that was rotating around a sun every thirty hours instead of the twenty-four hours on the earth. How would the body clock adjust? The answer is that the light from the sun would somehow synchronize the body's circadian clock, exactly what has happened in humans and other animals on Earth. Put simply, light enters the eye and hits the retina. The cells in the retina are stimulated in a way not that much different from the way a digital camera works. The visual information, instead of going to a flash card as in a digital camera, travels along nerves and ends up in the suprachiasmatic nucleus or the SCN. This is where the pacemaker cells reside. These cells are located above the optic chiasm, where visual information crosses over from one side of the nervous system to the other on its way to the part of the brain that processes vision. The SCN is the first place that information from the retina goes, which serves as a type of wake-up call telling the brain that it is morning, which in turn synchronizes the pacemaker cells. People who are blind because of problems between the eye and the chiasm can have serious difficulty in synchronizing their body clocks, and often have very severe sleep problems as a result. On the other hand, people with blindness because of problems in the visual cortex, the part of the brain that processes the information, may still have a normal circadian system.

Interestingly, circadian systems appear to be present not only in higher life forms, but also, for example, in plants. In fact, the first demonstration of a circadian rhythm was by a Swiss scientist by the name of De Mairan who set up an ingenious experiment using a mimosa plant that opened up its leaves at a certain time when it was sunny. He put the plant into a box so that there was no exposure to light, and the leaves still opened at the same time. This plant was able to keep track of time.

There are many time-related rhythms in biology that are not understood. Some biological rhythms can be measured in seconds (for example, breathing and heartbeat), while others have much longer cycles. Although the cycle we know the most about is the circadian rhythm, seasons of the year seem to play an important role when mammals become pregnant and when they give birth. One of the most mysterious cycles in biology is the menstrual cycle in women, which is reviewed in the next chapter. This cycle is about the same length as the lunar cycle and the timing system that results in the cycle, which averages twenty-eight days, is unknown.

What a Good Night of Sleep Feels Like

No matter what your circadian rhythm or body clock is, you should be able to recognize a healthy sleep pattern. With an excellent night of sleep you should feel wide awake and alert shortly after waking up, and for the remainder of the day. You are generally in a good mood and do not feel any need for a nap. An excellent night of sleep requires both quantity and quality (uninterrupted and the right amount of each stage).

You should not wake up feeling unrefreshed, as though you had not slept. You should not feel as though you must have one or more cups of coffee in order to be able to function. Struggling to stay awake while driving to and from places, falling asleep or feeling uncontrollably fidgety at movies, public meetings, or even in front of the TV are all signs that you may be sleep deprived. Furthermore, you should not feel as though you are about to fall asleep when reading.

If you do experience these symptoms, it indicates that the amount or the quality of your sleep is inadequate to keep you optimally wide awake and alert. You probably have a sleep problem if you are sleepy in the morning; feel tired all day; fall asleep when you don't want to; need to nap; and/or are irritable and moody when you awaken. It is important to note that boredom does not cause sleepiness. Boredom simply gives the sleepy person the opportunity to nod off.

As will become apparent later on in this book, there are other symptoms that may indicate that you have a medical problem. You should not wake up with heartburn, chest pain, shortness of breath, or an unusually fast or slow heartbeat. Waking up with a headache more than just occasionally or making frequent trips to the bathroom at night may also be signs of a medical problem. You should not wake up paralyzed or with severe sweating. Nor should you be committing any violent acts that injure yourself or others while you are sleeping. Bed partners should not be telling you that you stop breathing during sleep and that it is scary watching you sleep. If you have any of these symptoms, it likely relates to a medical problem that should be investigated.

You should also see a doctor if you sleep more than nine hours each night or less than five hours. Research has shown repeatedly that people who consistently sleep too much (more than ten hours a night) or far too little (fewer than five hours a night) have a higher death rate. However, the key issue is not the length of sleep. Rather we believe that such abnormal amounts of sleep are a symptom of a sleep or medical disorder that may cause or result in death.

The bottom line is that if you are not wide awake and alert the entire day, and if you have daytime sleepiness, or if you have the symptoms mentioned in the previous paragraph, you may have a problem.

We all sleep. Sleep is a state whose control and complexity we have only recently begun to understand. An excellent night of sleep can make a person feel wonderful and productive. A poor night of sleep or insufficient sleep leaves a person feeling exhausted and nonproductive; he or she may even pose a danger to others. Women are much more likely than men to have sleep problems. This is not just because some sleep disorders are much more common in women, but also because family responsibilities, menstruation, pregnancy, and menopause all can disrupt normal sleep.

Often, women do double duty. They are the first up in the morning and the last to go to bed at night. They work and they come home and are the primary caregivers in the family. They often organize and run the household, prepare meals, clean, and so forth. They need to be sensitive to spouses and kids, alert to problems and issues in the family, good listeners, empathetic, etc. If they lose sleep, the family can suffer. They can be cranky, irritable, and short-tempered with spouses and children.

A good night of sleep, on the other hand, allows a woman to start the day fresh with enough energy to take her through a long, full day. For a healthy lifestyle, a good night's sleep is as important as healthy eating and adequate exercise. The following chapters of this book will provide the information you need to recognize when you have a problem and what to do about it.

2

Sleep Through the Stages of Life

The Case of the Tired Lawyer

The lawyer sitting across the desk from me in my office was desperately seeking my help. She was not there to represent a client, but instead was telling me a sad tale about how, after giving birth to her first child, she could no longer function at the high level she expected from herself.

She noted how very sleepy she was every day when arriving at the office. Several cups of coffee did not help. She would start her day's work but found it difficult to concentrate. She would frequently nod off particularly when working at the computer. She was caught sleeping by one of the senior partners in the law firm who insisted that she take care of the problem or there would be professional repercussions. A sleepy lawyer would not be tolerated in a busy law practice.

The lawyer was about thirty-five years old. She exercised a great deal and considered herself to be in excellent physical condition. She had always been extremely successful at her work. But her life was now falling apart. Her once photographic memory was beginning to fail. She could not understand it. Was there a serious medical problem ruining her life? She was worried, but could not bring herself to say the awful words, "Do I have early Alzheimer's disease?"

Makeup could not hide the bags under her eyes, which were large and grayish. I asked her a series of questions, and discovered that the whole problem had begun roughly five months earlier with the birth of her first baby. She and her husband, also a practicing lawyer, had made a deal that she would wake up at night to take care of the baby during the week and he would take care of the baby at night during the weekends. Consequently, she had been losing one or two hours of sleep every weeknight. She had expected to be able to maintain her work at normal levels but she had been proven wrong. She had no idea that losing one or two hours of sleep could have such a devastating effect. However, she was relieved to learn that she did not have Alzheimer's.

What amazed me was that the sleepy lawyer was a well-educated person, but had no clue that her problems could be caused by sleep deprivation. Since neither she nor her husband knew much about the sleep patterns of babies, neither knew how long the baby would continue to wake up at night. She had no idea about what to expect and didn't know whether this was going to permanently impact her career. Most people know little or nothing about how sleep changes throughout the stages of life.

Sleep in Children

From birth, every child is unique and has individual sleep needs and patterns. The patterns change with time and the way the patterns change is unique. If a couple's first baby was a great sleeper, this does not mean that future children will be great sleepers. The parent who understands what to expect and learns the child's pattern can recognize when problems arise.

The First Year

Sleep patterns change tremendously in the first few months of life. At first, neither the baby nor the parents sleep through the night and the parents experience sleep deprivation. This can be a difficult time for all. It's also the time when a small number of mothers may experience postpartum depression, which can be very serious and often requires treatment. Not surprisingly, most parents only find relief once the baby begins to sleep through the night.

Birth to Two Months
What parents should expect. Most newborn babies have many sleep periods over the course of a twenty-four-hour day, most of which last between a half hour and three hours. As the newborn does not distinguish between day and

night, there are many awakenings for the baby and the parent throughout a typical night. By six weeks, nighttime sleep episodes become longer and a more regular sleep pattern usually begins. The baby will sleep a total of fourteen and a half hours on average, with the range being between ten to eighteen hours. Newborns spend about 50 percent of their sleep time in REM sleep during which they twitch and grunt. Boys may have erections. All of this is normal.

What parents should do to help baby sleep. First, learn the baby's language—that is, how he or she communicates signs of sleepiness. For instance, certain cries, fussiness, and rubbing of the eyes signal that the baby is sleepy. Parents should put the baby to bed when they see those signs and recognize the baby is tired. This would also be a good time for a sleepy parent to sleep, a situation rendered more difficult if it's not the first baby and other children require attention. Rocking the baby to sleep may not be a problem early on. By the end of the second month, however, most babies need to learn to fall asleep on their own.

What sleep problems parents should watch for. If the baby sleeps more than eighteen hours or fewer than ten hours per day, there may be a problem. If the baby is lethargic when awake, this is cause for concern. Additionally, if the baby snores loudly or obstructs or stops breathing repeatedly during sleep, she or he may have apnea. Check this out with the doctor. If the baby turns blue, get medical help immediately as this is a sign of low blood oxygen.

Two to Twelve Months

What parents should expect. The baby's nighttime sleep episodes gradually become longer. By four to six months of age he or she will temporarily wake up during the night but should begin to have the ability to fall back to sleep on his or her own. At two months a baby will take three or four naps over the course of twenty-four hours. By the end of the first year, most babies take two naps a day.

What parents should do to help baby sleep. A baby at this age should be put to bed on her or his back when ready to sleep. You can't put a baby to bed every time you see her yawn, and every yawn does not mean she's ready for sleep. You should learn when your baby will be sleeping and use that schedule so that you don't have to wait until she shows signs of sleepiness (rubbing of the eyes, fussing, repeated yawning) before putting her to bed. During the daytime, this might also be a good time for a sleepy parent to nap, especially if the baby is still waking up during the night. After you put the baby to bed, fight the impulse to check on her every time she awakens, as babies need to fall asleep on their own even in the middle of the night. If the baby begins to associate falling asleep with being held or rocked by a parent, you might end up with a baby who won't fall asleep without this assistance. Babies quickly learn, "If I cry, the parent will come and rock me." Parents learn, "Not again. If I don't go to the baby, she'll never fall asleep and I'll never get to sleep. I'd better go." Both are now trapped in a vicious circle. This is the time when it is natural for babies to learn to fall asleep on their own; parents should help them achieve this.

What sleep problems should parents watch for? Watch for the same problems that were mentioned for newborns: sleeping more than eighteen hours or fewer than ten; being excessively sleepy or nonresponsive while awake; and/or exhibiting loud snoring or obstructed or stopped breathing during sleep may be signs that the baby has apnea (contact the doctor). If the baby turns blue, get medical help immediately as this is a sign of low blood oxygen.

One to Three Years

By one year of age, children are still napping but most of their sleep is now occurring at night. Naps are generally quite regular. By the age of three, these naps are shorter, and by the time the child is five years old, naps are generally not needed.

Four to Thirteen Years

Children in this age group need at least two to three hours more sleep than adults (see Chapter 1). Over the years, I have seen several families who brought in children that were falling asleep in class; they could not understand it because the child was getting as much sleep as they were. Seven or eight hours of sleep a night are simply inadequate for a child. Parents and caregivers should become familiar with the amount of sleep that children of different ages require. Keep in mind that all children from birth through adolescence need more than the average amount required by adults.

Several sleep problems that begin when the child is much younger may become important issues in the years before adolescence. These include sleep-walking and bedwetting (enuresis). As seen in Chapter 14, sleepwalking is very common in children, and as in adults, may be made worse by sleep deprivation. Sleepwalking may be present from the time a child can walk but often becomes an issue later, for example when the child is invited for a sleepover. Sleepwalking generally becomes much less frequent as the child becomes older. If the sleepwalking episodes are not associated with anything dangerous, no treatment is usually required. Similarly enuresis often becomes a problem at ages five to ten years. The family should consult a pediatrician for advice on dealing with enuresis.

The Adolescent Years

Many adolescents go to bed late and wake up late. Before bed, many teens are involved in arousing activities such as chatting on the phone, playing video games, and surfing the Internet. In some children, the shift to a later sleep-wake cycle represents a change in the circadian body clock (see Chapter 8), and can have serious consequences. If the child's schedule results in the child falling asleep in class or performing poorly, the caregiver should step in and make sure the child does not stay up late, does not participate in arousing activities right before bedtime, and does not use excessive caffeine. (Some soft drinks have large amounts of caffeine—see Appendix B, page 293, for caffeine content of products.)

Certain symptoms deserve special attention. Besides the sleep deprivation caused by a lifestyle that interferes with and can replace sleep, adolescence may be a time when an adolescent's circadian clock becomes different from that of most other people and this may cause a problem (see also Chapter 8). When the circadian clock runs late, teenagers go to bed very late, have trouble getting out of bed to go to school, and sleep much later on weekends to catch up on sleep.

Sleep Disorders That May Start During the Teenage Years

- Sleep deprivation
- Abnormal circadian clock
- Sleep apnea
- Narcolepsy
- Movement disorder

If the teenager is extremely sleepy during the daytime and falls asleep at inappropriate times in spite of getting normal amounts of sleep, there may be a significant sleep disorder present—one that will require some evaluation. At this age, the possibilities include narcolepsy, which classically begins during the teenage years (see Chapter 13), sleep apnea (in a child who snores, the most common causes are enlarged tonsils and obesity; see Chapter 12), and some movement disorders (see Chapter 11). Teenagers who have an iron deficiency can also experience severe insomnia and daytime sleepiness, conditions that improve once the iron deficiency is treated.

Young Adults

Young adults, especially college students, are notorious for being sleep deprived. They stay up late and may have to get up early to go to class. They pull all-nighters to finish projects and prepare for tests. In college classes, especially when there are hundreds of students in the room, as soon as the lights dim, many start to nod off. Students who learn about the importance of sleep and practice healthy sleep habits, even during the college years, can significantly improve their ability to have a healthy, productive, and safe lifestyle.

Adulthood

Starting with puberty, there are huge hormonal and other biological changes that affect women (but not men) that can have dramatic and disruptive effects on sleep. The menstrual cycle, pregnancy, and menopause have such important effects on a woman's sleep that the topics are covered in the next three chapters.

Older People

Most older people are women. That's because women live longer than men. The 2000 U.S. Census reported that for every 100 women aged 75 to 84 there were only 65 men of the same age; for every 100 women aged 85 or older there were only 40 men of the same age.

What has also become clear is that measuring age only in terms of the number of rotations around the sun or years can be very misleading. When I was a medical student, the average male was dead by the age of 69, and the average woman by age 74. If you were more than 65 years old, you had a zero chance of getting into the intensive care unit if you became critically ill. There were very few people around who were in their eighties, nineties, and hundreds. Today, in spite of pollution, global warming, exposure to toxins in our food, genetically modified crops, and all sorts of catastrophes that have befallen the planet, the fact is that people in the developed world are living a lot longer and are a lot healthier than they ever were before. Therefore, we've had to rethink many of our definitions.

First, aging is very individual. Within a given person, some organ systems will age at different rates than others. In this section, the word *aging* refers to the deterioration in function related to time. In a given person, the joints and muscles may age a lot faster than the mind. People who are in their nineties can use computers and trade stocks on the Internet, read several newspapers a day, yet have trouble climbing stairs or going for a walk. On the other hand, there are many people whose intellectual abilities begin to plummet in their early sixties while their bodies remain fairly normal. Some people have diseases that seem to accelerate the aging process, for example diabetes; failure to treat the disease causes even greater acceleration. In this section, we will discuss sleep problems associated with aging. In Chapter 7 we will focus on how caring for an elderly parent or one with Alzheimer's disease can impact a woman's sleep.

Sleep in Healthy Older People

Healthy older people can have completely normal sleep—meaning they fall asleep quickly, sleep through the night, and are wide awake and alert the next day. A poll on sleep in older people released in 2003 found that many older people are sleeping better and longer than younger people. This same poll found that the better the health of older people, the better they slept. Though research has shown that older people may have less deep sleep, and may also produce less growth hormone during sleep, the impact of these research findings on health are not yet known. When sleep is abnormal in older people it is often because they have a medical condition that is interfering with their sleep.

Sleep in Aging People with Medical Conditions

As they age, all women will become menopausal, which causes sleep problems. Depending on lifestyle and genetics, they may develop medical conditions that affect their sleep. Many women develop high blood pressure, heart disease, diabetes, cancer, and depression; some have one or more of these conditions. The more conditions they have, the poorer the quality of their sleep. For example people with four or more of these conditions are five times more likely to complain of daytime sleepiness. These diseases are covered in greater detail in Chapter 15.

Napping in Older People

Some people, who do not develop any health problems as they age, will start to take naps in the afternoon once they retire from work. They may then find themselves having trouble falling asleep at night or awakening very early in the morning. Some of them have come to the sleep clinic complaining of these very early awakenings asking what they can do to promote their ability to sleep until the time they want to wake up. They are surprised to hear that these early awakenings may not be a problem if they are alert and functioning well during the daytime. Then they can continue on with their current pattern or try omitting the nap to see whether that improves their nighttime sleep. Thus, naps can be good or bad in older people.

Clues That an Older Person Has a Sleep Problem

Falling asleep in the daytime and doing so at inappropriate times and places is an extremely important clue that there is something abnormal with a person's sleep. An eighty-five year old woman brought her eighty-nine year old husband to the sleep clinic. He still had his driver's license, but she was increasingly terrified to drive with him, because he could not stay awake while driving. He had to take a fifteen-minute nap halfway through a thirty-minute drive from home to their country club. In this case, his excessive daytime sleepiness was a sign of sleep apnea, and he was also taking several medications that made him sleepy.

The Nursing Home

About 70 percent of nursing home residents are women. If you visit a nursing home during the daytime, you will often find lines of wheelchair-bound people who have nodded off. The residents of these homes seem to spend a great deal of time asleep. This may be due in part to the fact that they are not provided with enough exposure to natural sunlight, or the rooms may be poorly lit. This causes the body clock system, which is sensitive to light and helps orchestrate the sleep schedule, to malfunction. Some older people may start to sleep during the daytime and stay awake at night, or when they awaken during the night, they might start to wander.

Drugs Used to Treat Medical Conditions in Older People

Many of the common medical conditions of older people can lead to sleep problems, and many drugs used to treat the medical conditions can cause sleep problems. Chapter 17 covers the drugs that cause sleep problems. It is vital to remember that older people are more sensitive to the main effects and side effects of medications than younger people. Both the health-care provider and the patient should be informed about the side effects of every medication being considered. In other words, the benefit of these treatments should be considered relative to the side effects.

One should also make sure that the older person is instructed effectively with regard to both the dosage and medication regime. Sometimes aging patients' memories are not capable of tracking all of this information so it is helpful to have it all written down and accessible. A particular worry is patients who continue to take old prescriptions because the bottles are still around, while also taking updated prescriptions of the same drug. Such an unintended overdose of prescribed drugs can cause dangerous sleepiness.

Back to the Sleepy Lawyer

Although the two lawyers whose story began this chapter had sixteen years of university education between them, they knew very little about sleep and nothing about the sleep of children. The solution for the patient was to renegotiate and modify the deal she had made with her husband. In addition, and they certainly could afford it, they would have to bring in help to care for the baby at night in addition to their daytime child-care arrangement so that their daytime work could continue successfully. It was important for them to set priorities, particularly as neither one wanted to wake up at night and they did not want to impose on family members. They decided to hire a live-in nanny, which temporarily solved their problem. Soon after the nanny was hired, the problem was solved permanently when the baby at around seven months of age began sleeping through the night. Most couples would not be able to afford a nanny. They would have to split the nighttime duties fairly and sometimes enlist the help of family members to get them through this difficult period.

In this chapter we have seen that sleep is different in different stages of life and that not knowing what to expect can disrupt a family. In the next chapter we will see how hormones change during a woman's life and how this can interfere with sleep and cause problems that most men cannot even relate to.

3

How the Menstrual Cycle Affects Sleep

The Case of the Sleepy Woman with Irregular Periods

After suffering for almost five years from severe daytime sleepiness that made her unable to hold a job because she couldn't stay awake, a twenty-nine-year-old woman had reached the end of her rope. For months she had been awakening every morning with a headache. Her doctor felt that these headaches, combined with the sleepiness, were getting progressively more serious and having a negative impact on the quality of her life. Her doctor also noted that she had been snoring loudly ever since she was a teenager. She was referred to the sleep disorders center in hopes of getting to the root of both her snoring and her sleepiness problem.

On evaluation at the center, her examination revealed she was slightly overweight; at five foot five she was 160 pounds. What was more unusual about her was that she had much more facial hair than is normal for a woman and very hairy arms and legs as well as hair on her chest between her breasts. The medical term for this pattern of excess hair in a woman is *hirsutism*. When I asked whether her menstrual cycle was regular she was surprised but told me that her periods were actually very irregular, and for many months she had not had a period at all. But for what possible reason would I need to know about her menstrual cycle? What could it have to do with her sleep? In her case, it was everything.

She had an overnight sleep test, which showed she stopped breathing repeatedly, about once a minute, while she slept, a condition called *sleep apnea*.

When she was asleep the muscles in her throat were relaxed and the now floppy upper breathing passage became blocked, which caused her breathing to stop. Each time this happened, the level of her blood oxygen dropped to dangerous levels and to start breathing again her brain woke up in order to open up the breathing passage. This happened hundreds of times during the night. This disorder, much more widespread in men, causes severe sleepiness and can lead to headaches. This woman's sleep apnea was caused by a disease that caused her ovaries to produce too much male hormone and made her periods irregular.

The Menstrual Cycle

According to a 1998 poll conducted by the National Sleep Foundation that surveyed women about their sleep, about 70 percent of menstruating women report that their sleep is disturbed by symptoms associated with their periods. The poll found that the most common causes of disturbed sleep are bloating (in 50 percent of menstruating women), tender breasts (in 36 percent), headaches (in 33 percent), and cramps (in 28 percent). Surprisingly, these symptoms are not related to the age of the woman, and any woman from puberty to menopause can experience sleep loss due to these symptoms. On average, a woman can expect her sleep to be disturbed 2.5 nights out of every month. Even though the menstrual cycle is the most basic rhythm of a woman's life, millions of women have disturbed sleep due to menstrual symptoms.

As just described, reproductive or sex hormones have effects on many organs of the body, including the brain: an abnormal amount and type of sex hormones can be the cause of serious medical and sleep problems. For example, women are more likely to develop symptoms related to depression at times when the levels of these hormones are increasing or decreasing; for instance during puberty, in the days before menstruation, after giving birth to a baby, and right before and after menopause. Not coincidentally, depression is also associated with sleep problems. People with sleep problems are much more likely to be depressed or to eventually be diagnosed with depression.

As complex as an orchestral piece, the menstrual cycle requires the proper sequencing of hormones and activities in at least four different tissues of the body: the hypothalamus and pituitary gland, which are in the central nervous system; the ovaries; and the uterus. The cycle is made up of three distinct phases:

1. **Follicular phase.** This is the phase in which the follicle grows. One of the dormant eggs in the follicle in the ovary develops, and at the same time, the lining of the uterus begins to prepare itself for nourishing a fertilized egg.
2. **Ovulation.** The egg is released. On day 14 (in most women), midway through the monthly cycle, the egg is released and makes its way into the fallopian tube.
3. **Luteal phase.** The uterine lining thickens in preparation for possible fertilization. If fertilization does not occur, the lining of the uterus is shed. This causes the bleeding that occurs on the first day of the menstrual cycle.

Every woman is intimately familiar with the rhythms of her menstrual cycle but not every woman realizes how these three phases can affect the quality and quantity of her sleep. Simply put, the level of hormones fluctuates intensely, swinging between very low and high levels every single month in women of childbearing age, tremendously affecting many tissues of the body including the nervous system, which controls sleep. Disruptions in sleep can occur during the regular menstrual cycles, and more serious sleep problems can occur in three conditions linked to hormonal changes: premenstrual syndrome (PMS), premenstrual dysphoric disorder, and polycystic ovarian syndrome.

Sleep in Women with Normal Menstrual Cycles

Every woman who menstruates experiences three phases in her menstrual cycle. In most women who have regular periods, the menstrual cycle is not associated with sleep complaints, although research studies have found that there are subtle changes in sleep and in levels of daytime sleepiness. However, sleep is often disrupted most when hormone levels change most quickly: during ovulation and right before menstruation. At these times women may have a few nights of sleeplessness. On the other hand, they may not even notice any change, perhaps feeling only slightly sleepier.

Follicular Phase to Ovulation

Women typically experience their highest average sleep time in the early follicular phase. In the days before ovulation, the estrogen levels increase and the amount of rapid eye movement (or dreaming) sleep also increases slightly. Women sleep the least during ovulation. This is probably because of the effect on the brain of high levels of hormones that cause ovulation.

Ovulation to Menstruation

In the third phase of the cycle, there is an increase in progesterone, which among other things causes body temperature to rise. The number of brief awakenings is highest in the few nights right before bleeding starts, when levels of progesterone and estrogen are both dropping. Women might find themselves tossing and turning. In the late luteal phase, many women report that it takes them longer to fall asleep, they sleep less, and the quality of the sleep is poor compared to the beginning of the cycle.

Some women have painful cramps prior to and during menstruation, which can cause wakefulness. Many women find it hard to get to sleep during this time, and after they fall asleep they tend to have less REM sleep and a slightly elevated body temperature. Such women may be sleepier than normal at this time.

What About Birth Control Pills?

There are many different types of birth control pills and other types of contraceptives available. These pills control the menstrual cycle. The main effect of the pills is to prevent ovulation, so women who use birth control pills may not experience the mild effects on sleep related to ovulation. These women may still have symptoms related to menstruation, but in some women the symptoms might be less severe than they were before they began using the pill.

Premenstrual Syndrome (PMS)

Women with PMS have a variety of symptoms (for example, trouble sleeping, irritability, mood changes, and bloating) before menstruation. About 5 percent experience symptoms severe enough that they might interfere with their lives.

Most women who have PMS experience symptoms in the few days before the start of menstrual bleeding (the late luteal phase). Usually the symptoms end as soon as the bleeding starts or within two to three days.

How Is PMS Diagnosed?

To diagnose PMS, the symptoms should be present over several consecutive menstrual cycles and be severe enough to interfere with the woman's mental state and activities of daily living. But, even today, the diagnosis of PMS is somewhat tricky. This is because of the large number of symptoms that have been described over the years. The range of symptoms affecting almost all the organ systems of the body is staggering. Unfortunately, there is no standard test that can confirm this diagnosis. Women may go to various doctors, sometimes for years, before the correct diagnosis is made.

One can divide the symptoms of PMS into two general categories: those that affect the nervous system and those that affect other parts of the body. The nervous system symptoms include problems sleeping (which can be severe), mood swings, irritability, anger, headaches, memory loss, and tremors. The symptoms involving other parts of the body include breast swelling, fluid retention, muscle aches, nausea, and vomiting. Most women only have a few of the symptoms. Many women with PMS have trouble sleeping and may experience daytime sleepiness.

What Causes PMS?

Although there are many theories, the short answer is that we don't really know. Scientists have been unable to pinpoint a single mechanism that causes PMS. There are many hormonal and chemical changes that occur before menstruation. Each woman probably has a more or less unique combination of symptoms caused by a unique combination of chemical changes.

What Are Other Causes of Symptoms Similar to Those Found in PMS?

Because the symptoms of PMS are so varied, your doctor would consider several other disorders that may have similar symptoms. For example, symptoms such as sleeplessness, hot flashes, and being aware of a rapid heart rate might be found in hyperthyroidism (excess thyroid production). Tiredness might be caused by hypothyroidism (inadequate thyroid production). Some experts believe that in a small number of women, abnormal thyroid function may lead to symptoms of PMS. And, in some women, the sleep problems and mood swings might be a symptom of depression.

How Is PMS Treated?

As stated earlier, the mechanism causing PMS is not really known and may vary from woman to woman. Because there are so many differing symptoms, treatment for PMS is not specific but is based on the symptoms themselves with the expectation that the symptoms will get better on their own once menstruation begins.

General Measures

Women who notice it is taking them much longer to fall asleep or who are waking up frequently at night, should reduce caffeine intake as a first step and at the very least they should stop drinking coffee after lunch. Also, though many women believe that alcohol can help them fall asleep, it actually can cause them to wake up later on in the night. So women should avoid alcohol at night. Women who have repeatedly experienced disrupted sleep due to their menstrual cycle often expect to have a bad night's sleep before menstruation. Expecting a bad night causes stress and leads to a bad night. Women may benefit from learning relaxation methods that reduce the stress caused by the expectation of a bad night. If the sleep problem is very severe and does not respond to the treatments for PMS described next, the sleep problem may not be related to PMS. In that case, other types of problems as outlined in Chapter 10 should be considered.

Medications

There have been three approaches to the type of medication to help PMS and its effect on sleep:

- Relief of specific symptoms such as pain, which may interfere with sleep
- Change of hormone levels
- Prevention of the mood disorders before they occur

If you have been experiencing pain (e.g., tender breasts or cramps), your doctor might suggest an over-the-counter pain medication that has anti-prostaglandin properties (also called nonsteroidal anti-inflammatory medications or NSAIDs). In the United States, examples of NSAIDS available over the counter include those containing ibuprofen (Advil, Motrin, Nuprin, and Midol 200), and those containing naproxen (Aleve). Generic versions of these medications are also available. Check with your pharmacist. For bloating and water retention, your doctor may prescribe a mild diuretic (a "water pill").

The medications that change mood and hormone levels are powerful drugs and have potentially severe side effects. These must be taken in consultation with your doctor. Antidepressants known collectively as SSRIs (selective serotonin reuptake inhibitors; see Chapter 16) have been recommended in the luteal phase of the cycle (after ovulation). Oral contraceptives have been used to regulate the cycle. Other very powerful drugs that affect the levels of hormones have been used in cases of severe PMS include leuprolide (Lupron), and danazol (known as Danocrine in the United States, Cyclomen in Canada). These drugs can have very serious side effects. I do not recommend them if the main symptom being treated is sleeplessness. If the sleeplessness is indeed only caused by PMS it will improve in a few days.

The Food and Drug Administration (FDA) has not approved any of the drugs mentioned in the last paragraph for the treatment of PMS because they have not been adequately studied. The effect of long-term use of these drugs in PMS is not known, so the patient should discuss the pros and cons of the drugs with her doctor. Remember, the symptoms generally disappear once menstruation begins, so the best approach might be to take nothing. This is especially true if the woman is planning to get pregnant. If the woman becomes pregnant while taking these medications, she should contact her doctor at once.

Are Some of Your PMS Symptoms Severe? Is It PMDD?

If mood and nervous system premenstrual symptoms are very severe, it might be a more serious problem that has been called premenstrual dysphoric disorder (PMDD). If, in addition to the symptoms for PMS, a woman has symptoms of depression (hopelessness, severe sadness, or thoughts of suicide; see Chapter 16) or anxiety, wide mood swings, severe uncontrollable anger or irritability, and marked problems with sleeping, she may be suffering from PMDD. This woman may suffer from severe insomnia and have extreme difficulty falling asleep and staying asleep. She might awaken very early in the morning and not be able to fall asleep again. To diagnose a woman with PMDD or an underlying psychiatric problem that worsens before menstruation, a doctor should evaluate these symptoms.

Polycystic Ovarian Syndrome

Most tissues that produce one hormone are capable of producing other chemically related hormones. In polycystic ovarian syndrome (PCOS), the ovaries produce too much of the male sexual hormones (androgens). The high levels of male hormone in women results in low levels of follicle-stimulating hormone (FSH). As a result, the eggs in the follicles do not develop. The follicles swell and form collections of fluid called cysts. Many follicles with undeveloped eggs form cysts, hence the name *polycystic*. The ovaries sometimes increase in size quite dramatically to the size of a baseball, or even larger. The abnormal hormone levels cause two sets of problems: as shown in our twenty-nine-year-old patient, the woman may develop excess hair and other features normally found in males, and may experience accompanying problems with her reproductive system. Although it sounds rare, PCOS is quite a common disorder found in about one of every twenty premenopausal women. In about a quarter of teenage girls who don't menstruate, PCOS is the probable cause.

The most common symptoms of PCOS are male hair distribution, overweight, and problems with menstrual cycle or difficulty in becoming pregnant. The problem may first become apparent when a woman is being investigated for infertility. Women with PCOS, for example, may have facial hair or develop acne well past the teenage years, in their twenties and thirties, and might even develop baldness. Infrequent menstrual cycles and even complete cessation of menstruation are common in PCOS patients.

Women with PCOS also develop a resistance to the effect of the hormone insulin that lowers blood sugar. This may lead to diabetes in about 10 percent of women with this condition and an increased risk of cardiovascular disease. These women also have abnormal blood lipids which increases their risk for heart disease and because of the excess weight and the male distribution of the extra weight, they are much more likely to develop obstructive sleep apnea, a very severe sleep disorder characterized by repeated cessation of breathing during sleep.

In one study, 44 percent of women with PCOS were shown to have obstructive sleep apnea compared to 6 percent of women matched for age and weight. The women with PCOS stopped breathing more than forty times an hour while they slept. These patients snore, stop breathing during sleep, and experience daytime sleepiness. It is not just the weight that leads to the apnea, but the location of the fat tissue. These women had a male fat distribution. Excess fat distribution in males causes the waist to be increased more than the hip size. PCOS women had a larger waist-hip ratio than the other women. In other words, the waist size was out of proportion to the hips. As expected, the PCOS women had much higher levels of testosterone.

Treatment of PCOS

If you suspect you have this condition, see your doctor, especially if you want to become pregnant. Losing weight is very effective in helping manage the hormonal changes, and may help the sleep-breathing problem. With weight loss, male hormone production decreases and there will be an improvement in the body's ability to respond to insulin which is important in controlling diabetes. Sometimes even a relatively small weight loss can lead to dramatic improvement in the chance for a successful pregnancy or normal menstruation; it may also help relieve sleep apnea. If weight loss can't be achieved, an effective treatment to relieve sleep apnea is continuous positive airway pressure treatment (CPAP), which requires the woman to wear a mask over her nose while sleeping. The pressure delivered by the mask keeps the breathing passage open. Recent research suggests that the apnea may itself reduce the effectiveness of the hormone insulin. Reduced insulin levels or a decreased insulin effect play an important role in diabetes, and treatment of the apnea in PCOS may improve the diabetes in these patients.

Back to the Sleepy Woman with the Irregular Periods

Our twenty-nine-year-old patient's serious sleep-breathing disorder was caused by cysts in her ovaries that produced too much male hormone. She had the symptoms of PCOS. The male hormone also caused her to have abnormal periods, to be overweight, and to have a male distribution of body hair. To relieve the immediate problem of daytime sleepiness and headaches and improve her quality of life, she was started on CPAP and as a result, her morning headaches stopped within days. She is seeing a gynecologist to manage her menstrual problems. She is also trying to lose weight and she feels great. Why did her abnormal male hormone production cause such a serious sleep problem? Because sex hormones affect women's bodies in such profound ways that even sleep is affected. In this woman, abnormal sex hormones had caused a sleep disorder that had jeopardized her life.

Changes in sex hormonal function during the menstrual cycle, whether the cycle is regular, irregular, or absent, can have profound effects on a woman's sleep and in the case of PCOS can result in sleep apnea. Most women (more than two thirds) experience some form of sleep disturbance linked to menstruation. As we saw in the case of the sleepy woman with irregular periods, medical science has learned to better understand and help women with these problems. Women should be aware that menstruation causes sleep problems and PMS can make sleep problems worse. Happily, these sleep problems can be treated once they have been identified.

4

How Pregnancy Affects Sleep

The Case of the Sleepy New Mother

Three months after giving birth to her first baby, a twenty-nine-year-old woman came to the sleep clinic in a state of exhaustion. Although most new mothers can expect to be fatigued by the demands of caring for a newborn, this woman's lack of restful sleep was affecting the quality of her life and the care she gave her baby. More disturbing was the fact that her sleep problems had occurred during pregnancy and she and her doctor had unknowingly put her life and the life of her child at risk. I was not surprised to find out that her full-term baby was underweight at birth—only five pounds, ten ounces— and that she'd had two prior miscarriages.

As I took her history, more details emerged that unfortunately illustrate how many doctors are unaware of the serious health consequences of women's sleep disorders. She had been thirty or forty pounds overweight before her pregnancy. She had felt sleepy in the daytime for about ten years, but the sleepiness had become much more severe once her pregnancy began. When she was six months pregnant, she complained to her doctor about this problem. She explained that she had become uncontrollably sleepy, often falling asleep even when she did not want to. Also, her snoring had become much worse since her pregnancy began. In fact, her husband had noticed for at least five years that she stopped breathing during sleep. Her doctor told her that it was possible that she had sleep apnea. Unfortunately, this doctor also advised her that she should not have any testing or treatment for a sleep disorder during pregnancy as it would be much safer to wait until the baby was born.

Now that her son was three months old, her major problem was that she could not stay awake long enough during the daytime to care for the baby properly. She fell asleep while watching TV or reading, during conversations, and even sometimes when driving her car—in spite of drinking six to eight cups of coffee each day.

She had a sleep test to measure how many times she stopped breathing while she slept. The study revealed that she had very severe obstructive sleep apnea syndrome, which caused her to stop breathing 136 times each hour, and almost every time it stopped her brain awakened for a few seconds. When breathing stops, the amount of oxygen in the blood decreases. Correspondingly, her blood oxygen level dropped to very dangerous levels; she spent about 11 percent of her sleep time with her blood oxygen level below 80 percent, meaning that during these times, 20 percent of her blood was not carrying oxygen, which put great stress on her cardiovascular system. These are the types of oxygen levels one sees in people sleeping on mountains 15,000 feet high. And this problem was also what put her life and the life of her child at risk and was the probable cause of the baby's low birth weight.

The doctor's decision not to pursue treatment during pregnancy was dangerous. It highlights how important it is that women become more aware of the impact of sleep disorders on their health. Although pregnancy is often a time of great joy and excitement for a woman, it can also seriously affect her sleep. In fact, pregnancy can be associated with two sleep disorders and treatment of the disorders can have beneficial effects on the developing baby. It is important that women and their doctors know about sleep problems that affect women during normal, multiple-birth, and high-risk pregnancies.

Normal Pregnancy

Unfortunately for mothers-to-be, sleep problems are a normal part of pregnancy. The 1998 National Sleep Foundation Poll on Women and Sleep found that almost 80 percent of women report more disturbed sleep during pregnancy than at other times. Most of these women mentioned their frequent need to urinate as the main reason. The other reasons were due to the symptoms of pregnancy: tiredness, pelvic pressure, insomnia, lower back pain, restless sleep, leg cramps, and sometimes frightening dreams. These symptoms vary within the three trimesters of pregnancy.

"I found many short rests during the day and night was all I could do to com-bat my sleepiness. I don't think there was one night that I didn't get up about six or seven times to use the washroom or to get water or simply could not sleep while I was pregnant. I would sleep an hour, then awaken every hour during my whole pregnancy."

—Twenty-nine-year-old first-time mother

First Trimester

When they first become pregnant some women feel great. Others feel terrible. Some women's sleep remains normal, while other women have poor sleep from the beginning and become more tired in the daytime. The reason for this is probably the effect on the brain of the rising progesterone levels. Morning sickness, which is quite common in the first twelve weeks of pregnancy, can also cause women to awaken with nausea, sometimes before they are ready to wake up.

Second Trimester

During the second trimester many women experience fatigue or tiredness due to the demands on the body, the carrying of extra weight, and sleep problems related to the enlarging uterus. Some women may find that though they are tired and want to spend more time in bed, they are instead awake more of the time restlessly tossing and turning, trying to find a comfortable position. A more extreme version of this restlessness is in fact a medically diagnosable sleep disorder called restless legs syndrome (see Chapter 11 for a more detailed discussion). Restless legs syndrome is an uncontrollable urge to move due to unpleasant tingling sensations in the legs. Some women develop other problems that keep them awake at night such as cramps in their calves or back pains.

In the second trimester, women may start to experience heartburn at night, which may continue until the end of pregnancy. The heartburn is caused by acid from the stomach going backward into the esophagus, the tube that carries food from the throat to the stomach. One contributor to this acid reflux is the extra pressure on the stomach caused by the enlarging uterus. There are also muscles at the bottom of the esophagus that normally keep acid from backing up from the stomach. These muscles may not work as well during pregnancy. Eating (especially spicy foods) in the two to three hours before bedtime may bring on or exacerbate this condition.

Third Trimester

During the last trimester of pregnancy, a wide range of problems can disrupt sleep. Some women develop nasal congestion, which may cause them to snore for the first time in their lives and/or develop the symptoms of sleep apnea. Some women have marked worsening of the restless legs syndrome. Others are breathless in certain positions in bed, or have severe back pains that interfere with their sleep. Also, closer to the birth, breathing may become more difficult because the uterus enlarges to the point where it actually pushes up on the diaphragm, the major breathing muscle. As pregnancy continues, the woman's sleep becomes more and more difficult because the discomfort and the sensation caused by the baby's movements can lead to general overall restlessness. It isn't uncommon for the expectant mother to stay awake all night toward the end of pregnancy. In fact, I have seen some women who, in the twenty-four hours before going into labor, just could not sleep and sometimes started to demonstrate what can best be described as nesting behavior. For example, one woman, on the night before her daughter was born, used a sewing machine for the first time in her life and sewed curtains for the new baby's room. She never used the sewing machine again! Some scientists have suggested that the poor quality of sleep that women may experience during pregnancy gets them ready for the requirements of spending a great deal of time taking care of the newborn at night.

Sleep in Multiple-Birth Pregnancy

The sleep problems pregnant women encounter are magnified in those women who carry multiple babies. Giving birth to several babies has become more common due to advances in fertility treatments. Because the uterus can enlarge dramatically in women carrying multiple babies, the discomfort can be greater. Most women pregnant with more than one baby can only sleep on their sides. They can't sleep at all on their stomachs, and sleeping on their backs can result in breathing difficulties. The nutritional demands of the developing babies make iron or vitamin deficiency more likely. In multiple-birth pregnancies, it is much more likely that the mother might have to be brought to the hospital early and perhaps placed on bed rest to prevent giving birth prematurely.

After Birth

Giving birth causes a dramatic drop in a women's progesterone level, and other hormones start to kick in so that she will be able to breastfeed. After the baby is born, if there are no complications for the mother or the baby, the mother's sleep can return to normal fairly quickly, although "normal" is a relative term while she's doing frequent night feedings. However, if a caesarean section was required for delivery of the baby, substantial pain and discomfort after the baby's birth can contribute to poor sleep. During delivery, either caesarean or vaginal, blood loss may occur. Additionally, some women develop iron deficiency during pregnancy because the developing baby saps iron from the mother. The iron deficiency combined with the blood loss can lead to a low red blood cell count known as anemia. This can result in severe daytime fatigue in the new mother who is also suffering from sleep deprivation due to nocturnal feedings or the baby's crying. Not surprisingly, the mother's focus switches from her own sleep to the sleep of her newborn as described in Chapter 2.

Dealing with Sleeplessness in Pregnancy

Alongside the two sleep disorders that are often seen in pregnant women—sleep apnea and restless legs syndrome—the normal discomfort, pain, and the sensation of feeling the developing baby and its movements also can cause sleeplessness. However, there are some steps to take that may give the pregnant woman some much-needed relief.

First of all, I must caution you against using some remedies that you may have used to combat insomnia before pregnancy. Sleeping pills, alcohol, or over-the-counter medications are *not* recommended to help a pregnant woman sleep through the night. Scientists simply do not know the long-term risks to the baby that these medications or drugs might engender.

Some of the Thirteen Commandments for People with Insomnia found in Chapter 10, pages 127 and 128 may prove useful, and the additional suggestions reviewed next may help.

Short naps can be extremely helpful. If they are too long, they might interfere with nighttime sleep. A good time to nap is in the early afternoon, and the naps should be no longer than twenty or thirty minutes.

Women who get heartburn at night should avoid spicy food, acidic fruit juices, and alcohol. She should avoid big meals, and should probably not eat in the two to three hours before going to sleep. Even during the daytime these women should not lie down for at least a half hour after eating. Sleeping on several pillows or even in a recliner type chair might be effective if the heartburn is severe. Speak to your doctor if the heartburn becomes an important problem interfering with sleep. Your doctor might prescribe an antacid such as Tums, which will have the added benefit of providing a source of calcium. A glass of skim milk may offer temporary relief for a few minutes. Whole milk may actually cause more acid to form after initial relief. The woman should be careful not to drink too much milk to relieve heartburn as the extra calories may lead to extra weight, which can in turn lead to sleep apnea.

Perhaps the most effective way to improve sleep during pregnancy is to experiment until you find the most comfortable position for sleeping. Most women have to train themselves to sleep in a different position than they did before pregnancy. For instance, women who tended to sleep on their stomachs can no longer do this and women who slept on their backs might now find it too difficult to breathe. Also, sleeping flat on the back might result in the uterus pressing on the main artery of the woman's body, the aorta, which could reduce blood flow to the baby. For many women, sleeping on their side becomes the most comfortable position, and this will increase blood flow to the baby, because this will relieve pressure on the aorta. Those who are not used to sleeping on their sides might find that putting a pillow between their knees can improve their comfort level. Unfortunately there is no absolute remedy for pregnancy-related sleeplessness except giving birth.

Restless Legs Syndrome

Restless legs syndrome (RLS), which is described in more detail in Chapter 11, frequently occurs during pregnancy. Many women with RLS remember their first episode of the disorder occurring during a pregnancy. Women with RLS feel an irresistible urge to move their legs at bedtime. Moving or walking relieves this urge. In some patients, RLS is inherited. Women who have inherited RLS are much more likely to have increased symptoms of restlessness and a crawly sensation under their skin during pregnancy.

A study from the University of California published in 2001 researched the likelihood of developing RLS during pregnancy. None of the women studied had restless legs syndrome before they became pregnant, but by the end of their pregnancies, 23 percent of them were afflicted. They also had sleeplessness and a depressed mood. Those who developed restless legs syndrome were found to be iron deficient and/or folic acid deficient before becoming pregnant. These are known causes of RLS. So common sense mandates that women who develop restless legs syndrome during pregnancy have their iron status checked by a doctor. They should probably be prescribed a multivitamin preparation containing folic acid. If they have an iron deficiency, it should be treated. In addition to RLS, there is another reason for pregnant women to take folic acid. It has been shown that mothers who take folic acid have a reduction in the number of children born with a neurological malformation.

In most women, the restless legs syndrome goes away with childbirth, although for some women the symptoms brought on by pregnancy may go on indefinitely.

Snoring and Pregnancy

Some research studies have shown a frightening connection between snoring and a potentially dangerous medical condition called preeclampsia, a form of high blood pressure that can occur in pregnancy. The condition damages the kidneys, which causes a great deal of protein to be lost in the urine. Studies have found that pregnant women who snore are twice as likely to develop preeclampsia compared to those who do not snore. Also, women with this condition are twice as likely to have smaller babies if they snore during pregnancy. Affecting about 7 percent of pregnant women, preeclampsia usually begins after twenty weeks into the pregnancy. Blood pressure goes up causing damage to the kidneys. There may be few symptoms, as high blood pressure and kidney problems can be difficult to detect without testing. Early in the pregnancy, the woman might have headaches or severe swelling of the ankles. Thus, if a woman begins to snore while she's pregnant, she should have her blood pressure and urine checked, especially if she has headaches and swollen ankles. About one in twenty women with preeclampsia develop seizures as well as very severe high blood pressure and other problems. This even more serious condition is called eclampsia. Both conditions usually resolve soon after childbirth. Preeclampsia and eclampsia obviously require medical care but highlight the importance of talking with your doctor about sleep problems—even seemingly insignificant ones such as snoring.

Sleep Apnea

As described earlier, sleep apnea is a disorder in which a person stops breathing during sleep. Some women have sleep apnea before they become pregnant and the condition worsens during pregnancy. In other women, the apnea develops during pregnancy. The symptoms are quite similar to sleep apnea in nonpregnant women—mainly snoring, pauses in breathing during sleep, and severe daytime sleepiness. In addition to these symptoms, the woman might complain of other problems, such as getting up frequently at night to urinate.

It has been suggested that women with sleep apnea are more likely to have miscarriages. The danger with sleep apnea is that the blood oxygen level in the mother might drop to very low levels. Because the baby is dependent on the mother for oxygen, a pregnant woman with sleep apnea must be treated as soon as possible. The usual treatment would be a mask worn over the nose, which would increase pressure in the breathing passage, thus opening it. This treatment is called continuous positive airway pressure (CPAP). The system can be used by people who sleep on their sides, as pregnant women do.

Another important reason to treat women who have sleep apnea is that after the baby is born, the new mother will have many responsibilities. Treatment of sleep apnea will help ensure a good night's sleep so that the new mom can be wide awake and alert during the day to cope with the demands of a new baby. This is not easy for any woman, but is extremely difficult for a woman with untreated sleep apnea. For example, the very first woman I saw who had sleep apnea was diagnosed right after delivering a baby in our hospital. She could not stay awake and had to be started on emergency treatment, because there was no one else to care for her child.

Postpartum Mood Changes and Depression

Although new mothers are usually euphoric after giving birth, some women have changes in mood that can range from feeling temporarily blue to having an episode of full-blown clinical depression. Sleeplessness is a very common symptom of depression. It is believed that these abnormal moods are caused by reduction in the levels of the hormone progesterone. Women who have severe depression after childbirth very often have had prior depressive episodes, which may have gone undiagnosed. Postpartum depression can have devastating results (for example, suicide or harming the newborn) and new mothers who have depressive symptoms (see Chapter 16) should receive immediate medical attention.

Back to the Sleepy New Mother

After the first sleep test, which confirmed her severe sleep apnea, she was tested on CPAP to see whether the machine kept her breathing passage open and how much pressure was needed. The result was a dramatic improvement—her apnea episodes were gone. Her sleep became completely normal and her blood-oxygen levels never decreased to their previously dangerous depths. Two months later, after using the CPAP at home every night, she told me she felt great because the CPAP treatment was highly effective and she was no longer sleepy. "I can't sleep without it," she said. "Everyone says I'm better." With the assurance of a good night's rest, she felt better able to cope with her daily responsibilities.

The vast majority of women have problems with sleep during pregnancy. Sleeplessness can be mild or severe. Mild forms are often caused by having to go to the bathroom or by the discomfort from the enlarging uterus and movements of the baby. Severe sleeplessness may stem from disorders such as restless legs syndrome. In some pregnant women, snoring is a clue that preeclampsia or sleep apnea is present. These conditions may pose a danger to both mother and baby. Thankfully most sleep problems in pregnancy improve after the birth of the baby. The end of a woman's reproductive years, however, is not the end of a woman's bout with sleeplessness. After periods end and menopause arrives, sleep is often disturbed again. In the reproductive years, fluctuating sex hormone levels are often the cause; in the menopausal years, which we cover next, the lack of sex hormones is the main cause.

5

How Menopause Affects Sleep

The Case of the Sweaty Insomniac

Sitting in front of me was a fidgety, thin, and anxious fifty-one-year-old. Her family doctor had referred her to me because she had been complaining of a great deal of difficulty both falling asleep and staying asleep. Most nights after tossing and turning in bed, trying to get comfortable enough to nod off, she would fall asleep but then frustratingly, wouldn't sleep through the night. Instead, she would find herself awake several times, often covered in sweat, with the back of her head and her pillow soaked in perspiration. Sometimes, she awakened with her heart pounding, which frightened her. As a result of the poor nighttime sleep, in the daytime she always felt dragged out. Naturally, all this was affecting the rest of her life.

She could not pinpoint any cause for her sleeplessness. There were no problems at home or at work, nor could she attribute her sleeplessness to any problems with her mood.

Her family doctor had suggested sleeping pills, but she did not like taking pills and preferred to find an alternative way of treating her sleep problems.

Finally, she began to worry about this problem during the day, causing her to lose weight and she worried about it at night, which further exacerbated her difficulties in falling asleep. Only a few disorders commonly cause this constellation of symptoms. After I asked a few questions about specific symptoms, I knew I was on the correct path toward a diagnosis.

Menopause

Menopause refers to the ending of the reproductive phase of a woman's life, a transition experienced by all women. The term refers to the time after menstrual cycles have ceased. The time around which the production of estrogen starts to become irregular, fluctuate, and decrease is sometimes called the perimenopause. This may begin several years before menopause.

Menopause does not usually come on abruptly. At first menstrual cycles may become irregular or there may be increased time between periods. The amount of bleeding with each may vary. Most doctors agree that menopause is established if periods have been absent for a year.

The age at which menopause occurs varies. In some women, it may start in their early forties while for other women it may begin beyond the age of 50. In North America, for most women, the age of menopause ranges between forty-eight and fifty-five years with the average being roughly about fifty-one years. Women may also have early menopause because their ovaries were surgically removed for medical reasons. Women who have been treated for breast cancer are much more likely than other women to have menopausal symptoms, and the symptoms are particularly common in women who have been or are on tamoxifen. Tamoxifen is an anti-estrogen that counteracts the effects of the female hormone estrogen on breast cancer cells.

Menopause occurs when the ovaries no longer produce estrogen. Just as there were dramatic changes in organ systems during adolescence when the ovaries started to produce estrogen, the abrupt reduction of estrogen production during this later period in a woman's life also results in a wide variety of effects. When menopause occurs abruptly—for example, after surgical removal of the ovaries—symptoms can be quite severe. In other women, there are relatively few symptoms with menopause. Menopause is not a disease; it is a normal physiological state.

The Dreaded Hot Flash

In menopause, the way a woman's body regulates its temperature can change, often to her extreme discomfort. The hot flash is one of the most unpleasant symptoms of menopause; unfortunately it is experienced by between 80 and 90 percent of perimenopausal women. A study published in 2003 showed that women who smoke cigarettes or are obese are twice as likely as normal-weight nonsmokers to have severe hot flashes. When a woman experiences a hot flash she feels her body temperature increasing. In fact, it does increase by a small amount. This fools the hypothalamus, the part of the brain that regulates body temperature. Many scientists believe that reduced estrogen levels, especially if they are reduced rapidly, and release of some hormones from the pituitary gland cause the hypothalamus to respond as if the body is overheated. This in turn activates the mechanisms the body uses to rid itself of excess heat. These mechanisms redirect blood flow to the skin and cause sweating of the same type that occurs with vigorous exercise.

"At first, I did not realize my wife had a problem at all. I thought that I had a problem. I was waking up feeling really cold in the middle of the night and found, when I checked, that the thermostat was set much lower than normal. After a few nights of this I discovered that my wife had been setting the temperature much lower."

—Husband of a perimenopausal woman

The main mechanism the body uses to get rid of extra heat is a process called vasodilatation (*vaso* means "vessel" *dilatation* refers to enlargement of the size of the vessels). This means that blood vessels enlarge and increase blood flow to the skin. So even though the woman feels hot, her body is actually losing heat. It is this increase in blood flow that results in the sudden flushing sensation known as a hot flash. It will cause the woman to feel hot and flushed enough to be sweaty, which often is very uncomfortable. When this happens at night, the woman may experience night sweats that adversely affect her sleep. Both estrogen and progesterone replacement can stop hot flashes. There will be more about these treatments later in the chapter.

"My wife was no longer cuddling up next to me in the bed. She thought that there must be something wrong with me, that I was somehow too warm."

—Husband of a perimenopausal woman

The episode usually begins with the perception of feeling hot, then flushing of the face, which may then spread to elsewhere on the body. Some say that they become hot on their chest first and then it moves up. The average episode is roughly three minutes long, but can seem like an eternity to the woman. Usually, hot flashes are present for one to five years but some women experience them for more than ten years. Many women who experience hot flashes have more than ten episodes per day, which can be quite disruptive to their lives. Some women have episodes as infrequently as once every month.

At the end of the hot flash, there may be heavy sweating over the part of the body that had been involved in the flush. When these episodes occur during sleep, as they frequently do, the profuse sweating may bother women so much that they aren't able to get comfortable, or they might have to change their bedclothes. To make matters worse, at the end of the hot flash, the hypothalamus eventually registers that it has cooled the body too much, and so it activates mechanisms to increase the body temperature. This may lead to the woman feeling cold and clammy.

Other Effects

Hot flashes are a well known and familiar symptom of menopause but there are other effects that are due to the reduction of estrogen and progesterone in a menopausal woman's body. For instance, an important effect of reduction of estrogen is in the anatomy of the reproductive system, particularly in the vagina. This results in the walls of the vagina becoming thinner along with a decrease in the production of lubricating fluid. The result may be painful sexual intercourse and a loss of interest in sexual intimacy. Also, many women are subject to dramatic metabolic changes during menopause. Often this manifests as weight gain, which may increase the likelihood of or put a woman at risk for developing sleep apnea, a potentially dangerous disorder in which people stop breathing repetitively during sleep (see Chapter 12). Aside from estrogen, another important sex hormone that decreases with menopause is progesterone. This hormone is believed to have a protective effect against the development of sleep apnea. The combination of increased weight and decreased progesterone dramatically increases the risk of a woman's developing obstructive sleep apnea during menopause. Finally, another very important change due to menopause is that women are at increased risk for cardiovascular disease, cancer, bone fractures, and other conditions. As we will discuss later in this chapter, recent research has muddied the waters about whether hormone replacement prevents or worsens these problems.

Emotional Effects of Menopause Also Affect Sleep

One often overlooked issue is the impact of all the physiologic changes that occur at this time combined with external factors such as children leaving home and aging parents or other family members. Many women often may develop a mood disorder at this time. All these changes and the fluctuating hormone levels can cause emotional ups and downs.

"We finally realized what the problem was when she started to toss and turn, cover herself, uncover herself and simply not be able to get comfortable and she started to wake me up. She started to have nights that were abnormal to the point where she was having sleepiness during the daytime. This had never happened before."

—Husband of a perimenopausal woman

Menopause and Sleep Problems

More than one-third of women in North America today are menopausal or postmenopausal. Of those women, about 40 percent have sleep problems. A 2003 study reported that the highest rates of sleep problems were found in women whose menopause was caused by removal of the ovaries (48 percent of women with surgical menopause had sleep problems), and those late in perimenopause (45 percent). The rates of sleep problems in menopause were much lower in Japanese women (20 percent) versus white women (40 percent).

Women who are menopausal or postmenopausal are more likely to have insomnia than when they were premenopausal. A poll conducted on women's sleep in 1998 found that 44 percent of women going through menopause and 28 percent of postmenopausal women have hot flashes at night; on the average they had hot flashes three nights a week. This is severe enough to cause trouble sleeping or insomnia an average of five days each month. Not all groups have hot flashes to the same extent. The research study from 2001, mentioned above, reported the percentage of women between ages forty and fifty-five who had night sweats: African-American 36 percent; Hispanic 25 percent; Caucasian 21 percent; Chinese 11 percent; and Japanese 9 percent.

However, not all difficulty in sleeping is caused by hot flashes. Menopausal or postmenopausal women are more likely to have to go to the bathroom at night (43 percent) compared to premenopausal women (34 percent). Twenty percent of menopausal or postmenopausal women use prescription medications to help them sleep compared to 8 percent of premenopausal women.

Dealing with Sleep Problems Related to Hot Flashes

As smoking and being overweight make it more likely that a woman will have severe hot flashes, you should try to stop smoking and bring your weight down if you have these problems. Menopausal or postmenopausal women on hormone replacement drugs are less likely to have hot flashes during sleep. However, due to the perceived risks involved with such medication, many women first try to "sweat it out" without any treatment for their hot flashes. The symptoms usually improve with time, with episodes becoming less frequent and less severe. Women learn what works best for them, whether it's changing what they wear so they can remove layers when a hot flash comes on, or switching to lighter bedclothes, sheets, and comforters. Special fabrics that wick away sweat from the body and help keep athletes dry are now being used for women's bed clothes. Such fabrics include PowerDry (one retailer is www.menowear.com) and CoolMax (one retailer is www.hotcoolwear.com). Some women find that a drink of cold water when a flash begins may help and many will keep a large glass of cold water on their nightstand. If this doesn't give some relief or if you feel you need more help, it is probably time to seek information or help from your doctor.

What to Expect from Your Doctor

Postmenopausal women are at an increased risk for various medical conditions such as heart disease, high blood pressure, osteoporosis (bone thinning), and cancer. A woman seeking medical help should expect her doctor to measure her blood pressure and suggest or conduct the following tests: a pap smear, tests of blood lipids (cholesterol and triglycerides, which if abnormal increase the risk of heart disease), a breast examination, and often a mammogram. Depending on risk factors and your local medical community, the doctor may order bone density tests. This is because osteoporosis becomes such a common problem in postmenopausal women. Rarely, if the diagnosis of menopause is not clear, the doctor may order measurements of serum follicle stimulating hormone (FSH) and luteinizing hormone (LH). The levels of these two hormones, which change during the normal menstrual cycle, remain elevated when menopause has occurred.

Given the important research reported in 2002 and 2003 that has confused many patients and doctors, expect the doctor to review current research on hormone and other therapy, and discuss risks based on your personal and family medical history. Have you had cancer, stroke, cardiovascular disease, or blood clots in the legs or lungs? Is there a family history of cancer, osteoporosis, bone fractures, and cardiovascular disease? The doctor might order tests to check your lipid profile, to see if you are at increased risk of heart disease. All this information can be useful in deciding how to deal with the menopausal symptoms.

Hormone Replacement Therapy (HRT)

Until the summer of 2002, it was widely believed by medical scientists and the public that hormone replacement therapy effectively helped to prevent cardiovascular disease, osteoporosis, and other disorders that appear to be more common in postmenopausal women. Research published in July of that year in the *Journal of the American Medical Association (JAMA)*, however, concluded that there might *not* be a net benefit in using HRT. The research pointed out there may actually be a net risk. The research showed a small (but statistically significant) increase in myocardial infarctions (heart attacks) and stroke in HRT users, but a decrease in colon cancer and fractures. It concluded that there did not seem to be a net benefit in using HRT for the general population of postmenopausal women. Although there were more reported heart attacks in women taking HRT, there was actually no difference in death rate. A report published in *JAMA* in May 2003 found that in postmenopausal women aged sixty-five or older, HRT composed of estrogen plus a progesterone increased the probable risk for Alzheimer's disease.

Nevertheless, the best strategy for a woman who has severe sleep difficulties due to menopause is to discuss with her doctor the pros and cons of using HRT medication specific to her medical condition and symptoms. If life with hot flashes is unbearable and results in fragmented sleep and irritability, then it may be worthwhile to consider using this medication. Similarly, if sleep apnea were to come on abruptly with menopause, then it would seem prudent to see whether HRT might reverse the problem.

I wish there were a simple answer to the dilemma of whether to use HRT for most women who are having sleep problems caused by menopause.

Who Should Definitely Not Use HRT

There are some women who should not use HRT because they have a disorder that might be made worse by hormone treatments. For instance, some tumors depend on estrogen for growth. These include breast cancer, cancer of the endometrium (lining of the uterus), and melanoma (pigmented cancer of the skin). People who have had blood clots in their legs, especially if the clots have traveled elsewhere in the body, (for example, the lungs) should not use HRT because hormones increase the risk of these dangerous clots.

Women who have a strong family history of the disorders mentioned in the previous paragraph should discuss using HRT with their doctor. They should have available as much specific information about their own blood relatives' conditions as possible.

Alternative Treatments for Menopause Symptoms

Even before the recent research findings about HRT, many women were reluctant to use prescribed medications. Many women stopped using HRT when the findings were released. Thus, there is great interest in knowing what else might help.

"Natural" Treatments

There is a widespread belief among many people that a substance that is natural is by nature safer than a substance that has been manufactured or synthesized. One cannot assume that an estrogen-like product from soy or an herb is intrinsically safer than an estrogen-like product made in a lab or produced from chemicals obtained from the urine of pregnant mares. Women who have had breast cancer and are concerned about estrogen increasing their risk should be equally concerned about any substance claiming to have estrogen or estrogen-like properties.

Soy and Soy Products

Certain molecules in some plants can affect estrogen receptors in humans. These compounds, called phytoestrogens, which are chemically quite different than human-produced estrogens, are found in soy. Although there are more than a hundred publications in the medical literature about the use of soy in menopause, the results are contradictory. No detailed reports on sleep have been published. Very few randomized controlled trials (RCT) have examined the use of soy or other alternative treatments of menopause. This type of medical study compares the use of a treatment versus a placebo to see scientifically whether the specific treatment actually is more beneficial than no treatment.

Hot flashes are much less common in Japanese women. Some scientists believe that this may be related to the Japanese diet, which features a great many soy products. A study from Japan published in 1999 showed that not all soy products were the same in reducing menopause symptoms; it wasn't the amount of soy that was important, but the type of soy. In Japanese women the severity of hot flashes was reduced much more by their intake of fermented soy products rather nonfermented soy products. Examples of fermented soy products are miso and natto.

How much soy is needed? Research suggests using between 30 and 60 grams of soy daily. Examples of fermented soy products that you might find in a traditional Asian grocery (or perhaps your grocery), or sometimes a health food store include miso, natto, and tempeh. For most of these products ½ cup contains 12 to 16 grams of protein. Table 5-1 shows how much soy in various forms one would need to take to reach 30 to 60 grams. Note that the amounts are large and gastrointestinal side effects (gas and sometimes diarrhea) are common.

Table 5-1 Soy Protein in Various Forms

Product	Size of portion	Amount of soy protein	Calories in portion	Amount needed to reach 30 grams soy intake daily
Tofu	3 ounces	10 grams	90	9 ounces
Soy milk	1 cup	3–10 grams*		3–10 cups
Low fat			90	
Regular			140	
Soy flour	½ cup	20 grams	220	¾ cup
Soy protein isolate	1 tbs	12.5 grams	55	2½ tbs

*Read the labels of all of these products, as amounts will vary with manufacturer. Data in this table is based on a medical article by doctors Morelli and Naquin published in *American Family Physician*, July 2002.

Herbal Products

The following herbal products are used for menopausal symptoms: black cohosh, flax seed, dong quai, kava, chasteberry, and primrose. A medical article from Columbia University reviewed all studies published up to the end of 2002 regarding the use of plant products for menopause. The lack of long-term studies using natural products precludes recommending the use of such remedies because we do not know if they are safe when used for years or decades. There are no detailed studies on their effects on sleep.

Kava has been linked to a rare but potentially fatal liver problem. The U.S. FDA has issued a consumer alert warning people about this problem. Health Canada concluded that there was insufficient scientific support for the safe use of kava, which therefore posed an unacceptable risk to health. In Canada kava has been recalled from the market.

The Bottom Line

After talking to their doctor, and perhaps doing some research of their own, women seeking to treat sleep problems caused by night sweats and hot flashes should base their decisions on what they believe is right for them. Some authorities recommend the use of HRT for four years and then annual reevaluation. The individual woman must decide whether or not the sleep symptoms caused by estrogen deficiency are sufficiently severe and disruptive to warrant treatment. Although such treatment will improve the symptoms, she must take into consideration that she may be increasing her risk of cardiovascular disease and breast cancer. She should also take into consideration that HRT may carry with it the possible benefit of reducing risk of gastrointestinal cancer and problems related to osteoporosis. Each woman should take her own family history into account.

What about alternative treatments? Thus far no strong scientific evidence supports the use of any "natural" product for the long-term treatment of menopausal symptoms, and no research has examined the long-term effects of using these products. Until better data is available, women will just have to decide for themselves whether it is worth trying these treatments. Many women certainly do use them. In the next few years, as more scientific data becomes available, women should do online research; a good place to start is www.medlineplus.gov.

Other Disorders That Cause Sleeplessness in Postmenopausal Women

Whether they have hot flashes or not, many menopausal women develop insomnia. The reasons for this may be related to the fact that estrogen has many effects on the central nervous system. It is possible that the decrease of estrogen affects the centers of the nervous system that are involved with sleep.

Also, some diseases occur more frequently in older people and, thus, in postmenopausal women. These include:

- Mood disorders (Chapter 16)
- Movement disorders (Chapter 11)
- Painful conditions, including arthritis (Chapter 15)
- Diabetes (Chapter 15)
- Various cancers (Chapter 15)

Virtually any disease in this group—and often the medications used to treat them—may be associated with sleep problems. For a woman suffering from one or more of these conditions, the estrogen deficiency of menopause simply complicates an already troublesome part of life.

It is important to consider breast cancer in this chapter, not because it occurs more often in the postmenopausal period, but because the treatment of breast cancer often results in acute estrogen deficiency.

Breast Cancer

Breast cancer is a major problem for women before and after menopause. The treatment of breast cancer may result in estrogen deficiency. Women who are undergoing or have undergone treatment for breast cancer may have hot flashes that are often more severe than in women going through a normal menopause. In one study, two thirds of women treated for breast cancer had hot flashes; almost all developed insomnia and about a third developed a major depressive disorder.

In addition to the anxiety of first being confronted with a breast cancer diagnosis, the patient still has to face treatment, which often causes great emotional distress. Surgery, loss of a breast and the resulting damage to a woman's self-image, and the use of drugs that may lead to acute menopausal symptoms and hair loss can all lead to sleeplessness. Chemotherapy and radiation therapy can also lead to insomnia and daytime tiredness. Chapter 15 reviews sleep problems in medical conditions including cancer.

Breast cancer patients cannot use estrogen-containing medications (HRT) to stop the hot flashes because tumor cells grow more rapidly when exposed to estrogen; thus, these drugs may worsen the woman's prognosis. Many women have tried soy products, but the efficacy and safety of such treatments in breast cancer are not known. It is worth reemphasizing that we do not know at this time whether the estrogen-like chemical in soy is any safer than estrogen in pill form.

These patients may benefit from some of the treatments suggested for insomnia patients (see Chapter 10). In particular, treatment with a psychologist, pain medications, or sleep-promoting medications may help them sleep through the most difficult periods. Some patients who develop major depression may require psychiatric treatment. Recent research is beginning to focus on improving the daytime fatigue in these patients with wakefulness-promoting drugs such as modafinil (see Chapter 20).

Sleep Apnea

Although for many years doctors believed that sleep apnea was rare in women, this disorder is actually extremely common, affecting roughly 2 percent of adult women. Most women with sleep apnea are postmenopausal; the average woman with sleep apnea is about fifty years old. Harvard University research published in *JAMA* in 2003 suggests that by age fifty, women represent just about the same number of new sleep apnea cases as men. Just as estrogen and progesterone before menopause seem to protect women from cardiovascular disease, these hormones also seemed to protect women from sleep apnea. Progesterone, which is produced during the menstrual cycle, stimulates breathing, and estrogen is probably responsible for where fat is deposited in a woman's body. When premenopausal women become obese they tend not to have fat deposited in the neck that would increase the risk of apnea.

As a group, women with sleep apnea are older and heavier than are men with the disorder. A Pennsylvania study showed that sleep apnea was much more common in postmenopausal women (2.7 percent) compared to premenopausal women (less than 1 percent). The same group found that almost all premenopausal women, and postmenopausal women on hormone replacement therapy (HRT), with sleep apnea were overweight. While only half of postmenopausal women with apnea not on HRT, were obese. Postmenopausal women on HRT had apnea less frequently (0.5 percent of them) than postmenopausal women not on HRT. Thus, HRT seems to protect against developing sleep apnea. Other researchers have found that apnea is much more common in postmenopausal women, affecting perhaps 10 percent of them.

A recently discovered hormone, leptin, which is produced by fat cells may stimulate breathing in obese women and prevent them from developing apnea. It has been suggested that in extreme obesity, the breathing centers of the brain no longer respond to the leptin. A research group in Australia reported that breathing failure in massively overweight women may be caused by resistance in the brain to the effects of leptin.

Treatment of Sleep Apnea in Postmenopausal Women

Women with symptoms suggesting sleep apnea are evaluated exactly as men are, and they receive the same treatments. The focus is on using CPAP, encouraging weight loss, and avoiding alcohol. See Chapter 12 for more details. An obvious question is whether postmenopausal women with apnea should be treated with hormones. There are several articles in the medical literature that could be considered pilot studies, or reports of individual cases. Most of the authors concluded that there may be a benefit in treating such postmenopausal women with hormones (especially estrogen). One paper suggested that progesterone may not be important. Several research studies now suggest that the treatment of apnea in postmenopausal women might include HRT. Large randomized studies are needed to establish whether HRT works and what constitutes the correct dosage. That's one more item for modern medicine's to-do list.

Back to the Sweaty Insomniac

Only a small number of disorders could explain the symptoms of the woman with insomnia who woke up in a sweat and with her heart beating rapidly. A strong possibility was that these symptoms were due to perimenopause. She underwent blood tests to rule out excess thyroid secretion as a cause of her symptoms; this disease can cause night sweats (see Chapter 15). She had a sleep test, which did not demonstrate that she was suffering from restless legs syndrome or dangerous cardiac rhythms during sleep.

Her thyroid function and the amount of iron in her body were normal. She did not have an abnormal heartbeat when she slept or while awake. However, her heart rate increased when she woke up in the night. The most impressive part of her sleep study was not the many squiggly lines on her chart, but the video that showed her tossing and turning and constantly changing her position. Even when she slept, she was pulling her blanket off and then on, looking frustrated when she awakened during the night. At the end of all this testing, the most obvious diagnosis was the one that was on top of the list in the first place: she had perimenopausal symptoms. Her estrogen levels were dropping and she was experiencing a sleep disorder typical of women in perimenopause. Basically, she was having hot flashes and sweats while she slept. We discussed treatment options including hormone replacement therapy. All the media stories about the potential dangers of hormone replacement treatment had spooked her and she was reluctant to use any medications. She elected to sweat it through.

Hormone levels affect women's sleep throughout their lives. Women and their doctors are beginning to understand the relationship between hormones and sleep. In the next few chapters we will see that besides the sleep problems caused by hormones, women also have roles in the family and the twenty-four/seven world that can adversely affect their sleep.

PART II

DO I HAVE A SLEEP PROBLEM?

6

How to Tell If You
Have a Sleep Problem

The Case of the Tired Man with Cancer

There are times when a doctor thinks, "I wish I had been consulted on this case earlier." This was one of those times. The man sitting in front of me had been complaining of tiredness for about two years. His wife confirmed his lack of energy. At first his family doctor simply had assumed he was depressed. After treatment for depression didn't work and routine blood tests revealed nothing unusual, the symptom was simply ignored. The man and his wife were resigned to his being tired. The symptom continued and became more and more severe, and after about a year his wife insisted that the doctor do more tests. One of the tests revealed blood in his stools. This quickly led to the diagnosis of colon cancer and the patient had surgery. The patient had been referred to me because he had insomnia, and his doctor assumed that the insomnia was caused by anxiety over the cancer diagnosis.

The patient and the doctor had interacted many times in the two years, but were really not communicating. Had they been communicating, the cancer might have been picked up much sooner.

People who think they have a sleep disorder try to describe their symptoms using words that are familiar, but those words often mean something quite different to a doctor who is trying to interpret the symptoms. This miscommunication might stand in the way of a correct diagnosis, and it is often a major obstacle for women seeking help for their sleep problems.

In this chapter you will learn how to tell if you have a sleep problem, and how to tell your doctor about it. We will review the best words to describe symptoms of sleep disorders to help make sure that you and your doctor are speaking the same language. I will also provide you with some tools to help you learn whether you have a sleep disorder. These tools are only guidelines and they are not perfect. If you believe that you may have a sleep problem, you should seek help from your doctor.

Sleepiness

"I am tired," "I have fatigue," "I have no energy," "I am exhausted" are all phrases that patients often use to describe how they feel when discussing a sleep problem with a doctor. For most people, the word *tired* refers to a physical lack of strength, a feeling that it takes too much effort to engage in any activity or remain alert. You might feel this way after a hard day of skiing or doing yard work—or if you had a medical condition that made you physically weak. People with lung or heart diseases might also use the word to describe their inability to perform certain activities because of breathlessness.

To sleep scientists, the word *fatigue* refers to a lack of strength or an inability to perform daily tasks as a result of prolonged activity. The activity could be physical or mental. Patients more commonly use the expression *no energy*, which is vague. Many people say they have *no energy* when they actually mean they are very sleepy. Some doctors may hear these words and interpret the symptoms to mean excessive sleepiness and refer the patient to a sleep clinic. However, other doctors who hear these same expressions of symptoms might interpret them to signal depression and end up treating the patient for that.

Rather than use these words, you should describe what actually *happens*. For example, rather than saying "I am tired," tell the doctor something like: "I always fall asleep watching TV," "I fall asleep at my computer," and so forth. Unless you and your doctor are talking the same language, you might very well be misdiagnosed.

But how can you tell if you are sleepy? You are sleepy if you have the urge to fall asleep at the wrong time and place. One commonly used questionnaire

Figure 6-1 Epworth Sleepiness Scale

Using the following scale, circle the *most appropriate number* for each situation.

0 = would doze *less than once a month*

1 = *slight* chance of dozing

2 = *moderate* chance of dozing

3 = *high* chance of dozing

Situation	Chance of Dozing			
Sitting and reading	0	1	2	3
Watching TV	0	1	2	3
Sitting, inactive in a public place (e.g., a theater or meeting)	0	1	2	3
As a passenger in a car for an hour without break	0	1	2	3
Lying down to rest in the afternoon (when circumstances permit)	0	1	2	3
Sitting and talking quietly to someone	0	1	2	3
Sitting quietly after a lunch without alcohol	0	1	2	3
In a car, while stopped for a few minutes in traffic	0	1	2	3
Add the eight numbers you have circled	**TOTAL**			

to gauge sleepiness in adults is the Epworth Sleepiness Score developed by Dr. Murray Johns at the Epworth Hospital in Australia. In Figure 6-1, circle the number (0 to 3) that describes how likely you are to fall asleep in different situations. Then add up the eight numbers you have circled.

People who have a total score of more than 12 are as sleepy as people with sleep apnea. People with a score of more than 15 are at very high risk of falling asleep when they don't want to. Figure 6-2 shows the range of values seen in about 90 percent of people. I have seen some sleep apnea patients who score 3 and others who score 24. Of course people who are sleep deprived and are medically normal might have very high values as well.

Some people do not believe that they are sleepy if the sleep disorder has come on gradually. Because they have become accustomed to feeling sleepy,

Figure 6-2 Range of Epworth Scores

Normals	Less than 9
Obstructive sleep apnea (Chapter 12)	6–17
Narcolepsy (Chapter 13)	14–20
Insomnia (Chapter 10)	0–6
Movement disorder (Chapter 11)	5–13

they may believe that what they feel is normal; consequently, they may actually deny the symptom. Even if such a person denies being sleepy, research has shown that he or she may be a hazard behind the wheel or at risk for injury.

Other Faces of Sleepiness

A patient may be feeling that something is not right, but may be unable or unwilling to confront these feelings or experiences that may be the direct result of inadequate sleep or a sleep disorder. For instance, you might complain of poor memory and concentration and inability to focus, but not recognize that the root of these problems is sleepiness. Although you may not see it, other people may notice that you are sleepy.

Some people when they are sleepy develop irritability and sometimes a personality change. They might become angry easily or for no reason. They might not interact with others at social occasions or might appear disinterested. Some people with more severe sleepiness may demonstrate automatic behavior during which they perform activities that might at first appear normal but actually are inappropriate. For example, a woman experiencing that level of sleepiness might find herself loading the dishes into an oven instead of a dishwasher. She will not generally have any memory of this type of robot-like behavior. I have seen patients who, while in the state of automatic behavior, have committed violent acts on others and their property without any memory of the incident.

Some people experience a form of sleepiness called sleep drunkenness. After awakening, these people have much more difficulty becoming alert than the average person. This grogginess might continue for several minutes to an hour or more. This is common in severely sleep-deprived people.

A doctor has to sort carefully through these behaviors as described by their patients to discover the sleep deprivation that may possibly be caused by a sleep disorder.

Other Symptoms of Sleep Disorders

Being sleepy or being unable to fall asleep are not the only symptoms of sleep problems. There are many types of sleep disorders. In the next section, I describe symptoms that provide clues to some of these sleep problems. Some of the symptoms are those of disorders that might require treatment or referral to a sleep clinic.

Dreaming While Not Quite Asleep

Some people, in the minutes before falling asleep and sometimes in the minutes directly after falling asleep, may sometimes have very frightening dreams that include sounds, visually rich images, and even sometimes sensations in various parts of the body. These dreams are called *hypnagogic hallucinations*. They are not normal. People don't normally dream unless they have been asleep for about ninety minutes. However, a sleep-deprived person may have hypnagogic hallucinations, and they are quite common in people who have narcolepsy (see Chapter 13). If you experience this type of half-awake hallucination more than once or twice a month, discuss this symptom with your doctor.

Paralyzed on Awakening

Sometimes people awaken during the night, and notice that they cannot move. Usually this is because they have awakened from a dream, although they might not remember the dream. This symptom might last a few seconds to a few minutes, can be frightening, and can lead to a fear of falling asleep (see Chapter 14). The feeling of paralysis sometimes occurs in people without any other symptoms of sleep disorder and is generally not considered to be a medical problem. However, it is also a common symptom of narcolepsy (see Chapter 13). If you have this symptom and are also sleepy in the daytime, you may have narcolepsy and you should discuss the symptom with your doctor.

The "Weird Stuff"

Sleep behaviors can range from an insignificant incident to a probable symptom of a serious sleep disorder that requires treatment (see Chapter 14). Some of these behaviors are described in this section; if any of these is affecting your life, you should definitely discuss it with your doctor.

• *Sleepwalking* and *sleep talking* are very common, especially in children (Chapter 14). Unless the child does something dangerous, it is not something that requires medical attention.

• *Sleep terror* or *night terror* is a symptom in which people get out of bed during the night or sit up in bed and scream and sometimes sweat. Their eyes are wide open. This is a variant of sleepwalking, and as awful as it sounds, it is not dangerous. It is sometimes also found in people with sleep deprivation.

• Some people are *confused and disoriented* when they awaken from sleep. This symptom is more common in the elderly who might also wander during the evening or at night (see Chapter 7). This latter symptom has been called *sundowning* or *nocturnal wandering*. This is a symptom that should be brought to the doctor's attention since it might be a symptom of Alzheimer's disease or related to other factors that might be treatable.

• Everybody has had the experience of awakening from a *nightmare*. This is common and can be very frightening for children—and sometimes for adults. This symptom is not believed to be very significant (see Chapter 14). However, if the nightmares are frequently very similar, are violent in nature, and are extremely disturbing, they might be a symptom of *post-traumatic stress disorder* (see Chapter 16). This symptom should be brought to the doctor's attention, since the patient may require treatment.

• Some people react physically to or act out their dreams. When this happens, the dreamer might actually react to the dream by striking out and sometimes hurting his or her bed partner. This is a symptom of *REM sleep behavior disorder* (RBD), which can be quite severe (see Chapter 14) and usually requires treatment.

• Some people can't stop moving when they sleep. They toss, turn, get up and walk around, fidget, and twitch during sleep. Some even exhibit movements as bizarre as simulating riding a bicycle. These are symptoms of a possible *movement disorder* (see Chapter 11). If people have such movements and have insomnia or daytime sleepiness, they might require treatment.

• Sometimes people will have a disorder called *head banging* in which they repeatedly bang their head into a mattress or a pillow or even a wall, or move other parts of their body in a repetitive manner. As bad as it sounds, this is a movement disorder that does not have important consequences except that in a small number of people it may result in self-injury (see Chapter 14).

The symptoms that were just reviewed might be unimportant (sleepwalking, sleep talking, head banging), or they might require evaluation and treatment (reacting to dreams, repeated nightmares, violent movements). Sleep paralysis and hypnagogic hallucinations might be symptoms of narcolepsy, which requires treatment. If any of these symptoms are affecting your life, it is best to seek medical help.

Noises in the Night

In the previous section, I described behaviors that might indicate sleep problems. In this section, I describe noises that people make while they are sleeping. These noises might be unimportant or they might be markers of a severe sleep problem. Sleepers do not hear the noises they make, but the noises can impair the sleep of a bed partner.

Snoring

Snoring is a noise that is familiar to everyone, so your doctor will understand what you mean if you use this term. However, describing the snoring as accurately as possible can be helpful. For instance, snoring can be loud or soft. Ask your bed partner to tell you about the level and frequency of your snoring and then let the medical practitioner know (although he or she may not ask) how many nights a week you snore, for what proportion of the night, whether the snoring is more common in one position, and whether alcohol makes it worse.

Awful Silences

Snoring is most often continuous; it does not seem to change much over the course of a night. However, some people have episodes of silence between snores. These silences, particularly if they are long, can be quite frightening and disturbing to the listener. This is because the snorer has actually stopped breathing. Periods of silence are a symptom of sleep apnea (see Chapter 12) and should be described to a doctor.

Snorts and Gasps

Some patients, especially women with the upper airway resistance syndrome (see Chapter 12) might not snore continuously, but have episodes of snorting that might be quite brief and not especially loud. Snorting and gasps may also be a sign of sleep apnea (see chapter 12) and should also be described to the doctor. At the end of episodes of apnea and at the end of the silence, the person might exhibit very loud snorting, gasping, or deep breathing.

Looking at Patterns with Sleep Diaries

A sleep diary is a tool that helps you document your sleep habits and patterns. It can help identify patterns that may be disturbing sleep and may help you and your doctor pinpoint a sleep problem. Using such a diary, one might find, for example, that sleepiness commonly occurs after the weekly late evening aerobics class. With children, you might discover that there is a problem with the body clock (see Chapter 8). Observing the sleep schedule might illustrate that, during the week, the child falls asleep very late, and then sleeps much later on the weekend, suggesting the body clock is running late. Following are some types of diaries you might use to help you identify a sleep problem.

Using the NSF Sleep Diary for Adults

The NSF Sleep Diary in Appendix 1 takes only a few minutes each day to complete. We suggest you keep it in one convenient place, such as on your bedside table. Complete the diary for seven consecutive days, or copy it and use it for a longer period of time. Then, look over the diary to see if there are any patterns or practices that may be contributing to your sleep problems. Discuss these with your health-care provider; bring the completed sleep diary with you to help you get the most out of your visit.

Using the Cognitive Therapy Diary for Adults

This diary, which is shown in Chapter 19 (Figure 19-1), should be filled in every morning at the same time and might be used as part of cognitive behavioral treatment for insomnia. After filling it in for a week or two (make copies), you might see a pattern of behavior that can both identify a sleep problem and lead to a treatment plan. Bring a copy of the diary with you when you see your health-care provider.

Using the NIH Sleep Diary for Children

The National Institutes of Health has created the Garfield Star Sleeper website at www.nhlbi.nih.gov/health/public/sleep/starslp, which has information about sleep disorders for children, parents, teachers, and pediatricians. From this site you can download a sleep diary designed for children to use (www.nhlbi.nih.gov/health/public/sleep/starslp/parents/diary.htm).

Back to the Tired Man with Cancer

It turned out that the tired man with cancer was actually sleepy. That is the symptom that he first noticed. He had used the word *tired* and the doctor had not asked him about his sleep. It turned out that the insomnia had actually preceded the cancer diagnosis by about a year. The patient had developed an irresistible urge to move his legs at bedtime and this interfered with his falling asleep. He had a textbook case of restless legs syndrome (RLS), but his doctor had not read the textbook. Iron deficiency is a cause of RLS. The RLS came on because the patient was developing an iron deficiency caused by a slowly bleeding colon cancer. The insomnia and sleepiness were thus symptoms of the cancer. He was still iron deficient when I saw him. The iron medication would probably take care of the insomnia. Hopefully, the cancer hasn't spread. This case highlighted to me the importance of using the right words and making sure the words are understood.

In this chapter, you saw how important it is to be able to know whether symptoms affecting sleep require medical attention and how to communicate these symptoms to the doctor. Questionnaires and diaries can be very helpful in identifying a sleep problem. For many women who have difficulty sleeping, however, a bed partner may be the cause of the problem. In the next chapter, I review how disorders in family members can make a woman's life miserable.

7

My Family's Sleep Problems Are Keeping Me Awake

The Case of the Snorer Who Didn't Have a Problem

Patients almost always come to the sleep clinic with someone accompanying them. Children come with parents, husbands come with wives, and the very elderly come with a spouse or a child, very often their daughter. Sometimes, the challenge with a new patient is figuring out whether the patient is actually the one who's having the problem, as seen in the following case. I have heard variations of this case hundreds of times, but each patient is unique and each one presents special challenges.

A husband and wife came into my examination room. The husband took the seat closest to my desk because he considered himself the patient. I asked the husband a long series of questions and only one of them had a positive answer: Yes, he snored. But he had never been observed by his wife to stop breathing during sleep; he had no abnormal sleepiness during the daytime; he never fell asleep when he did not want to, and had no trouble staying awake at movies or plays. He had no other medical problems that could be determined by asking a large number of questions. He did not smoke. His caffeine intake was reasonable. He had alcohol once in a while and the snoring was worse after the alcohol.

I glanced at the woman and saw that she was looking at the floor. The bags under her eyes were clearly visible. I turned to her and asked how her husband's snoring was affecting her. After a few minutes, it became apparent that the husband was not the one with the problem. The real patient was the wife. She related how much difficulty she had falling asleep because of the snoring

73

and she said she felt terrible during the daytime. However, it did not seem to register with her husband as they briefly started to argue about how bad the snoring was. Her husband said that it couldn't be all that bad because it didn't wake him up. I asked the husband if he would have come to the clinic if his wife had not insisted. He replied, "No." It was now evident that the snorer who thought he did not have a problem had a huge problem—his wife, and possibly, his marriage.

Sleep Problems in the Home Affect a Woman's Sleep

As the above case illustrates, a sleep problem in a family member can interfere with a woman's sleep. Typically, the woman is the one who takes on the responsibility of caring for the children, the spouse, and the elderly parents when they need help. In addition, it is often the woman who suffers when children have sleep problems or her spouse has a disorder such as sleep apnea. A woman's sleep is often even disrupted by the family pet. All these can cause a woman to be very sleep deprived, which can make her life miserable. This chapter will review how women can recognize and manage their own sleep deprivation and their family's sleep problems.

Although the disorders discussed here are covered elsewhere in the book, this chapter deals with them from a different perspective. Three universal truths I've discovered about sleeping are:

1. There is perhaps nothing more comforting than watching a loved one sleep comfortably and peacefully.
2. There is perhaps nothing more distressing than observing a loved one's struggle to breathe or battle to achieve restful sleep.
3. There is perhaps nothing more frustrating than a family member doing something annoying or disruptive to your sleep that is not dangerous but keeps you awake.

Families in the Third Millennium

There have been dramatic changes in the American family in the past three decades. There has been a large increase in the number of divorces; people are marrying later; the birth rate has decreased as the use of birth control has increased; and more couples are living in common-law or same-sex relationships. The March 2000 census reported that the number of married-couple families decreased from 87 percent of families in 1970 to 69 percent in 2000. Single-mother families now make up 26 percent of the total, while single-father families make up 5 percent. More people are living alone. The percent of households with more than two people has decreased from 54 percent in 1970 to 40.4 percent in 2000.

When we talk about family roles, we must keep in mind that the family has changed, and roles that were traditionally represented by one parent might switch to another family member such as a grandparent. Because of divorce and because many women are choosing to have children without being married, there are now a large number of single-parent families.

Problems with Bed Partners

When people share a bed or sleeping quarters, one person with a sleep disorder can severely disrupt the sleep of others. In a barracks setting, for example in a prison or military accommodation, the sleep of many can be disturbed. Most often, though, only one bed partner suffers.

Snoring

Snoring is a noise that occurs during sleep when tissues vibrate as air attempts to flow through an obstructed breathing passage. The sound can vary from an almost soothing whisper to an astonishingly loud noise that can be heard throughout the entire house. People frequently deny that they snore because they cannot hear themselves doing it. But for anyone in the vicinity, the noise can be a form of torture. In this section, let's assume that the snorer is a male with no other health problems.

I recently interviewed a military officer whose wife left him to return to her family in Texas. One of the main reasons she left was that she simply could not stand his snoring and had been unable to get adequate amounts of sleep. People who don't sleep properly are tired, irritable, and snappy; some women in this situation actually have clinical responses consistent with depression. In some cases, this may make it difficult to maintain a marriage.

When I treat snoring in a person who does not have a serious health problem such as sleep apnea, what I am really treating is the impact of the noise on the family and others who might suffer as a result of the snoring. Thus, the goal is not to improve the snorer's health, but rather the health of the person most affected by the snoring—the listener! The question becomes one of just how invasive treatment should be when it is not for the purpose of alleviating a health problem in the snorer. Should the treatment for the snorer include surgery, which has its risks and may be associated with a great deal of pain? The interests of both the snorer and the person affected by the snoring must be considered.

The most reasonable approach in this situation is to start with the treatment that is most likely to result in a permanent cure. I counsel snorers to work on reducing their weight (if appropriate) and to avoid alcohol, which is known to make snoring much worse. The best thing you can do is encourage your snoring partner not to drink alcohol before bedtime.

What else can be done? There are really only three or four treatment options available.

Get to Bed First
Some women reason that if they fall asleep before the snorer does then they will not be awakened by the snoring during the night. This may be worth trying, but I doubt that it will be effective on a regular basis. By the time people come to my office such measures have failed.

Adjust Your Bed Partner's Sleep Position
Typically people snore most when they are flat on their back. You can encourage your snorer to sleep on his side by gently pushing on his side or elbowing him in the ribs. There are all sorts of gadgets that you could try. Sleeping with backpacks or a tennis ball sewn onto the back of the pajamas to keep the snorer on his side has been recommended, but this approach seems unreliable, and it might cause a sore back.

Wear Earplugs
Interestingly, recent research shows that the spouses of people who snore very loudly actually have impaired hearing, suggesting that loud snoring can pos-

sibly damage the hearing system. So apart from being beneficial for your own sleep, you may want to invest in earplugs to prevent hearing damage. Earplugs are the simplest solution and work extremely well for some women. There are many different types of earplugs on the market. Find the type that fits best, is the most comfortable, and is the least likely to fall out of the ear during the night. It will likely take a couple of nights to get used to wearing them. Earplugs are sold in drug stores, stores that sell industrial and safety clothing, and some stores that sell loud machinery such as chainsaws. The earplugs designed for industrial use can be less expensive and probably more effective than some of the earplugs at other types of retail stores.

Try Separate Beds

Sleeping in separate beds might seem excessively expensive or ineffective. However, it might be worth trying because some snorers also move a great deal in order to keep their breathing normal. Thus, it is not always the noise that keeps the bed partner awake; sometimes it's the movements associated with the breathing.

Especially if they have slept together for many years, some couples view sleeping in separate beds as some sort of failure. However, for many, it is the only way they can cope with their bed partner's problem.

Sleep in a Separate Room

Desperate to fall asleep, some women jab their husbands, hoping to get them to stop snoring. Most eventually learn that this is a temporary solution. Some simply leave the bed and find a quieter place to sleep. Ironically, they sometimes do this because they are afraid that their sleeplessness might awaken their deeply asleep and snoring husband. Sleeping on a couch is not terribly comfortable and eventually many women take over another bedroom—often the most distant one from the bed partner. Incidentally, this is not guaranteed to work; some snoring, particularly at a very low pitch, can be heard throughout a dwelling.

Buy the Property Next Door

Although I mention this in jest, I bring it up because I had one couple (actually it was the woman who snored), who did exactly this because the snoring could be heard everywhere in the house. They bought the house next door and that is where the woman slept. Certainly that was better than contacting a lawyer.

When Both Bed Partners Snore

Contrary to expectation, a real problem occurs when both members of a couple snore because a contest seems to develop to see who will fall asleep first. In these snoring relationships, the couple keeps waking each other up and after a while one of them usually retreats to another room to snore in peace. One of them may even learn that sleeping in a comfortable chair is not so bad and that they sleep much better in a semi-upright position. They are not imagining this. When people are in this position they snore less and even some people with sleep apnea will have much more normal sleep when they sit rather than lie down to rest.

An important bit of advice for couples who snore is to avoid getting into the habit of using something to knock yourself out so that you don't hear the snoring. Sleeping pills and/or alcohol may turn snoring into sleep apnea. Sleeping pills and alcohol relax the muscles of the throat that keep the breathing passage open and will worsen breathing.

Stopping Breathing

Although snoring can be very annoying to the listener, there is probably nothing more disturbing than thinking and believing that the loved one lying in bed next to you is about to take his last breath and die. Many people cannot get used to sleeping next to someone who stops breathing on a regular basis. They are always listening, waiting to hear their partner take an effective breath. This very common problem is covered in depth in Chapter 12. The bottom line is that a person who stops breathing can keep a bed partner awake. The solution to the problem is not to wear earplugs, or to move to a different room, but to insist that the person who stops breathing receives proper medical evaluation. If this is your situation and your bed partner is diagnosed with sleep apnea and is treated with a continuous positive airway pressure (CPAP) device, you will undoubtedly prefer the white noise of a CPAP machine over the sound of your bed partner.

Tossing and Turning

Your bed partner tosses, turns, gets out of bed, walks around, gets back into bed, and takes half an hour to several hours to fall asleep. Meanwhile, you are lying there angry and frustrated because you are not getting to sleep. Finally, he falls asleep, but your problems are not over. He twitches every twenty or thirty seconds. Sometimes there is a slight movement of the bed-clothes or an actual kick. Sometimes he may be sweating a great deal. This is a description of what it is like to sleep with someone with a movement disorder (see Chapter 11). Most patients with this disorder can be treated, but if the treatment doesn't work, the couple may opt for separate beds.

Teeth Grinding

It is very difficult to describe the sounds of bruxism, or teeth grinding, except to say that it sounds like there is a chipmunk in bed with you making one of the most annoying noises you have ever heard. At first, when you hear the noise, you cannot believe that it is coming from a person. You can try the same techniques used for snoring: earplugs, changing bedrooms, and so forth. The best approach is to encourage your bed partner to go to a dentist to be fitted with a mouth guard that will minimize the damage that grinding can inflict on his teeth—and your sleep. The teeth grinding can become so severe, that it can wear down the teeth so that they no longer function well and might actually have to be removed.

Talking During Sleep

Some people intermittently speak gibberish, moan, and/or make all sorts of strange noises while they sleep. This does not represent anything serious, and in most cases the bed partner becomes used to it.

Singing the National Anthem

Yes, one person gets up from bed, sings the national anthem as loudly as he can, and then goes back to bed and has absolutely no recollection of the event until he's told about it the next morning. This is a form of sleep talking and should be ignored.

Sleepwalking

Your bed partner may sleepwalk without your even knowing that it has happened. Some sleepwalkers get out of bed, walk around, and even go to the kitchen (where they might even eat), all while sound asleep. They end up back in bed eventually with no recollection of what they have done. Other people might find themselves awake in some unusual location in the house. Most of the time, this is not anything to be concerned about because the activities are not dangerous. However, there are a couple of things you can do to reduce sleepwalking by your bed partner. Sleepwalking occurs more often after people have consumed alcohol and when they are sleep deprived. Make sure that your bed partner gets the right amount of sleep, and does not drink alcohol before going to bed. If your bed partner does dangerous things while sleepwalking, it is time to seek medical help.

Having Sleep Terrors

Your soundly sleeping bed partner suddenly lets out a bloodcurdling scream and sits bolt upright, pouring sweating, with eyes wide open and glazed. This behavior, also called night terrors, would severely frighten anybody within earshot. The next morning, your partner has no memory of what happened. This story is typical of someone who is having sleep terrors. Believe it or not, this disorder is not dangerous. It is a variant of sleepwalking and is treated in the same way.

Having Nightmares

Your bed partner wakes up sweating, heart pounding, breathing hard, frightened from a terrifying dream. If this happens infrequently, once a month or less, this might not be a problem worth treating. If the nightmares are frequent and involve a recurrent, violent dream, you should encourage your partner to be evaluated by a doctor. The person may be suffering from post-traumatic stress disorder (Chapter 16). Sometimes people might be having panic attacks that wake them (Chapter 16). Women who sweat a great deal when they sleep might be going through menopause (Chapter 5), have an overactive thyroid gland (Chapter 15), or be suffering from a chronic medical condition. These symptoms should be checked out by the doctor.

Hitting While Sleeping

Patients with REM sleep behavior disorder (covered in more detail in Chapter 14) physically react to what they are dreaming. If they are dreaming that they are being attacked, they might actually attack their bed partner. They may punch the walls, throw objects, or jump out of bed, and might easily hurt themselves and others. This is a serious condition and should be treated by the doctor.

Sleep Problems in Children

Because the woman is usually the main caregiver in the home, sleep problems in children can result in her losing sleep. Such problems occur in children of all ages, and the types of disorders that may occur vary with age.

Birth to Twelve Months

Of course everyone in the home loses sleep when a new baby is first brought home from the hospital. Until the baby begins to sleep through the night and does not require feedings at night, the parents, especially the one who does the night feeding, can expect to be sleep deprived. This is normal.

As mentioned in Chapter 2, sleep problems in children usually result in parents' sleep being disrupted. However, according to Dr. Jodi Mindell of the Children's Hospital of Philadelphia and author of *Sleeping Through the Night: How Infants, Toddlers, and Their Parents Can Get a Good Night's Sleep*, parents can begin to help their baby develop positive sleep habits as early as three months of age. These practices will help a baby to naturally start sleeping for long stretches at night. The three key things are to:

- Develop a regular sleep schedule that is the same every day.
- Establish a consistent bedtime routine.
- Put the baby to bed drowsy but awake.

A baby who can soothe herself to sleep at bedtime will be able to fall back to sleep on her own when she naturally awakens at night. However, some problems do arise in the first year that can impact the entire family.

Colic

At around two weeks of age, about 10 percent of newborn babies start to have unexplained episodes of crying that might occur on a daily basis. These episodes can last for hours and can occur at any time, which causes a great deal of distress to the parents or caregiver. Pediatricians often use the "Rule of 3" to judge whether a baby is colicky. That is, crying lasts for three hours or more per day, three days or more per week, for three weeks or longer. Colic often starts at one to two weeks old and ends by age three or four months. Between the episodes of crying, the baby seems absolutely fine. The noise of the crying and the distress that it can cause in the mother can interfere with much needed sleep.

Medical science has not found the cause of colic, but some important facts are known. Colic is not caused by gas or abdominal pain, and it is certainly not the result of bad parenting. If the child does have a large amount of gas and/or problems with excessive diarrhea, she may be allergic to cow's milk. Generally, the episodes of colic will start to decrease after a month or so and are usually gone by the time the baby is four months old. However, these few months can be torture for the parent. Although most parents try cuddling and rocking the baby early on, it soon becomes important for parents to try to normalize their child's sleep habits; otherwise the baby may not be able to fall asleep on her own. Establishing a healthy sleep pattern is essential to good sleep. Parents should make sure that their baby wakes up at roughly the same time every morning and goes to bed at roughly the same time every night. It appears that some children who have colic have trouble sleeping even after the colic is gone. This may be related to not having established a regular enough sleep schedule. Although colic can be bad news, the good news is that not every child develops it—and it does go away.

SIDS

Caregivers should know about this important problem and steps that can be taken to reduce the risk. Sudden infant death syndrome (SIDS) is the unexpected death of an infant who appeared perfectly healthy. It strikes one out of every thousand babies and has devastating effects on the family. SIDS is more common in babies who are born prematurely and those who are very small at birth. The time of highest risk is when the baby is between two and four months old. Roughly 90 percent of babies who succumb to SIDS die before they reach six months of age. Research has shown that in the United States, the rate of SIDS might be twice as high for African American babies compared to the rest of the population. The reasons behind this discrepancy are unclear, although many scientific articles have reported that it may be due to unsafe sleep surfaces, bed sharing, or other socioeconomic factors. Sleeping on the back, pacifier use, and breastfeeding have been reported to reduce SIDS.

Causes of SIDS. Although the precise mechanisms that lead to SIDS are as yet unknown, SIDS deaths usually occur while the baby is sleeping. One theory that might explain some cases of SIDS is that babies' nervous systems are not adequately developed so that they are not able to respond when they stop breathing or when their blood oxygen levels dip.

A big breakthrough has occurred within the past few years based on research showing that babies sleeping in the facedown position are more likely to die of SIDS. It has been estimated that one third of SIDS cases are related to sleeping on the stomach. Smoking by the mother before or after the birth of the baby has been linked to an increase in the risk of SIDS. Infants who are breastfed are less likely to die of SIDS. The following recommendations are based on research studies.

1. The baby should be placed on her back to sleep. If the baby has breathing problems or excessive spitting up of milk with feeding, this should be discussed with the doctor.
2. There should be no exposure to cigarettes either before or after birth. Smoking by the pregnant mother and smoke exposure after birth have been linked to an increased risk of SIDS.

3. Bedding should be firm.
4. To reduce the possibility of the breathing passage being blocked parents or caregivers should remove extraneous objects from the crib. This means beanbags, cushions, sheepskins, pillows, and stuffed animals should be removed whenever the baby sleeps.
5. Some studies suggest that sharing beds may increase risk.
6. The parents or caregiver should make sure the baby doesn't overheat. This can occur if the room is too hot, the baby is wearing too many clothes, or the bedclothes are too heavy, especially if the baby has a fever and/or illness such as a cold or other infection.

Since the campaign to have children sleep on their backs began, there has been a 40 percent reduction in the number of SIDS deaths. Besides reducing SIDS, sleeping on the back has been reported to reduce episodes of fever, stuffy nose, and ear infections. However, there is still much to be learned about this mysterious and devastating syndrome.

One to Three Years

For most children, sleep during these years is not a problem. The children have usually established a regular sleep/wake pattern and almost always sleep through the night. Of course, there are always exceptions to the rule, and some of these are covered in this section.

When the Child Can't Fall Asleep Without a Parent

If a child has learned to associate sleep with being held or rocked, she may have a great deal of difficulty falling asleep on her own. Some children will crawl into the parents' bed or insist on sleeping in the parents' room. Failure to deal with this problem when the child is young can have long-term implications. I recall a couple in my office several years ago asking me for strategies on how to remove their thirteen-year-old son from their bed.

Dr. Richard Ferber from Harvard University has written a book, *How to Solve Your Child's Sleep Problem*, which helps parents deal with this problem by teaching children how to fall asleep on their own. This approach works for many families, and I recommend this book very highly. The basic principles are as follows:

1. Establish a nightly routine before bedtime that is relaxing to the child. This could include taking a bath, rocking, singing, or storytelling.
2. The child should be put to bed in her own crib and in her own room (if possible) while she is awake and beginning to show signs of sleepiness. The important part of the technique is that the child learns to fall asleep on her own.
3. The parent or caregiver should leave the room once the child has been put to bed. This is the most difficult part. If she cries, the parent or caregiver waits a bit before going into the room. If the caregiver does go into the room, the visit should be brief and the child should not be held, fed, sung to, or rocked. The amount of time before going into the child's room should become longer and longer on progressive nights. In this way, the child learns that crying only brings a brief visit from the parent, which means she will have to learn to go to sleep on her own. With consistent adherence to the process, it usually takes about a week or sometimes two, although it is a time that can be very difficult on the family.

Getting a slightly older child who is sleeping in a parents' bed to move can be more complicated. The child may claim to be frightened to sleep alone. Is "frightened" an excuse or is the child really frightened? One technique that sometimes works when the child is using the excuse of being frightened is to offer to let the child sleep on the floor next to the bed. After a while, the child will learn that sleeping on the floor is a lot less comfortable than sleeping in his own bed. If the child really is frightened, this might not work, and the child will have to be reassured. If neither of these options works, you might have to seek professional help. The first step is to check with a pediatrician.

Children at Any Age

Some of the problems that might occur in an adult bed partner mentioned earlier in the chapter can be present in children. These include sleep talking and sleep terrors. Snoring in children is not usually caused by obesity, and if it is present, the cause should be determined by a doctor. Most often snoring or sleep apnea in children is caused by enlarged tonsils and adenoids.

Why Is the Child Snoring?

A child that snores loudly and stops breathing during sleep may have obstructive sleep apnea. If the child has large tonsils or is obese, these problems will probably have to be dealt with.

I have seen many adult snorers whose sleep apnea was caused by an abnormal jaw; often it turned out that their children also snored and had small jaws. If a parent with a small jaw has sleep apnea, his or her snoring child should be evaluated by a dentist or an orthodontist, as the obstructed breathing pattern may also be due to an abnormal jaw structure. If a child has a very small jaw, orthodontics can often improve the jaw structure and might help reduce the chance of significant sleep apnea years later. The first evaluation visit to an orthodontist is often free.

Elderly Parents

Sleep in older people can be quite normal. As reviewed in Chapter 2, sleep in older people becomes abnormal as they develop medical conditions or as a result of medications. Women frequently lose sleep caring for ill family members. This might include caring for people who have had a stroke, are on breathing machines, are incontinent, or require that someone administer medications to them at night. All these situations can have a terrible effect on a woman's sleep.

Alzheimer's Disease

Alzheimer's is a medical problem that many people fear. Because the woman is usually the caregiver in her family, she is the one who most often deals with a family member with Alzheimer's disease. Eighty-four percent of caregivers of Alzheimer's patients are women, and on the average the caregivers are sixty-five years old. Women are also more likely to develop this disease. Alzheimer's is what scientists call a neurodegenerative disorder, meaning there is degeneration of the nervous system. Most of the time, this degeneration in Alzheimer's patients is caused by an accumulation of a chemical called amyloid in the brain, which appears to choke off normal brain cells. The disorder may progress very rapidly or there may be a gradual but progressive loss of brain function (including the ability to sleep) over a period of many years.

The statistics concerning Alzheimer's are staggering. In the United States, there are two to four million people living with Alzheimer's. It has been estimated that between one in ten and one in twenty of all people over seventy, and perhaps half of people older than eighty-five have Alzheimer's. Because women live longer than men, many more women have Alzheimer's than men. It has also been suggested that within a given age group a woman is more likely to have Alzheimer's than a man. For example one study from Denmark estimated that of 100 women age ninety or older, eighty had Alzheimer's; in contrast, of 100 men age ninety or older, twenty-four had Alzheimer's. In addition to the primary symptoms of the disease, 42 percent of Alzheimer's patients are depressed.

More than 70 percent of those with Alzheimer's disease live at home, and they put a great emotional and financial burden on their families and cause many sleepless nights for the caregiver (very often the patient's daughter). The average patient lives about eight years after diagnosis. Some researchers have stated that the single most important reason why patients with Alzheimer's are institutionalized is because they wander at night and do not sleep. Their caregivers cannot cope with these nighttime activities in addition to their own sleep deprivation.

Dealing with Sleep Problems in Alzheimer's

It is beyond the scope of this book to review in detail all the sleep issues in Alzheimer's. Several resources are given at the end of the book. People with severe Alzheimer's may spend a great deal of time awake at night, and many may reverse their days and night, sleeping fitfully all day and remaining awake all night. In addition, some Alzheimer's disease patients may experience *sundowning*.

Sundowning occurs in about one in five institutionalized older people—and most institutionalized people are women. Sundowning takes place usually in the late afternoon or early evening. The person might become agitated and have hallucinations or episodes of anxiety. It is believed that this symptom might be related to a breakdown of the circadian clock or may be due to poor quality sleep.

Tragically, there is as yet no cure for Alzheimer's disease, but new medications are available that seem to slow the pace and might result in some improvement in brain function. These drugs can cause nausea, vomiting, diarrhea, and insomnia, however, and their effect on Alzheimer's patients' sleep patterns has not been widely studied. Sometimes patients may be given other medications, such as antidepressants, that also might cause insomnia. Recent research suggests that exposure to light during the daytime may be helpful in improving nighttime sleep. The theory is that this may be helpful in resetting the person's circadian clock. Some scientists have recommended the use of melatonin. Several studies have suggested that melatonin at a dosage of 6 to 9 mg may be effective in improving sleep and treating sundowning in Alzheimer's patients. Despite extensive research, much remains to be learned about Alzheimer's disease, its effect on sleep, and the most effective treatments.

The Caregiver in Alzheimer's Disease

Taking care of an Alzheimer's patient at home is very stressful and can have a profound impact upon the caregiver's sleep. The caregiver often has to coordinate medical care (medications, doctor visits) and personal care (hygiene, laundry, feeding, etc.). The caregiver must make sure that she receives sufficient sleep. If she is sleep deprived, she should seek help and find out what resources are available.

Back to the Snorer Who Didn't Have a Problem

It became apparent to all three of us that although the snoring patient did not have a medical problem, his wife had a *big* problem. To improve her sleep and to save the marriage something would have to be done. We discussed different options and we settled on the husband wearing a dental appliance that kept him from snoring. He wears the appliance every night, and now his wife sleeps through the night.

In this chapter you learned about how sleep problems in family members can negatively affect a woman's sleep, and what she can do about it. A teenager who has to be dragged out of bed to go to school can also disrupt the family. In the next chapter you will see that some problems with sleep are not diseases at all, but are the result of a body clock that is different from that of most people.

8

My Body Clock Is Different

The Case of the Night Owl

The woman sitting in front of me was in her mid-twenties but looked quite haggard. She was obviously very tired. The bags under her eyes were a grayish blue, her eyes were bloodshot, and she had difficulty focusing on our discussion. I sometimes had to ask her the same question several times. She told me that it was taking her three to four hours to fall asleep every night and she could not get out of bed to be at work by eight the next morning. Even the several alarm clocks she used didn't help; she slept through them. She had her mother call her, but she couldn't rely on the phone. Sometimes the ringing would fail to rouse her. The effect of all this was that her performance at the office was becoming unsatisfactory and she felt she was at risk of losing her job.

She first became aware of these symptoms when she was a teenager. She would stay up past midnight and get up late the next morning. Many mornings her mother would have to drag her out of bed to get her to school. Then, once she got there she couldn't stay awake for morning classes. Consequently, she had a lot of difficulty in school, and she barely managed to graduate because she missed so many classes and had poor grades. She was determined to go to a university, but she had to take courses in the afternoons to cope with her sleepiness. She finally came to the sleep clinic because her work schedule was exhausting her and she was seeking a solution to the problem. Were there any pills she could take? My question to her was whether she ever felt wide awake and alert. She answered: "Weekends. I don't understand it." That was the clue I needed.

Disorders of the Body Clock

In Chapter 1, I described the mechanism located in our brains that sleep scientists call the *circadian clock*. One of the many functions of this clock is to control the time of day when we are sleepy, and the time when we are alert. In some people, the clock runs *slow*, and as a result, they tend not to become sleepy until later at night. In some people, the clock runs *fast* and they feel sleepy earlier in the evening. And in still others, the clock seems to work erratically. These circadian rhythm differences among the general population are not a disease. In fact, these people are perfectly healthy. Problems arise when their circadian rhythm is on a schedule that may not be in sync with the demands of society and their lifestyles.

Delayed Sleep-Phase Syndrome: The Night Owl

For people with this syndrome, the night owls, the clock seems to run three or four hours or more late. It is as though one lives in Boston, but the internal circadian clock behaves as though it were in Seattle. These people just don't feel sleepy until one to three o'clock in the morning or sometimes later. During the week, they have tremendous difficulty getting out of bed if they have to wake up at a normal hour to get to work or school; during the day they remain drowsy enough that they might actually nod off in class or at work. However, on weekends, people with this problem generally are able to sleep in until noon or even later and wake up feeling alert and refreshed. The night owl complains of trouble falling asleep and difficulty getting up (see Figure 8-1). It is usually a parent who drags the student with delayed sleep phase out of bed to go to school. Because the parent may be more aware of the situation, she or he may also be the first to insist that the night owl see a doctor.

People who have delayed circadian rhythm frequently go to the doctor complaining of insomnia because they cannot fall asleep at a normal time. Simply put, their internal clock will not let them sleep until it's time, and this

Figure 8-1 The Night Owl's Delayed Clock

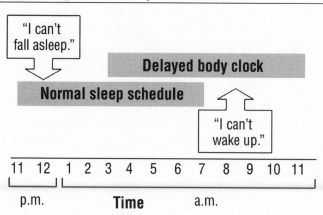

is as much a physical characteristic as their hair color and eye color. It is just the way they are. It is not normal or abnormal; it is just different from most other people. Though they may be comforted that they don't have a disease, unfortunately the way their body clock tells time can cause a major problem in their daily lives.

Coping with the Delayed Clock

Dealing with children or family members with body clock irregularities can be quite problematic, especially for parents of school-age children. Getting these children through school may be a huge challenge as it puts stress on the routine that most parents use to keep everyone in the family on schedule. Parents can try communicating with and educating school officials/teachers regarding the physiological need to adhere to a different sleep schedule and why this is important for a student's school performance. Requesting and receiving some schedule adjustments can help the student cope. Specifically, such students would benefit from classes that begin in the afternoon. In my experience, some school systems are very accommodating while others are very resistant to changing anything to do with student schedules. However, if the school will accommodate the child's scheduling needs, this can be a good first step in reducing the stress on the student and the family.

Probably the best way for women to cope with delayed sleep phase is to find a career with work hours that are in sync with her body's schedule. Some of my patients with a delayed clock have been very successful in the entertainment business and in service industries such as restaurants because the workday begins later. Today, there are many jobs for people who want to stay up late and sleep in. In addition to their career, night owls may have relationship issues caused by their sleep pattern. Conflict may occur in couples where one is an early bird and the other a night owl. When 10:00 p.m. rolls around, one partner may be ready for sleep while the other is ready to rock and roll. Night owls would probably be happier in relationships or marriages with other night owls. Interestingly, the offspring of night owls are also frequently night owls so a genetic component might be involved in delayed sleep phase.

Treating the Delayed Clock

Two approaches can sometimes effectively change the circadian rhythm. *Chronotherapy* adjusts the person's sleep schedule so that they go to bed two hours later every couple of days until they work their way around the clock. For example, if a person feels like a good time to go to bed is at 2:00 a.m., a schedule is devised so that in the first two days she goes to bed at 4:00 a.m., then the following two days at 6:00 a.m., and so on. (Obviously for people going to school, this can only be tested during holidays.)

Here's how it works: once the person works her way around the clock, she should stop at a desirable time and then consistently choose this time to go to bed. In practice, this method has worked for some people, but if they stay up late for one or more nights, sometimes they fall right back into their old routine.

Another treatment, sunlight exposure, might also be effective. The body uses light to synchronize the circadian clock. Research has shown that morning exposure to bright light from either natural sunlight or commercial lamps can help to rouse people who have delayed body clocks. In far northern and southern locations, during winter, the sun may rise fairly late and so electric lamps might be used in the mornings to replace and simulate the sun. These are the same lamps that are used to treat seasonal affective disorder (SAD), which is also called winter depression. It seems to be brought on by insufficient sunlight in winter. This method can help people regulate their internal clock, but if they stop using the lights, they will likely fall back into the same undesirable sleep pattern. Sunlight exposure and/or chronotherapy are treatments worth trying, although they may or may not be effective over the long term in the real world.

What About Using Melatonin?

Melatonin, a supplement billed as the "hormone of sleep" was extremely popular several years ago in treating sleeplessness and, in particular, circadian rhythm problems. I am reluctant to recommend melatonin for reasons I will address in more detail in Chapter 20. The bottom line is that melatonin might work for some people, but the long-term implications of its use in children and teenagers have not been adequately studied.

Advanced Sleep-Phase Syndrome: The Lark

The other side of the coin is the person whose clock runs early (see Figure 8-2). This person might get tired early in the evening, by 9:00 p.m. or earlier, and be unable to stay awake. She may typically wake up between 4:00 and 6:00 a.m. This type of person may report symptoms of insomnia, and complain of waking up too early and not being able to fall asleep again. It is as though she lives in Los Angeles, but her clock is on New York time. When she seeks medical attention, it is because she believes that her early morning awakenings can't be normal. She wakes up when everyone else is asleep, and she figures that there must be something wrong with her.

These people usually do not have problems in the workplace, but they have major problems in fulfilling social obligations. For example, they are usually too sleepy to attend evening parties and family get-togethers.

Coping with the Advanced Clock

People with advanced circadian rhythms are often very successful in some endeavors and indeed for some represent the ideal schedule. Benjamin Franklin recommended going to bed early so one could get up early. In fact, he thought sleep was a waste of time. Farmers, surgeons, anesthesiologists, and nurses frequently have this kind of schedule; often they self-select themselves into those careers. In most places of the world, the day shift for nurses begins at 7:00 a.m. and for the anesthesiologist and surgeon, the drive in from home to work usually occurs before dawn. They are frequently already in the operating room at 7:00 a.m.

Figure 8-2 The Lark's Advanced Clock

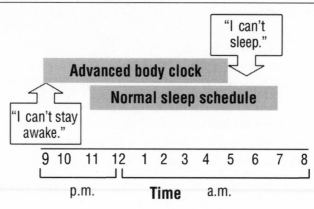

Treating the Advanced Clock

What about the people who wake up very early because they have become very sleepy early in the evening? Explaining the body's physiology to these people tells them that there is nothing wrong with them and they most often simply accept the fact and do nothing.

When There Doesn't Seem to Be a Clock at All

Some people do not seem to become sleepy at all at night or they sleep at random times over the course of a twenty-four-hour day. It is believed, for example, that Leonardo Da Vinci took catnaps every few hours throughout the day. This is sometimes seen in people who have suffered damage to the part of the nervous system that controls the circadian clock as well as some people with psychiatric disorders. Parents should be aware and concerned if their teenager starts to have such a sleep pattern; one cause of these problems could be the use of "street" drugs (see Chapter 17).

Jet Lag

Your body clock can also feel broken when you suffer the effects of jet lag. Unknown until the mid-twentieth century, jet lag can present a big sleep problem. It has only been in the past thirty years that large numbers of people have been flying very long distances in high-speed aircraft. Flying from New York to Paris requires shifting several time zones and many people have noticed that their body clocks become disoriented and confused. Currently, millions of people cross time zones every day. For some it is part of their job. The flight crew of a commercial aircraft is a perfect example. Most have learned to cope with jet lag in their daily lives whereas an ordinary traveler still has to learn.

Many people don't realize that jet lag only occurs when crossing time zones; flying north and south, even great distances does not cause jet lag. The impact of jet lag on a passenger's sleep depends on the direction flown (east or west) and the number of time zones crossed. Since the world conveniently has twenty-four time zones, if you cross twelve time zones it does not matter whether you travel by going east or west. If you travel any other number of zones you will experience a different impact on your sleep if you go east or west.

Going East

When you fly east, you typically "lose" time. On a typical eastbound flight, for example from New York to Paris, the flight might be seven hours long. Your flight leaves around 9:30 p.m., and you arrive in Paris at 10:30 a.m. You'll notice that though it is midmorning in Paris, your body feels like it is the middle of the night—you feel as if you have lost six hours. And that feeling is exacerbated by the conditions you experienced on that seven-hour flight. If you were lucky, you slept for four hours. The first hour in a flight is full of commotion. The last hour of the flight is full of announcements. The middle of the flight has meals and movies. Paris is one of the most exciting and romantic cities in the world, but it is hard to enjoy when your body clock is confused and you are dead tired from the trip to get there.

Going West

Flying East to West (for example, San Francisco to Tokyo) presents a different challenge because the traveler "gains" time. The twelve-hour flight often leaves between noon and late afternoon, and arrives in the late afternoon or

Figure 8-3 Flying East

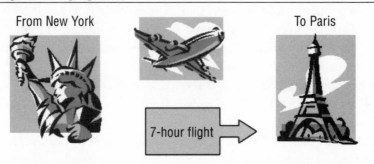

From New York

To Paris

7-hour flight

When you leave, your body thinks it is 9:30 p.m. and it is 9:30 p.m. outside.

When you arrive seven hours later, your body thinks it is 4:30 a.m. but it is 10:30 a.m. outside.

evening. If you changed your watch to Tokyo time, it will seem like you landed four hours after you took off, except that it is the next day. Your body will think it is about midnight—time to go to sleep, but it is only 5:00 p.m. in Tokyo. Experienced travelers will try to sleep on such a flight and many will take a sleeping pill (one of the short acting ones), very soon after boarding the aircraft. By the time they land, go through security, and get to their hotel destination, it is night time again and usually they are exhausted enough to fall asleep at an appropriate time to wake up at an appropriate time the next morning.

How to Defeat Jet Lag

The following suggestions are based on both scientific articles and interviews with flight crew members who have learned how to cope with jet lag. At the end of this chapter are tips from a true expert on jet lag, a flight attendant who has flown overseas hundreds of times.

Advice for Going West to East

For example, New York to Paris. When you get on the plane, reset your watch to the local time of your destination. Get as much sleep as possible on

Figure 8-4 Flying West

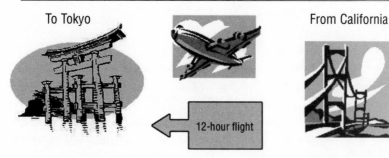

To Tokyo

From California

12-hour flight

When you arrive twelve
hours later, your body
thinks it is midnight
but it is 4:00 p.m. outside.
It is also the next day.

When you leave, your
body thinks it is 12:00
p.m. and it is 12:00 p.m.
outside.

the plane. Tell the flight attendants you do not want food or interruptions.
Use an eyeshade and earplugs. Do not drink alcohol. Some people have suggested taking melatonin or a short-acting sleeping pill at roughly the sleep
time at your destination.

When you arrive, try to adapt your schedule to the schedule at your destination. So if you arrive early in the morning, expose yourself to sunlight
(this will help reset your body clock) and try to avoid taking a long nap right
after you arrive. Doing so may lengthen the adjustment time you'll need. Some
flight attendants have told me that when they arrive at their destination, they
go for a workout even though they might be dead tired because the exercise
jazzes them up for a few hours. That way, they can stay awake for the day and
sleep that night at the normal local bedtime.

Advice for Going East to West

For example, Paris to New York. When you get on the plane, reset your
watch to the local time of your destination. Do not sleep too much on this
seven- to eight-hour flight; a short nap may do. Watch the movies. When you
arrive, try to adapt your schedule to the schedule at your destination. So if
you arrive early in the afternoon, try to avoid taking a long nap right after you
arrive. You should be very tired when bedtime finally arrives. You have had a

long day. (For a much longer flight—for example, San Francisco to Tokyo—try to have a much longer sleep soon after takeoff).

Advice for Going East or West

If you have an important meeting at which you must be sharp and articulate, it is probably not a good idea to schedule the meeting for the day you arrive. About ten years ago, I attended a medical meeting in Cairns, Australia. For most of the participants, this was a very long trip. The North Americans flew west. The Europeans flew east. For most people travel time was twenty to thirty hours. A meeting was held on the first day and most of the attendees were exhausted. As soon as the first speaker started and the lights were dimmed, almost the entire audience fell asleep. Imagine a room full of sleeping sleep specialists who snapped awake when the lights came on between presentations. The following day nobody could remember any of the presentations, although they had very likely been excellent. Sleep specialists should know better than to schedule a session for the date of arrival.

Returning home in either direction will again result in a shift of the circadian clock. Travelers can count on taking several days to recover from a short trip and to return to their normal schedule, and up to a week or more to recover from a very long trip. Don't schedule anything important for several days after you return.

Sleeping Pills

Sleeping pills are not recommended for trips of eight hours or less. The reason is that if one takes a sleeping pill and is then awakened four to five hours later, the drug may still have an effect, and the person may have a nasty hangover, be disoriented, and have poor memory. About fifteen years ago an article was published in the *Journal of the American Medical Association*, which described what happened to three people who had flown to Europe from North America. They each took a sleeping pill and had some alcohol on the flight. Long after they had arrived, they realized that none of them had any memory of what they had seen and done for the ten hours following their landing. However, for long-haul flights, a sleeping pill (see Chapter 20) may help passengers fall asleep and keep distractions from waking them up.

Melatonin

Although many experts recommend against the chronic use of melatonin, there is much less concern about its occasional use in alleviating jet lag. Many experienced travelers use melatonin for this purpose. However, melatonin is not available in all countries and manufacturers use varying amounts of melatonin when producing over the counter preparations.

One well-respected expert recommends taking 3 mg of melatonin at the bedtime of your destination. So, if you are flying from North America to Europe as in the earlier example, you would take the pill right before takeoff. You should wait until you are absolutely sure the plane will be taking off. If the flight is delayed or canceled, you might find yourself in a very groggy state.

Northwest Flight Attendant Swen Salgadoe's Expert Tips on Easing Jet Lag: What to Do After You Arrive

In my career as a flight attendant people have often asked me, "How do you deal with jet lag?" I normally answer by saying that I simply do not get it, but I suppose it is more accurate to say that I'm used to it because I've dealt with it over and over again. Here are some ways to ease jet lag and get back into a normal schedule or adapt to a new time zone:

Stay awake. If you arrive at your destination and it's still daylight there, try to resist the temptation to nap. If you must nap, force yourself to get up before the sun sets. Splash cold water onto your face and promptly head outside for some fresh air.

Make plans. Go out with friends—this will give you an incentive to resist cuddling back into that warm and inviting bed. They will be eager to see you. Don't let them down.

Exercise. As counterproductive as it may seem, nothing wakes up a tired body more than a good thirty to forty-five minutes of heart-pumping cardio action. If you work out during the day, when nighttime approaches, you will have a much more restful sleep.

Drink lots of water. And I mean *lots*. The urge to go to the bathroom often naturally helps you stay awake.

Eat light. But be sure to consume enough to fuel your body. Heavy meals rich in carbohydrates will make you want to sleep. Pass on the pasta, bagels, and ice cream. Eating high-fiber foods such as apples and peanut butter will give you energy and prevent constipation.

Drink coffee. Enjoy as much as you'd like, but if you like it sweet, use a sugar substitute to avoid taking in excessive carbohydrates. Avoid coffee in the few hours before the local bedtime.

Have fun. Do something you love. Staying awake is such a mental activity. Talk on the phone, e-mail a friend, dance, garden, cook, shop, etc. Doing activities you enjoy will distract you from your physical exhaustion. Avoid sedentary activities such as reading, watching TV, or knitting, which will most likely make you fall asleep. Stick with activities that involve your body *and* your mind.

Resisting the urge to give in to jet lag is as easy as you make it. Although you should exercise and consume a healthy diet, you must also have a personal incentive to stay awake. A lot of planning, discipline, and thought go into easing jet lag. Hopefully using this advice will help you have a pleasant transition into the time zone of your next destination.

Back to the Case of the Night Owl

This woman had a classic delayed sleep phase syndrome. Her slow-running body clock kept her from feeling sleepy so she could not fall asleep until 3:00 or 4:00 in the morning. As a result, during the workweek, she felt as if she were operating in a daze. But on weekends, because she slept in until 1:00 to 2:00 in the afternoon, she felt great. Although I explained to her that her problem was not a disease, she wanted to try to have a "normal" schedule. The first treatment we tried was chronotherapy. She took a couple of weeks off from work and every night she went to bed two hours later until she worked her way around the clock and began falling asleep around midnight. She also needed to go out every single morning as early as she could to be exposed to natural sunlight. At first this worked very well, but a few weeks later, she stayed up late at night at a party and went right back to her original sleep pattern. It was evident that the chronotherapy approach was not going to be effective in the long run.

I again reminded her that she did not have an illness. I advised her to identify with her own slower circadian rhythm just as she does with her hair color and personality. I recommended that she might have a better quality of life if she looked for a job that started in the early afternoon. She took my advice and switched careers. She has for years now successfully worked afternoons and evenings. When last I saw her she was quite content with her life. She had married another night owl. She had adjusted and no longer considered her circadian rhythm a problem.

Irregularities in a woman's body clock or circadian rhythm can cause her difficulty in falling and staying asleep. Sometimes the irregularity is caused by a body clock that is different from that of most of the population. Sometimes the problem is caused by a body clock that has been confused by travel. However, the good news is that women with problems caused by their body clock are usually healthy in spite of their tiredness. They just have to find the right method to deal with their situation—whether that means changing jobs so they can accommodate their sleep schedule or committing to using chronotherapy and sunlight exposure treatment to try to maintain a regular schedule. The next chapter shows how your lifestyle and work schedule can also cause difficulty falling asleep and staying asleep.

9

Sleeping in a World That Never Sleeps

The Case of the Sleepy Bus Driver

At the clinic, some people come to see me whose sleep complaints must be addressed almost instantly, such as pilots, air traffic controllers, commercial bus drivers, long-haul truck drivers, and others whose jobs leave no room for errors or nodding off.

One morning the person in my office was a woman in her early thirties who worked as a public transit bus driver. She had severe daytime sleepiness and was finding it difficult to stay awake on the job. After her supervisor had witnessed her nodding off on a few occasions, she sought help. We needed to evaluate her to determine whether she had a disease that was making her sleepy and therefore jeopardizing her ability to drive a public bus safely.

To diagnose the problem, I began by asking her the usual medical questions to see whether she had the symptoms of the major sleep disorders that normally cause sleepiness (for example, sleep apnea, narcolepsy, and severe insomnia). She did not. Then I asked her about other possible medical conditions, including thyroid disease and diabetes, which might be associated with her sleepiness. She had no symptoms of those maladies either. However, once she started to describe her daily schedule, I knew I'd found the cause of her sleep problem. She didn't have a disease that was making her sleepy and therefore a danger to the public, but rather her work was making her sleepy and making her a danger to the public. I'll describe her problem at the end of this chapter.

A Twenty-Four/Seven Risk to Health

What if you knew that something you were doing increased your risk for all these things: breast cancer, abnormal menstrual cycles, automobile accidents, preterm birth, preeclampsia, miscarriage, infection, sleep difficulties, obesity, abnormal blood lipids, and cardiovascular disease? You would certainly want to know about it. I'm not talking about ingesting a poison. I'm talking about shift work and night work. More and more information is coming to light about the links between work schedules and health risks.

Many studies demonstrate the connection between shift work and women's health problems. A study from the Fred Hutchinson Cancer Research Center in Seattle in 2001 reported that women working the graveyard shift (midnight to morning) had a 60 percent higher incidence of breast cancer. A 1996 study of Norwegian radio and telegraph operators showed that late-shift work was associated with a 50 percent higher incidence of breast cancer. One study of nurses done at the University of Washington in Seattle in 2002 showed that just over half of them had menstrual problems when working these shifts. They also reported sleeping approximately one hour less when working nights compared to days, and had difficulty falling asleep during the day when working nights.

A 2000 study from the University of Michigan concluded that women who had worked shifts or nights had a 24 percent increase in preterm births. And a study from Norway in 1997 showed that shift work increased the risk of preeclampsia (hypertension and increased protein in the urine during pregnancy) by 100 percent. In a 1996 study from Sweden, a marked increase in late-term miscarriages was found in women working nights. A similar conclusion was reached in 1993 by a study reported from McGill University in Montreal, which showed a strong link between work schedule and pregnancy loss. Furthermore, studies show that in women there is a link between symptoms of depression and increased alcohol consumption and late or rotating shift work.

Shift work may also increase the risk of cardiovascular disease. A study from Sweden in 2001 reported that women shift workers had a 71 percent higher incidence of three markers of abnormal lipids linked to cardiovascular disease. According to another Swedish study, women who worked permanent overtime (by more than five hours a week) were almost twice as likely to die with in five years than women not working overtime. Many studies have examined the relationship between shift work and cardiovascular disease; on the average the studies have shown a 40 percent increase in risk for these workers.

A study from Harvard University in 1992, involving 635 nurses, showed that those who had rotating shifts had twice the risk of falling asleep driving to or from work, and double the risk of reporting an accident or an error because of sleepiness. The connection between the sleep disruption caused by shift work and women's health problems is too strong to ignore.

But what accounts for this increased health risk? Why should working shifts increase risks of breast cancer? At night the body continues to regulate hormones. Some hormones such as melatonin are secreted primarily during sleep. Some recent studies have suggested that melatonin might inhibit some cancers. When someone works at night and is exposed to light, there might be a reduction in melatonin production. Though we don't know yet the precise link between breast cancer and other diseases and shift work, a great deal of research is being done on the impact of the twenty-four/seven world on women. This world may improve industrial productivity, but society, especially women, may be paying too high a price.

Blame Thomas Edison, the Great War, and Henry Ford

If this book had been written a hundred years ago, this chapter probably would not have been necessary. Electricity was not widely available, the telephone was not yet in widespread use, and there really wasn't a whole lot to do after it became dark except go to bed. Even reading was not so easy because one was forced to use either gas lamps or candles. People slept at least an hour more each night on average than people now sleep in North America.

In October 1878, Thomas Edison applied for a patent for electric lights that was approved in April 1879. The first public demonstration of the electric light bulb took place only a few months later on the last day of 1879. Guess where the first Americans lost sleep because of the electric lights? New York City. In 1882 one square mile of New York City received electric power; there were only 52 customers on the first day. Very soon after, however, electric utilities sprang up all over. Electricity came to the White House while Benjamin Harrison was in office (1889–1893). In 1892 General Electric, now one of the world's largest companies, was formed to first generate power and later to produce light bulbs. By the mid-1930s about 90 percent of urban America and 10 percent of rural America had electricity. Within a decade almost everybody in America had it. The night had been conquered. People could now easily control light. The world would never be the same. Starting with the light bulb there have been several trends that have contributed to sleep deprivation among American women.

Trend 1: The Sun Never Sets

New York is famous for being the city that never sleeps. In reality, ours has become the world that never sleeps; in virtually every city of the world there are many people who are working all night in jobs that simply did not exist in the nineteenth century.

In the twentieth century, as electricity and artificial lighting became available, industrialists decided that it was a lot more productive to keep factories and machinery running twenty-four hours a day; they simply had to hire people to work the extra two shifts every day. In 1922 Henry Ford introduced the twenty-four-hour assembly line. Every major industry seemed to adopt this method in an attempt to increase market share, improve productivity, and of course, make more money. The number of industries that never shut down is truly staggering. Because there were people out there who were awake, working, and going to and from their homes in the middle of the night, we soon had the phenomenon of all-night businesses including radio stations, television stations, grocery stores, gas stations, as well as all the companies that serviced those businesses. Since you never knew when you might want to make a telephone reservation for an airline, or you might want to talk to tech support about your computer or your dishwasher, call centers sprang up all over the world. These are industries that employ tens of thousands of people you never see, you have no clue where they live when you speak to them, but they are always cheerful and ready to help you with your problem. Thirty minutes before I wrote this, I had driven by a large bank call center near my house. The stand-alone building was perhaps fifty yards by fifty yards and was filled with cubicles and computer displays. It was 9:30 at night, but cars crammed the parking lot. People from all over the country were doing business with this bank by telephone.

The other important trend in this world that never sleeps is that people want instant service and, in some industries, instant transactions. This has been made possible by the electronically networked world. One can make a reservation for an airline ticket at 4:00 a.m. using the Internet. A commodities trader in Chicago might leave home in the northern suburbs at 3:00 a.m., arrive at the workplace at 4:00, and trade commodities on the London, England, market.

The bottom line is that there are now millions of jobs that require working at hours normally reserved for sleep. These working hours play havoc with the body clock, family life, and perhaps many other things we haven't even thought of yet. This is progress?

Trend 2: All Men—and Women—Are Created Equal

During World War I women were not allowed to serve in the theaters of war, but they were needed to do the work to keep nations running and to manufacture the armaments. In addition to more traditionally female jobs such as nursing, these women worked in factories, on farms, and in administrative jobs. It became clear that a woman's value to society in the workforce equaled that of a man. In the past century women have made enormous strides in their ability to get the same jobs as men. This includes all those jobs that are part of the twenty-four/seven world. Women are now long-haul truck drivers, airline pilots, surgeons, police officers, soldiers, and firefighters to name a few.

Trend 3: Options, Options, Options

Children today have activities available to them that simply were never available to previous generations. Parents have to manage their children's busy time and activities as much as their own. When I was growing up, the only after-school activity that was generally available was piano lessons. Now some children have access to every activity imaginable from rhythmic gymnastics to martial arts, debating, chess, and dozens of other clubs. Then there are lessons such as ballet, theatre, and skating. And let's not forget the appointments with doctors, dentists, and orthodontists. These are all activities that can take up a lot of time and, because there are only twenty-four hours in the day, they might lead to sleep deprivation. Consider ice hockey. If a child is on an ice hockey team, chances are that he or she has played many games that began at 6:00 a.m. Often this is when ice time is available. The entire family might have to leave home at 4:00 or 5:00 a.m., in the dark, to take the child to the game.

Trend 4: Some Things Never Change

In spite of great strides that women have made in the world of careers and work, in most families, it is the woman who deals with a majority of family- and household-related functions. It is still the woman who usually keeps track of the health status of all the family members, knows the shoe sizes of the children, and makes arrangements for lessons. It is usually the woman who enrolls the children in schools and stays up late at night making their lunches and cleaning the kitchen. Now before you accuse me of perpetuating sexual stereotypes, I do admit that there are some families in which the men play the roles I have just mentioned, or at least share some of these responsibilities. It's also true that in this generation men are much more likely to assume those roles compared to previous generations. There are a large number of families with a single-male-parent head of the household, but the number of women in charge of single-parent households is at least four times greater. The bottom line is that in most families, whether there are children or not, one person really has two jobs: a daytime job, which may have a terrible schedule, and a night and weekend job keeping the household going.

Trend 5: Sleep Deprivation Has Negative Consequences

In current North American society, people are overworking, and it goes almost without saying that the more they work, the less they sleep and the worse they feel—and the more likely they are to be sick. For example, a study published in 2003 that collected information about sleep and health from 71,000 nurses found that those sleeping fewer than five hours were 45 percent more likely to develop a cardiac disease when followed for ten years. The link between sleep and health was also obvious in the 2002 National Sleep Foundation *Sleep in America* poll. This poll of 1,010 adults aged eighteen and older found that the less people slept the more likely they were to feel poorly. People sleeping more than six hours on a weekday were more likely to feel optimistic and satisfied with life, while those getting fewer than six hours were more often tired, stressed, sad, and/or angry.

This same poll found that just over 50 percent of U.S. adults admitted to having driven a motor vehicle while being drowsy in the previous year. Males were much more likely than females to admit to drowsy driving, as were young adults (ages eighteen to twenty-nine) and adults with children in the home. Twenty-two percent of males and 12 percent of females admitted to having fallen asleep at the wheel in the previous year! Understandably, there is growing concern by many sectors of society about the performance of sleepy people.

No one wants their pilot to have alcohol on his or her breath or droopy eyelids. It's no fun imagining that your air traffic controller might be taking

Tragedy on the Road

The woman sitting in front of me at the clinic had very severe insomnia. The reason for her insomnia at first glance seemed obvious. Some sort of accident had crippled her. She was in a wheelchair, and her feet pointed in different directions, so one could conclude that she had broken bones that did not line up when they healed and the pain was likely causing her sleep problems.

As she related her story it became apparent that her insomnia was not so straightforward. One morning about a year earlier, she and her husband were driving on a two-lane highway to their cottage. A car drifted across the median, came toward them and crashed into their vehicle. Her husband was killed instantly and she lost consciousness. The woman spent many months in a hospital being treated for multiple fractures of her legs, pelvis, and arms. What bothered her the most, she said, was not the pain but getting over her husband's death. The driver in the vehicle that drifted over the center line had fallen asleep at the wheel. He had been awake all night and was on his way back to the city. My disabled patient's insomnia was caused by a drowsy driver who destroyed her life. She felt she would never recover from her injuries or her grief.

sedatives for anxiety or be unable to concentrate because she is coming off a twenty-four-hour shift. You do not want your doctor to be unable to focus because she was in the operating room the entire night before your appointment. Thousands of different jobs require alertness, but in these twenty-four/seven times, sleepy people can lose attention and fall asleep on the job. The consequences can be disastrous.

Steps to Improve Sleep in a World That Never Sleeps

The world is still obsessed with speed, communications, productivity, and global competition. It is unlikely that this will change any time soon. Quality of life is simply not an important enough priority in our society. I have colleagues who spend two to three hours a day commuting to and from work in horrible traffic. They make up for it by getting fancy, comfortable cars, but math wins the day. If you spend two hours a day driving and you go to work forty-eight weeks a year, you have spent 480 hours on the road in one year. Some people choose to avoid rush hour by leaving their homes at 4:30 to 6:00 a.m. and leaving work after 6:00 p.m. These people hardly ever see their kids. They never see the family in the morning, and only have a short time with their loved ones in the evening because they go to sleep at 9:00 p.m. How does that enhance quality of life? But take heart—there *is* hope. There are steps people can take to improve the quality of their lives in this world that never sleeps.

Making Choices About How You Spend Your Time

First, make a realistic inventory of your values and priorities. Then chuck the items on your list that are not all that important to you. Once you're down to two or three important values, it is then time to see whether your lifestyle and your life fit with those values. Are you spending time on your priorities? If a woman's most important value is to be with her children and her lifestyle ensures that this is virtually impossible, then the lifestyle and schedule must change. I have used this approach many times with people in their forties who have sleep problems that are related to severe obesity. I remind them that if they remain morbidly obese, and have a severe untreated sleep disorder, they are unlikely to be alive for their children's high school graduation and probably will not live to see any grandchildren. If this is important to them, they need to address the problem and develop and plan to lose weight and/or treat the sleep disorder. If spending two to three hours a day in a car or having a job with terrible shifts does not fit with your important personal values, you must make an effort to change your lifestyle. The money may simply not be worth it.

Making Career Adjustments

If your work schedule is having a negative impact on your well-being (you are always tired, irritable, and in a terrible mood) or you have poor health (diseases made worse by stress, including heart disease, high blood pressure, gastrointestinal disorders, infections, and diabetes) you should consider changing your schedule or finding a new career path.

Dealing with Shift Work

The third step to improving your life in the twenty-four/seven world if shift work cannot be avoided is to maximize the amount of sleep you get.

In thinking about how to cope with shift work, it is important to address the question of how to get the right amount of sleep so you can be healthy, not endanger yourself or others, and still be productive in your work and in your life. The first decision you might have to make is whether or not shift work is for you. Remember that when staying awake nights, people are battling their body clock, which is telling them to go to sleep. It is as though they are subjecting themselves to jet lag every few days. On the other hand, over the years, I have met people who are more naturally inclined to do shift work. They are night owls and they love to stay awake at night. They frequently end up working the night shift in hospitals and elsewhere. Some people can change and work different shifts without a great bother. For other people staying up late or working at night is torture. Their work life is miserable. Their personal life is miserable. People need to decide whether the advantages of shift work (a job, perhaps extra pay) are worth the tradeoff. For instance, the morning host of a radio station in a huge American market used to have to get up at 4:00 a.m. in order to get to the radio station to start his shift. After years of having this prestigious well-paying job he decided that he'd had enough of going to bed at 8:30 in the evening and getting up while it was still pitch dark. He was sick of having no life. He is much happier now with a less prestigious job with normal hours.

Sleeping at Home During the Daytime

If you need to sleep during the daytime, make sure that the home environment is conducive to sleep. This might involve investing in some heavy blinds that darken the bedroom. Perhaps get an answering machine or voicemail. If you're not on call, simply turn off the phone's ringer. When sleeping during the daytime, you might find that the only quiet room is some forgotten spot in the basement.

You need to communicate with everyone in your family and all your friends so that they understand your requirement for sleep and respect your schedule. Additionally, you could write a note to your neighbors asking them to respect that you have a job that requires shift work and that at times it will be necessary to sleep during the day. Politely request that they not make noise that might disturb your sleep. You might even give the neighbors a schedule of which days might be a problem, especially if you work a rotating-shift schedule. Thank-you notes and reminders will usually win their cooperation and understanding. Do whatever you need to do to ensure that noisy distractions of any kind are minimized. If some noises are unavoidable (you live near an airport or near a bus route), earplugs might be very helpful.

Exploring Various Kinds of Shift Work

If you are considering shift work, you should try to find out what type will be the best for you. A *fixed shift* is one with a regular schedule in which you always work at the same times. For example, you might work five nights in a row from midnight to 8:00 a.m., have two days off, then work another five nights in a row, and so on. A *rotating shift* is one in which you work a few days at one shift, have a few days off and then switch to another shift. The number of days you work in each shift can vary, and the direction of the shifts can vary. For example, one schedule might be working four nights in a row on nights, then having three days off, then working four day shifts in a row. In this example, the rotation was clockwise. A rotation that goes days (8–4 p.m.) ➤ evenings (4 p.m.–midnight) ➤ nights (midnight–8 a.m.)

is a clockwise rotation. A rotation that goes backward from days (8–4 p.m.) ➤ nights (midnight–8 a.m.) ➤ evenings (4 p.m.–midnight) is a counterclockwise rotation. If there is no pattern or you are asked to come in at random (this is common in long-haul truck drivers), the schedule is simply referred to as irregular. A split shift is one in which the workday is split by a few hours of no work (more accurately no pay) usually in the middle of the workday. You might be paid for four hours, not paid for four hours, then paid for another four hours. Thus, you are being paid for eight hours even though you are away from home for twelve.

In general, fixed schedules are better than rotating schedules for establishing a regular sleep pattern and lifestyle. Rotating schedules are better if the rotations are clockwise. In general, avoid work schedules that do not allow sufficient time to deal with family issues or social time. If a woman has no choice but to work, what is the best shift as far as her family is concerned? When there are preschool children, an evening or a night shift means that it is usually easier to get relatives to help care for the children in the home. When a woman works evenings or nights, the father is twice as likely to be the primary caregiver.

Handling the Workday

At work, don't leave the boring stuff to the end of the day; you may find it difficult to finish up. If you are doing dangerous work or work that lowers risks for others (for example, a heavy machinery operator, a ship pilot, an air traffic controller) make sure that there is a system in place that allows you to be relieved for a rest if you become too sleepy. You may even ask coworkers to let you know when you seem to be losing alertness. You will do the same for them. Try to stay in well-lighted areas if possible. Eat healthy and nutritious meals and snacks.

If you have a terrible work schedule, you should try to change it, but know that it may be quite a challenge to accomplish. This might involve talking with the employer, or the union, to see what compromises and changes can be made. Make your employer aware of the impact of shift-work schedules on the health and productivity of their employees. Find out whether the work schedules violate labor laws. Find out where the schedule originated. Did it come from the employer, the union, a consultant—or was it the result of a labor negotiation? In many situations, the schedule may have been the same for decades and there is no person or organization that takes current responsibility for it. Some companies may be prepared to change schedules based on new scientific information.

Find out what other employees think about the work schedule. Check to see whether other similar industries have better schedules. Arm yourself with the appropriate research and any materials you can gather to present your case. Approach your employer, not with the problem, but with a proposal for a solution. Involve your coworkers so that together you might be able to come up with a better work shift schedule, or you might suggest that the company consult with experts to advise them on how to improve schedules. If the information is presented in a positive way that would enhance the productivity of the workplace, reduce absenteeism, and improve the health of the workers, you increase your chance of a positive response. There is no chance of a positive response if you make no effort to change the work schedule.

Napping at Work

If it can be arranged, napping at appropriate times during work may be a lifesaver for shift workers, especially for those on irregular shifts. Check to see if your employer has a napping policy. A short fifteen- to thirty-minute nap can dramatically improve alertness for several hours even for someone who is very tired. More and more airlines, for example are beginning to allow copilots to nap on long-haul flights. Make sure that the nap is not too long; if you fall into a very deep sleep you might wake up groggier than you were before the nap. While other people are having doughnuts and coffee during a break, consider finding a place to sack out.

Finishing a Shift, Going Home, Going to Sleep

If you have finished a night shift and are going home, the following might be helpful. First, consider a carpool if that can be arranged. Besides saving on gas, having multiple people in the car helps the driver to remain alert. Some employers might actually be prepared to provide taxi transportation home for some shift workers, if it is not safe to drive home. Wear wraparound sunglasses if it is sunny outdoors, particularly if you plan to sleep as soon as you get home. Exposure to bright light in the morning may reset the body clock (see Chapter 8) and make it difficult to sleep. Avoid heavy meals and alcohol before sleeping. Having a big dinner at breakfast time will make it harder to sleep and might result in weight gain. Alcohol might actually wake you up within only a few hours (see Chapter 12).

Using Drugs to Fall Asleep
In general, using sleeping pills to try to fall asleep is not advisable when trying to adjust to a difficult shift work schedule. We simply don't know how safe it is to use such medications over months and years and even decades. Using alcohol for this purpose is also problematic.

Using Drugs to Stay Awake
Some people will use caffeine in its various forms, or even take stimulant medications such as amphetamines or methyl phenidate (see Chapter 20). Although drugs have the potential to improve performance temporarily and make people more alert, they may negatively affect nighttime sleep and cause insomnia in the long run. Recently, there has been great concern that amphetamines may result in poor judgment when used to maintain alertness. Late in 2003, the FDA panel that reviews drugs recommended that modafinil (Provigil in the United States and Alertec in Canada; see Chapter 20), a wakefulness promoting drug, could be used to treat sleepiness in shiftworkers with sleep problems.

What Are You Entitled To?
If you are working shifts, it is important for you to know what you are entitled to and what protections you have under the law, through your union, and via your employer's written policies. Most communities operate under federal laws or local regulations that protect workers. Some industries, such as aviation, are very closely regulated. Others have regulations that are sometimes loosely enforced—for example, in the trucking industry or in medical training facilities. One set of regulations may actually act counter to another set of regulations. For example, in some communities doctors in training might spend more than a hundred hours a week on duty; hospitals might argue that these doctors are "training" and not really "working," which they may claim justifies their ignoring other labor laws. In 2003 the organizations that regulate medical training programs have begun to enforce schedules that do not permit trainees to work more than 80 hours per week. Not all areas are improving, though. At present, a pilot may not be on active flight duty for

more than eight to ten hours per shift, but a surgeon may operate on you even if he or she has been awake for thirty-six hours.

Back to the Sleepy Bus Driver

The bus driver I mentioned at the beginning of this chapter described her workday to me. Every day, she awoke at 4:00 a.m. to make lunches and get things organized for her husband and children for the day. At 5:00 a.m. she left her house to go to the bus terminal and would start working at 6:00 a.m. Her morning shift was a total of four hours and she was finished by 10:00 a.m. Between 10:00 a.m. and 3:00 p.m., she hung around the bus terminal because she did not want to spend two hours going back and forth to her home. Her afternoon schedule, which took place during the afternoon rush hour between 3:00 and 6:00 p.m., lasted for three hours. After she returned to the terminal, she made her way home arriving there at roughly 7:00 p.m. Besides being absolutely exhausted when she got home, there was very little time to have a family life and also obtain sufficient sleep. She normally went to sleep at around 10:00 p.m., so on the average, she slept only six hours a night. No wonder she was a wreck and could barely stay awake while operating the transit bus. After we discussed various options, I contacted, on the patient's behalf, her union and her employer to see whether anything could be done about these shifts. In my opinion, such a schedule was endangering her and the public. There was absolutely no interest by either the union or her employer to do anything about these split shifts. The employer told me that the shifts were controlled by the union. The union head told me that it was too bad that she could not handle the schedule, but better work schedules were reserved for drivers with more seniority and she would have to work for several more years before the schedule would change.

The patient and I discussed the pros and cons of these shifts and she decided that her health and her family were too important to her and that she would have to change careers. This was not the first time, nor will it be the last time, that I have encountered an appalling lack of knowledge about the health consequences of shift work by people who were in a position to help the employee, and who should have known to do so.

In previous chapters we saw how a woman's biology (menstruation, pregnancy, and menopause), and her many roles in the home can cause problems with sleep. In this chapter we saw how a woman's many roles in a world that never sleeps can bring about sleep deprivation and health problems. The next few chapters review the sleep disorders that can have devastating effects on a woman's life.

PART III

CAN'T SLEEP, CAN'T STAY AWAKE

10

Insomnia

The Case of the Woman Who Wouldn't Sleep

A patient in her seventies had been referred to me by her family doctor because of insomnia. The woman was thin and looked nervous. She had not combed her hair. She told me it usually took her three to four hours to fall asleep; once she finally did fall asleep she would wake up an hour or two later and be unable to sleep again. In response to my questions, she said she did not have continuous movement or restlessness in her legs either at night or in the daytime. Nor was she particularly fidgety in the daytime. She did not toss and turn causing her bedclothes to become a mess. In fact, she said that she was perfectly still in bed whether she slept or not. She did not know whether she snored because she lived alone. When she did fall asleep, she sometimes awakened from a terrible nightmare drenched in perspiration. I asked her whether she was frustrated at not being able to fall asleep quickly, and she said no. Her difficulty maintaining sleep throughout the night had gone on for so long that she was used to it. When she awakened from sleep, she did not have acid in her mouth, heartburn, hunger, chest pain, shortness of breath, or any unpleasant sensation. I was stumped until I asked her how long she'd had the problem and whether she could remember when it started. When she told me that she remembered the exact night, I knew that I was on the right track.

What Is Insomnia?

For most people insomnia is *not* a disease. It is a complaint or symptom that usually indicates something else is wrong. Insomnia is a symptom that has many underlying causes including any of the following: psychological disorders, psychiatric disorders, medical disorders such as diseases of the heart, lungs, kidneys, disorders occurring in the transitions of a woman's life (such as menarche and menopause), as well as side effects of medications. Thus, if you have trouble falling asleep and/or trouble staying asleep one of these may be the underlying cause that requires treatment:

- Premenstrual syndrome (Chapter 3)
- Pregnancy (Chapter 4)
- Hot flashes (Chapter 5)
- Complex home life (Chapter 7)
- Body clock differences (Chapter 8)
- Our twenty-four/seven world (Chapter 9)
- Restless legs syndrome (Chapter 11)
- Medical conditions (Chapter 15)
- Psychiatric conditions (Chapter 16)
- Medications (Chapter 17)

The rest of this chapter reviews issues that are important to all people with insomnia. It focuses on the types of insomnia that are not associated with other conditions.

Is There a Problem?

There are times when what is perceived as an abnormal symptom may actually be considered within the normal range. People sometimes go to their doctor with a symptom that may be causing them distress but isn't an actual problem. What these people require is reassurance that nothing is really wrong. For example, I have seen many people who feel that taking thirty minutes to fall asleep is very distressing; others who take thirty minutes to fall asleep have no complaints. For some, any delay in falling asleep seems endless. Most of the patients that I have seen who suffer from insomnia take more than forty-five minutes to fall asleep.

Over the years, I have seen many patients who have told me that they only sleep six or seven hours a night; they therefore assume they must have insomnia. Many request that I prescribe sleeping pills because they have read that they should be sleeping eight or nine hours each night. I then ask them how they feel during the daytime and how productive they are. If they tell me that they feel wide awake and alert and they are functioning at a high level during the daytime, I tell them that they are among the lucky people who can get along with less sleep than the rest of the population. Though there are recommendations for the ideal amount of sleep, there is no single number that defines the optimal amount of sleep for each person within the entire population. For every individual there seems to be an optimal number. However, although some people know their optimal amount of sleep, others are unsure and so they often perceive a lack.

If you are uncertain about how many hours of sleep you need, you should carry out the following experiment. For the next two weeks, record the amount of sleep you had during the night and rate your daytime functioning at the end of the day on a scale from 1 (worst functioning I've ever had) to 10 (best functioning I've ever had). You can rate how you performed at work, in your hobbies or other activities, in relation to your family, or some combination. After two weeks, look at the relationship between your nightly sleep and your next-day functioning. Pay specific attention to whether or not your sleep is highly associated with your next-day functioning. Some people notice, for example, that there are days they function very well on relatively little sleep and on other days they function poorly despite obtaining a relatively large amount of sleep. Conducting this type of experiment can serve as a way to judge the impact of sleep on your daily life.

Is Your Environment the Problem?

Some people have trouble sleeping not because they have a medical problem, but because their environment is problematic. Too much light in the room can keep people awake or wake them up early in the morning. This is most often solved with good window shades. Excessive noise from outside the house (buses, cars, or airplanes) or from inside the house (music or television) can keep people awake. It may also be very difficult to fall asleep if the temperature is too hot or too cold. Whenever I travel and stay in a hotel, I always ask for a quiet room away from elevators and ice machines, but I also ask for a room without a feather pillow or down comforter. Why no feathers?

Is the Bed the Problem?

I learned many years ago, when I was a child, that I was allergic to feathers. A person waking up in the middle of the night with a stuffy nose or sneezing might also be allergic to feathers in the bedding. Is the bed comfortable? Many people have beds that are too firm for them. Others don't realize that mattresses and even bed frames should be replaced, and they end up trying to sleep on a bed that is lumpy or has a huge crater in the middle. Another problem is trying to sleep in a bed that is not the right size. Be aware that your teenager may suddenly outgrow the standard single bed he has been comfortable in for many years. You should take particular care to find a bed you and your partner will be comfortable in. A short "test drive" in the store may not be enough time to determine if a bed is right for you; always make sure you can return or exchange the bed before you buy it. When you are traveling (at a hotel or in a friend's home) don't be afraid to ask about the brand and model of a bed that you find is particularly comfortable. You spend one-third of your life in your bed—take the time to make sure it does not cause a sleep problem.

How Common Is Insomnia in Women?

Insomnia is not just a problem among overstressed and overworked North Americans. Insomnia is widespread in every country in which it has been studied, including France, Germany, Great Britain, the Scandinavian countries, Australia, and Japan. In all these countries, certain patterns emerge. Insomnia is common and it is more frequent in women and older people. For example, one study from Sweden determined the percentage of thirty-eight-year-old women who had sleep problems and compared this with the percentage of the same women who had sleep problems twenty-two and twenty-four years later. When they were younger, 17 percent of the women studied had sleep problems; when the same women were older, 35 percent had sleep problems.

Around the world, research has shown that insomnia is more common in women than it is in men. For example, an American poll reported in 2002 found that more than half (58 percent) the adult population suffered from insomnia a few nights a week or more; 63 percent of those reporting insomnia were women. Thirty-five percent of the adults in the sample reported that they had symptoms of insomnia nightly or almost every night. According to the survey, insomnia seems to be more common in households with children, in people who are in poor health, and in shift workers. Compared to people who had insomnia a few nights a week, those people surveyed who rarely or never had insomnia tended to consider themselves full of energy, optimistic, happy, relaxed, satisfied with life, and peaceful. People not getting enough sleep believe that they are likely to become impatient and irritable and to make more mistakes.

A Japanese study in 2000 showed that insomnia in women was associated with never having married, being widowed, or being unemployed. Among men, insomnia was more common in those who were older, those who had never married, and those who were divorced or separated. Compared to 3.5 percent of all men in the same study who were using sleeping pills, 5.4 percent of women were using such medications. The use of sleeping pills was much more common in those who were older, were widowed, or who had never married.

The bottom line is that insomnia is very widespread and is more frequent in women than men. It is more common in the unmarried, divorced, or separated; the elderly; and those under stress. People with insomnia tend to feel much less positive about their lives than those who do not have it.

Psychophysiological Insomnia: Learned Insomnia

When you develop insomnia as a result of one of the problems such as stress or pain that will be discussed later in the chapter, you should learn ways to manage or minimize the symptoms; otherwise you may develop behaviors that keep the insomnia going, even though the original cause of the problem is no longer present.

Say, for example, that a woman suffers a painful back injury that prevents her from falling asleep. In the days and weeks following this injury, she finds it very difficult to fall asleep and eventually becomes very frustrated about not falling asleep: she tries harder and harder to fall asleep but that doesn't work. She begins to associate her bed and her sleep with a time of frustration. By now, her injury has healed. Yet she continues to have insomnia, which is not caused by the pain, but is instead perpetuated by a new problem, the patient's learned behaviors. She now associates the bed with not sleeping. Although she is very tired upon going to bed, when she enters the bed, she immediately feels wide awake and alert—a very clear sign that the bed has become a cue for sleeplessness. This has been called learned insomnia (see below). Because her sleep is very poor, she attempts to keep alert during the day by drinking excessive amounts of caffeine. However, consuming caffeine, especially close to bedtime, can worsen the insomnia. Therefore, other factors maintain the insomnia even though the original cause is no longer present.

What Does a Drooling Dog Have to Do with Anything?

Those of you who have taken a psychology course have no doubt heard of Pavlov's dogs. Pavlov (at the turn of the last century) did an experiment in which he rang a bell and then presented food to a dog. Initially the prospect of food made the dog drool and Pavlov then measured the drool. This was done over and over again—Pavlov rang the bell and presented the food—which reinforced the dog's drooling in response to the bell. Eventually the dog drooled and behaved as though food were coming whenever it heard the bell, even when no food was presented. The dog's behavior (i.e., drooling) proved that it now associated the bell with food. The significant finding was that the dog learned this behavior. This is why a conditioned or learned response to a situation is often called a Pavlovian reflex.

People often develop this type of conditioned or learned response. For example, some people enjoy going to a movie and eating a big bag of popcorn. Over time, if they continue to go to movies and eat popcorn, they will find that the very act of going to the movies elicits an urge to eat popcorn. For many people, even if they have just had a large dinner prior to going to the movie, the first thing that they notice upon stepping into a theatre is the urge to eat some of that delicious popcorn.

The same conditioning process can occur with regard to sleep. After repeated nights of sleeplessness and frustration when lying in bed, the sight and feel of your bed can begin to elicit those very same feelings (i.e., frustration, arousal). Another example is that many people have trouble falling asleep before going on a trip. Anxiety about waking on time or anticipation causes you to toss and turn; you just can't get comfortable waiting until it is time to get up. Then, you go on the trip, come back and everything is fine. Before the next trip, exactly the same thing happens and eventually you connect going on a trip with not being able to sleep the night before.

When there is an expectation of a bad night's sleep, it follows that there will be a bad night of sleep. This is an example of psychophysiologic or learned insomnia. Unfortunately, this vicious circle is surprisingly common.

So, if you experience insomnia very rarely or just before particular events, you most likely have nothing to worry about. However, if you have trouble falling asleep most nights and then have frustration, anxiety, and difficulty in functioning the following day, you have cause for concern.

How Does One Deal with Psychophysiologic Insomnia?

First, all people with sleep problems should follow some basic rules.

The Thirteen Commandments for People with Insomnia
1. Use the bedroom for sleep and sex only.
2. If you can't fall asleep, after fifteen to twenty minutes get out of bed and do something else that is relaxing.
3. Avoid any activity that might cause your brain to be excessively aroused before going to sleep. That means no arguments, no discussions about money or major problems, and no exciting TV or books. Avoid any vigorous activity for four to five hours before going to bed (however, sex seems not to present a problem).
4. Do not consume heavy or spicy meals, which might cause heartburn or discomfort. You do not want to feel too full or hungry before bed.
5. If you use an alarm clock turn it away from you. Avoid checking the time throughout the night. Better yet, get rid of it.
6. Have a relaxing ritual at bedtime, for example, reading nonarousing books.

7. If there are caregiving duties during the night (children, elderly parents, pets), share the duties or get help.
8. Avoid daytime or evening naps (especially in the four to five hours before bedtime). If you must take a nap, make sure that it is not more than ten to twenty minutes.
9. Get plenty of exercise but not too close to bedtime.
10. Restrict time in bed. Spending more time in bed than you need actually worsens your sleep.
11. Try having a warm bath or a hot drink (without alcohol or caffeine) to help you relax.
12. Cut down or eliminate cigarette smoking. Limit caffeine dramatically and if the insomnia is severe, avoid caffeine after lunch. Reduce your consumption of alcohol, which can actually disrupt sleep.
13. If you are taking medications and have insomnia, check with a doctor to make sure that it is not the medication that is causing this symptom.

Stress and Insomnia

Any type of stress can result in difficulty falling asleep and staying asleep. Examples of acute or situational stress that can cause insomnia include an exam, a meeting, or a trip the next day. Examples of chronic stress might include marital strife, separation, or divorce; financial difficulties; illness in oneself or family member; or problems in the workplace. Some stresses are completely out of a person's control and related to factors completely out of the person's environment. For example, the acute stress Americans felt after September 11, 2001 resulted in a huge increase in cases of insomnia in the United States. The use of medication to help sleep at least a few nights a month increased from 11 percent of the population to 15 percent. Other examples of this type of stress are unstable international politics that might lead to war or a downward spiral in the overall economy that might lead to financial loss and unemployment. Human sleep can be affected by something as intimate as a personal relationship or something as impersonal as a war thousands of miles away.

For most people, sleep returns to normal when the factor causing the stress is removed (unless there are psychophysiologic factors at work). In a situation in which the stressful situation is expected to be very brief, but the sleep disruption is severe, medication can be effective. You should speak to your family doctor about what types of medication are available, the benefits and disadvantages of each, and their costs. Some information about these medications is provided in Chapter 20. Insomnia related to most stressful situations is expected to improve without treatment; therefore, most people get through the difficult period without drug treatment.

In most situations, even when stress occurs over months or years, sleep does return to normal. However, there are cases in which the insomnia continues long after the stress is over. I have seen people in my clinical practice who suffered enormous stress that was still causing symptoms of insomnia fifty years later. For example, many Holocaust survivors continue to have trouble falling asleep and staying asleep. Many still suffer from terrible nightmares. Some of these people also suffered from post-traumatic stress disorder, a serious psychiatric condition that is discussed further in Chapter 16.

When a stressful situation is not improving and insomnia continues, you need to get help to deal with the stress. As a first step, look to your close friends, family, or clergy. Do you have a support system of people you can trust with whom you can discuss your problem? Talking with them about your situation might alleviate some of the stress and, therefore, the insomnia. If the situation is too severe, consider seeking help from your family doctor, a counselor, or a psychologist. Sometimes a social worker can help, particularly one who has access to social and other services.

What to Expect from a Doctor

When you go to a doctor, do not expect the doctor to ask about your sleep as part of the routine medical evaluation. This question simply does not come up often enough. If you're experiencing insomnia, don't be surprised if you have to bring the issue to the doctor's attention.

Your doctor should take the time to explore your stressful situation and do an assessment to see whether clinically important depression or a medical problem is present (see Chapter 15). What the doctor should not do is simply write out a prescription for a sleeping pill or an antidepressant without any further exploration of the insomnia.

Over the years many women have been referred to me for insomnia after being told by their doctors that they were depressed. Many of these patients were being treated with antidepressants, although it turned out some were not depressed at all. The worst example was a woman who had developed insomnia on a business trip to Boston in the mid 1970s and was started on medications for depression that she was still taking thirty years later. Tragically, the medication she was taking was not a sleeping pill or even an antidepressant, but an antipsychotic medication that a doctor prescribed to her in error at the very beginning. She had gone to several doctors and had the prescription refilled more than a hundred times, and none of the doctors questioned why she was on this particular medication. This poor woman had basically been in a fog for most of her adult life because of an error in her initial diagnosis and treatment. If you are prescribed a pill to help you sleep, you must ask what the pill is. Find out whether it is a sleeping pill or an antidepressant—and whether it is approved for use for the treatment of insomnia. Sometimes doctors use medications to treat insomnia that have not been approved by the government. If you are prescribed an antidepressant, ask whether you are, in fact, depressed, how long you will be on the medication, and what will constitute a cure.

As you will learn in Chapter 16, insomnia is a common symptom of depression. Women with insomnia not caused by depression and women who are depressed often share a number of common experiences (such as loss of interest in their usual activities, depressed mood, lack of concentration, reduced memory, fatigue, sleep disturbance, loss of energy, lack of motivation, and irritability). They usually differ dramatically on other features, however; people who are depressed also might have extremely low self-esteem; extreme and inappropriate guilt over past events, wrongdoings, or failings; a high degree of self-blame; a disturbed appetite; and they might consider suicide.

Don't be surprised if the medical practitioner refers you to another doctor (perhaps a psychiatrist) or a psychologist. Most doctors do not receive sufficient training on how to deal with the psychologically stressful situations that may give rise to sleep disruption. Referral to another colleague is not a weakness on the doctor's part, but rather a strength. It proves that the practitioner knows his or her limitations and can see when it is appropriate to refer the patient to a specialist.

The Less Common "True" Insomnia

So far in this chapter, insomnia has been discussed as a sleep complaint or a symptom that requires attention and treatment. However, some people's insomnia is still a mystery. For 5 to 10 percent of the total population of people who have insomnia, the cause of their problem remains unknown, and scientists say they have true or primary insomnia. It is believed that people with this problem are born with an abnormal sleep-generating system.

Most people with this condition have had it most of their lives. They frequently claim to have been terrible sleepers as children, as teenagers, and as adults. Their parents say that they were terrible sleepers even when they were babies. They fussed and had tremendous difficulty falling asleep and sleeping through the night.

People with primary insomnia sometimes have parents or siblings who have exactly the same sleep problem, which is why this type of insomnia is believed to be inherited in some people.

Treatment

Because we do not know the cause of the problem, treatment addresses the symptoms rather than the cause or disease in this type of insomnia. Some experts have reported good results with using a very low dose of antidepressant medication at bedtime. These people might also do well with hypnotic drugs (sleeping pills), which are reviewed in Chapter 20.

Fatal Familial Insomnia

This is a very rare and fatal condition that has been described mostly in Italy (although rare cases have been reported elsewhere in the world, including countries in Europe and in North America) and has involved only a very small number of families. This disorder is caused by a prion, which is a chemical that is not a virus but behaves like one. The chemical takes over the machinery of the cells to make copies of itself. Prions cause mad cow disease and, in humans, a disease called Jakob-Creutzfeld disease. In this disease, there is progressive damage to the nervous system. People eventually lose their ability to sleep. The disease has always been fatal because there is no successful treatment. However, this disorder is so rare that you do not have to worry about it. I only mention it to point out that insomnia can in extreme cases be associated with death.

Back to the Woman Who Wouldn't Sleep

When the woman told me about the exact night her problem started, the story sent a chill down my spine. She had been living in an apartment with her son who was in his twenties in a part of the city where there is a great deal of crime. One night, the night that would change her life forever, two men broke down the door to her apartment in an attempt at robbery and ended up killing her son with a knife. After this happened, the woman became obsessed with personal safety. She tried to stay awake as long as possible every night to make sure no one would break into her apartment. The times that she woke up in a sweat from a dream were terrifying for her because her dream concerned the stabbing of her son. After a while, she developed a fear of falling asleep. It actually did not bother her a great deal because remaining awake meant that she would not have those awful dreams. I knew I was out of my depth—my training is in internal medicine, pulmonary medicine, intensive care, and then sleep disorders—I am not an expert in psychiatric conditions. This patient was a woman with a psychiatric condition who required expert help. The solution for her was not going to be a sleeping pill, but rather a detailed psychiatric assessment and treatment by a specialist. I referred her to another doctor, and she has apparently done well. This woman's case reinforces the notion that insomnia is not a disease, but rather a symptom of something else. To "cure" the insomnia you have to find out what else is going on.

Insomnia has many different causes and can be very distressing. The goal in treating insomnia is to find the cause and then to treat the cause. In the next chapter we review restless legs syndrome, a very common cause of insomnia that most doctors don't know anything about.

11

Restless Legs Syndrome

The Case of the Doctor's Wife Who Couldn't Stop Moving

I was having lunch in the hospital cafeteria when one of my colleagues asked me whether it would be worthwhile to have his wife evaluated for a sleep disorder because she had not slept properly for approximately thirty years. In fact, he was skeptical as to whether anything could be done for her because she had this problem for so long. I suggested that it was worth pursuing.

When I saw the doctor's wife in the clinic, she told me a story that was familiar to me. During her third and last pregnancy, thirty years earlier, she developed an irresistible urge to move her legs when she tried to go to sleep. She couldn't stop moving. She tossed and turned and found the only way she could alleviate this discomfort, if only temporarily, was to get up out of bed and walk around. Consequently, she had severe difficulty falling asleep and staying asleep. She no longer slept with her husband because the tossing and turning and recurrent awakenings disturbed him. She had little or no energy in the daytime and frequently fell asleep at inconvenient times. She did not want to start on sleeping pills and believed that nothing could be done to help her. After interviewing and examining her, I ordered some simple blood tests and after receiving the results, knew I had found my answer.

Recognizing Restless Legs Syndrome

The sleep disorder this woman had is called restless legs syndrome (RLS). The abnormal and excessive movements of RLS can interfere with normal sleep. It has been called the most common medical problem you have never heard of. It is the second most common sleep disorder and affects 15 percent of the general adult population and 10 percent of the female population, yet doctors hardly ever diagnose it. It is much more common among older people, affecting 30 to 40 percent of people as they age. It is very likely that you or someone you know has this syndrome. The disorder seems to run in some families. Sometimes RLS may be caused by other medical conditions, including iron deficiency, but in many cases the cause is never found.

Symptoms at Night

At the sleep clinic, we first assess a person's symptoms. Most people with RLS complain of insomnia or restlessness at bedtime. Some will only have repetitive twitches at night. Almost all RLS sufferers have trouble falling asleep and more than three quarters of them have trouble staying asleep. People with RLS are fidgety; like the doctor's wife, they toss and turn all through the night trying to find a comfortable position. Yet these patients often have difficulty in verbally expressing their symptoms. They experience discomfort in their legs and sometimes in their arms. Some patients describe this discomfort as an irresistible urge to move their legs; some describe a creepy crawly or drawing sensation sometimes on the surface of the skin, and at times, below the skin. Often, patients will say it feels as though insects are crawling below the skin. Others describe severe burning, itching, buzzing, or hot sensations in their feet or legs. I have heard some patients say they have "crazy legs." Most patients find some relief of these symptoms by moving around or walking. For many, the urge to move their feet or to walk is irresistible. Some people fan their feet at night or apply cold wet towels to their legs.

You might expect that once people with restless legs syndrome fall asleep, their brains would relax and their sleep would become normal. Unfortunately, this is not the case. In roughly 80 percent of women with restless legs syndrome, twitches in their legs and less often in their arms, occur about every twenty to forty seconds. These twitches are easily detected in the sleep disorders laboratory. When more than five twitches per hour are present, the patient is diagnosed with periodic limb movements in sleep (PLMS). A wide range of movements can occur in patients; sometimes these twitches are so subtle that we record their electrical activity but do not see any movement. Unless a patient undergoes an overnight sleep study, it would be difficult to diagnose PLMS as they wouldn't be able to notice this often imperceptible twitching. The bed partner may complain that the patient has a movement or a twitch every twenty to forty seconds. In other cases, the movements are subtle; sometimes only the big toe moves. Some people look as if they are riding a bicycle in their sleep. Others might kick or strike their bed partner with their hands. Usually the bedclothes are a mess in the morning. Thus, most RLS patients really have two problems: the unpleasant sensations that keep them from falling asleep, and the movements that awaken them or their bed partner.

"I became pregnant in December 1951. Within a month I discovered I couldn't sit still in movies or church and I was walking until three and four in the morning until exhaustion finally let me sleep. I was unable to describe what was happening in my legs. Try to describe the sensation of crawly things under your skin from the knee down, usually starting with a tingly feeling around the knee and then periodic jerks that caused the legs to jump. I had a very loving and sympathetic husband but eventually we ended up in twin beds.

"Over the years it gradually got worse, especially with the start of menopause. I feared for what I might do I got so exhausted and frustrated. I wondered how I could function with so little sleep. I began to panic. My thought at one time was: 'Thank God I don't live in a high-rise—anything to end this.'"

—EO, seventy-four, RLS sufferer, undiagnosed for forty years

Sleeping next to a person with this syndrome is not terribly pleasant. The bed partners of RLS sufferers have told me that sometimes it feels like sleeping beside a wriggling fish and that the patient may also kick or hit them. The bed partner might also develop insomnia because of the RLS sufferer's excessive movements. Frequently, couples start to sleep in separate beds and even in separate rooms.

Sometimes RLS patients inform us that when they were very young they were considered "squirmy" or restless children and were poor sleepers from the very beginning. The youngest child that I have seen with proven RLS was eight years old.

Symptoms in the Daytime

Although people complain that their symptoms are the most severe at bedtime, some patients develop an irresistible urge to move their legs or to walk around when they are sedentary or in situations that require that they sit still. For example, you might go crazy if you have to sit as a passenger in a car for an extended period of time and might insist that the driver stop the car so you can get out and walk around. You might also find it difficult to sit still in a movie theater; your constant fidgeting may irritate people around you. Even when simply sitting in a chair, you might continuously move your legs or tap your heel.

Some people with RLS fall asleep at the wrong time and in the wrong place during the day and this is the reason why they seek medical help. Their main complaint isn't the movements, but severe daytime sleepiness, which can drastically impact their personal and professional life. Even when they fall asleep, the continuous disruptions and movements result in poor sleep quality and sleepiness the next day. And some people have the awful combination of being overwhelmingly sleepy and yet unable to sleep.

"I had to stay still for a bone scan. It was forty-five minutes of sheer torture. Finally they tied my legs down with elastic bands and then had to hold them in place because the spasms were so strong."

—EO

RLS in Your Family

You will have little difficulty in recognizing RLS in yourself. What about in others? Asking a family member that you suspect has this disorder about symptoms at bedtime may be the most direct way to find out if there is a problem before deciding to seek medical help.

A movement disorder in your bed partner will probably be obvious. The person with RLS tosses and turns and may get out of bed and return several times a night. Even when these people sleep, they may change positions and have repetitive twitches or movements of the legs and sometimes the arms. Sometimes they will even kick you. Another sign is that some RLS patients sweat profusely. Thus, sharing a bed with one of these individuals is simply not a whole lot of fun.

"It is hard for me to sit still in the evening because my right leg either jerks or gets a bone-tickling feeling that necessitates moving my leg. I usually don't feel energetic when I get up in the morning, no matter how much sleep I have had. For at least the past twelve years I have been able to pretty much sleep anytime, anywhere. As soon as I am inactive, I can fall asleep. In college I would fall asleep in class, even in small classes of less than ten. It was very embarrassing but I could not stay awake no matter how hard I tried. I would frequently go to the library for the sole purpose of sleeping in between classes. It was very easy for me to fall asleep anywhere, even sitting up with my head on a hard desk."

—CM, age thirty

There is no data about how common RLS is in young children. As I mentioned earlier, I have seen it in children as young as eight years old. One clue suggesting a movement disorder is if the child is a very restless sleeper. If your child or teenager tosses, turns, and changes positions constantly and the bed is a huge mess in the morning, it is possible that a movement disorder is present. It is also possible the child has a sleep-breathing disorder (see Chapter 12). If your child falls asleep in class, a movement disorder might be the cause.

A great deal of research has recently examined the relationship between attention deficit hyperactivity disorder (ADHD) and restless legs syndrome. For example, one study reported children who were performing very poorly at school had severe insomnia and were found to have restless legs syndrome and low iron levels. When the iron levels were corrected, all the symptoms vanished and grades improved in school. This is important information for parents who definitely do not want their children taking medication unnecessarily; many people are concerned about the increasing rate of ADD and ADHD diagnoses in the United States.

Restless legs syndrome and periodic limb movements in sleep are extremely common in the older population. The reasons for this are not entirely clear at this time but may in part relate to the fact that many older persons have medical conditions that predispose them to the conditions. Movements may be more common in those with Parkinson's disease, arthritis, anemia, diabetes, and heart disease. As in younger people, difficulty falling asleep and staying asleep may be a clue to a movement disorder.

Causes of RLS

The next step at a sleep clinic would be to discuss the possible causes of the patient's RLS, including a checklist of other medical conditions that could be associated with it. The cause of the excessive movements during the daytime, their increase at bedtime, and the repetitive twitches are just now beginning to be understood by the sleep medicine community. The impulses that cause the increased movements appear to arise in the central nervous system. And the impressive regularity of the twitches, (see Figure 11-1) suggests that some pacemaker in the nervous system is involved. For example, we know that in some patients, the irrepressible movements occur even when the part of the spinal cord that controls the legs is separated by injury from the rest of the nervous system. Thus, at least in some people, the pacemaker that causes the twitching may be in the spinal cord.

Other clues about what causes RLS come from knowing which type of medications suppress the movements. First, drugs like Requip, Mirapex, Permax, and Sinemet that increase the amount of dopamine or attach themselves to dopamine receptors in the nervous system have been successful at treating RLS and suppressing the twitches. Dopamine is one of many chemicals the nervous system uses to send messages between cells. This suggests that a person with reduced dopamine levels may be more likely to develop RLS. As will be discussed below, factors that may reduce dopamine in the central nervous system may also be important. For example, iron is involved in the production of dopamine. Reduced iron levels in the body, which is quite common in women, may be associated with RLS.

Medical Conditions

In many patients, RLS does not seem to be associated with any other medical condition. It sometimes runs in families. There are some medical conditions in which it often appears. The following conditions are linked to RLS: iron deficiency, anemia, folic acid deficiency, B_{12} deficiency, osteoarthritis and rheumatoid arthritis, diabetes, kidney problems, or depression. Having one or more of these medical conditions may increase the chances that you will have RLS. If, after reading the list of possible associations, you suspect you have RLS, you should check with your doctor.

Restless legs syndrome may occur in people with anemia, a reduced level of red blood cells, especially if it is caused by iron deficiency. Recent research makes it clear that iron deficiency even when there is no anemia may still cause RLS. Women are particularly at risk of developing anemia and iron deficiency because of the repeated loss of blood during the menstrual cycle. This can result in iron deficiency if the diet does not replace the lost iron. We have also found that people who donate blood frequently may be at greater risk of developing anemia and restless legs syndrome. Very often, women first notice restless legs syndrome during pregnancy. About one quarter of pregnant women have RLS by the third trimester. The iron in the developing baby obviously comes from the mother, so if her dietary intake of iron does not keep up with what the baby is taking, then iron deficiency will occur. During pregnancy, RLS may also be caused by a deficiency in folic acid. Folic acid is one of the B vitamins, which also plays a role in DNA synthesis and the production of red blood cells. RLS may also be more common in people with low blood vitamin B_{12}, one of the B vitamins that play a role in the synthesis of DNA and red blood cell production. Some families with RLS tend to have low vitamin B_{12} levels. The problem may lie with inefficient absorption of the vitamin.

At any given time, millions of North American women diet to become or stay thin, which may result in their not getting enough nutrients from food. A diet deficient in certain nutrients such as iron and vitamin B_{12} may cause

RLS or worsen the already existing disorder. At the sleep clinic, we have seen RLS caused by low levels of iron in women who avoid red meat or are strict vegetarians.

Studies have reported that RLS is more common in diabetics. This is due to the effect diabetes has on the nervous system. When it has been present for many years, diabetes can damage nerves. This is called neuropathy, which is believed to be a cause of RLS. About half of all patients with kidney failure who are treated with dialysis have RLS; severe insomnia can result because the excessive movements keep the patient from falling and/or staying asleep.

At the sleep clinic, we have also found that RLS is more common in people with diseases such as osteoarthritis or rheumatoid arthritis. Interestingly, we have found this disorder quite frequently in people waiting for implantation of artificial joints. We do not yet know the reason these diseases are linked to RLS. The RLS might represent a reaction to the pain from these conditions.

"RLS has caused me to be deprived of restful sleep for several years, though I didn't know it. I noticed that I was more emotional than other women, and that my fuse was shorter too. I was diagnosed with depression and have been on medication for several years now. Before that, my emotions could change on a dime, regardless of the time of month. In relationships with the opposite sex, my difficulty in controlling my emotions was confusing and scary to my boyfriends, who didn't know what else to do but conclude that I wasn't the one for them. In turn, this has caused me to be afraid to be real with others, as I am afraid I will scare them away."

—CM, age thirty

Unfortunately, women with RLS are too frequently being diagnosed with depression, and are being treated with antidepressants. In some cases they may actually be clinically depressed, but often the patients have not been asked about the symptoms of RLS before they are treated for depression. This happens because women with severe restless legs syndrome might be very sleepy during the day. Her desire to sleep all the time and her disturbed sleep at night can be interpreted as a symptom of depression. The fact is that women are diagnosed with depression twice as often as men; it is easy to see how RLS-related sleepiness might be mistaken for depression by a doctor. However, this may lead to patients being treated for the wrong condition. Equally important, is that some of the drugs used to treat depression such as tricyclic antidepressants, can actually make RLS worse in some people. If you or someone you know is being treated for depression, it is important to talk to the doctor about the possibility of RLS.

Diagnosis

The right treatment can only be prescribed when the right diagnosis is known. This requires an interview and examination and, often, medical tests.

Clinical Interview and Examination

Unfortunately, many doctors do not ask patients about their sleep or about symptoms of RLS. Thus, many women remain undiagnosed or are misdiagnosed. For example, out of 287 people ultimately diagnosed with RLS, only one of them actually had been referred by their doctor to the sleep disorders clinic for specific treatment for RLS. We have seen many patients who actually had RLS but were labeled as having chronic fatigue syndrome and/or fibromyalgia. RLS is perhaps the most common medical condition that doctors don't diagnose. So if you suspect you have a movement disorder, consult your family doctor. Make sure you tell the doctor taking the clinical history about your symptoms of RLS. It is usually diagnosed this way.

Blood Tests

At the sleep clinic, we take a medical history of the patient followed by a complete clinical interview. If we believe that the patient may have RLS, we order blood tests to see whether anemia is present. Red blood cells contain a pigment called hemoglobin that carries oxygen. When the number of red blood cells or the amount of hemoglobin is too low, it means that anemia is present. Three factors—iron, B_{12}, and folic acid—are involved in the production of red blood cells and are also believed to play a role in causing RLS. Iron is found in the red cells and in the bone marrow where the red cells are produced. Iron is also carried by ferritin, the body's major iron-storage protein. The most reliable way to detect iron deficiency, other than examining a bone marrow specimen, is to run a complete blood count and measure the ferritin level. Even when the complete blood count is normal, the body's iron stores might be reduced. The range of normal ferritin levels is wide, but even within the normal range, the lower the ferritin level, the more likely it is that the person is iron deficient. The National Institutes of Health recently suggested that a ferritin value less than 50 ng/ml in a person with RLS indicates that iron deficiency may be a causative factor. Therefore, iron replacement treatment is recommended. One setback with the ferritin level test is that ferritin may be elevated when the patient has some acute or chronic illnesses; thus, masking an iron deficiency.

Tests That May Help in RLS Management

- Complete blood count to check for anemia
- Studies (ferritin, serum iron, total iron-binding capacity) to check for reduced iron levels
- Vitamin B_{12} level
- Folic acid level

If the blood test reveals that anemia is present, and an iron deficiency isn't indicated, then a lack of folic acid or vitamin B_{12} may be playing a role. B_{12} deficiency and folic acid deficiency can also be diagnosed with blood tests.

Sleep Study

If a particular sleep disorder cannot be diagnosed with a clinical interview and examination, the person might need a sleep study. To monitor movements, activity of the anterior tibialis muscle (the muscle over the shins) is recorded. The sleep study may reveal that the patient takes a very long time to fall asleep, tossing, turning, and trying to find a comfortable position. There is an increase in activity of the anterior tibialis muscles while the person is awake. Once the person falls asleep (which may take hours), we frequently

Figure 11-1 Sleep Recording in RLS

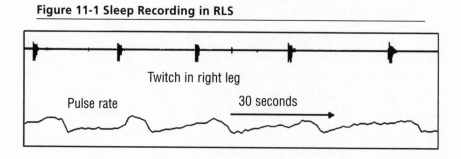

detect the repetitive twitches in the muscles that occur every twenty to thirty seconds. These periodic limb movements in sleep (PLMS) are found in about 80 percent of RLS patients. Although the diagnosis of PLMS is established when there are more than five repetitive twitches per hour of sleep, most patients actually have many times that number. Most RLS patients have between thirty and a hundred twitches per hour of sleep. When we observe the patients during the sleep test, we can usually see the repetitive movements. Figure 11-1 shows about two minutes taken from a sleep recording. It shows a twitch occurring in the right leg about every twenty-five seconds. With each twitch, there occurs an increase in the pulse (heart rate).

Sometimes patients complain to their physicians about daytime sleepiness; they do not have prominent symptoms of insomnia or restlessness at bedtime but have the repetitive twitches during the night. A sleep clinic evaluation will establish that many of these twitches are linked to brief awakenings of the brain. These short awakenings not only change the brain waves, but they also temporarily increase the heart rate. So the quality of sleep decreases and this may cause sleepiness during the day. If sleepiness is your main problem, you should ask your doctor whether a sleep test is appropriate. The sleepiness could be caused not only by the movements, but also perhaps by a coexisting problem such as sleep apnea (see Chapter 12) or narcolepsy (see Chapter 13).

Treatment

The type of treatment used will depend on how severe the problem is and what is found with the tests. Sometimes no cause can be determined.

If a Cause of RLS Is Found

At the sleep lab or in your family doctor's office, once you have been diagnosed with RLS, your treatment can be determined. First and foremost, the doctor should try to determine the cause and then treat it. After doing the medical interview and administering the tests discussed earlier, the doctor should prescribe the appropriate treatment. We do not recommend that people treat themselves. Self-treatment without a correct diagnosis can be dangerous. For example, although iron deficiency may be the result of heavy periods, pregnancy, and so on, it could also be the result of a serious medical condition such as colon cancer or an inflammatory bowel disease. Taking large amounts of iron if you do not have a severe iron deficiency may lead to serious medical problems. The good news is that when treated correctly improvement can be dramatic. However, it has been my experience that if the iron deficiency has been present for many years, the RLS may not resolve with iron replacement.

So if your doctor says you're iron deficient, the cause of the iron deficiency should be determined. Is it due to gastrointestinal bleeding? Is it due to heavy periods, poor diet, or excessive blood donations? If iron deficiency is the cause of RLS, your doctor should prescribe iron usually in the form of tablets to be taken for several months. Only about 1 percent of iron taken by mouth is actually absorbed, so it takes a long time to replenish iron stores in the body. Many preparations or multivitamins contain so little iron that they do not actually replenish the body's iron stores. The doctor should recommend a preparation that contains enough absorbable iron. Some people, particularly children, have trouble taking iron tablets. Fruit-flavored liquid iron preparations are available, but they are more expensive. In rare cases, injections of iron can stabilize an iron deficiency.

Some people with RLS have a vitamin B_{12} deficiency because they do not absorb B_{12} properly from the gastrointestinal tract. These people require repeated B_{12} injections to treat the deficiency.

Some studies show that folic acid or iron deficiency may cause RLS during pregnancy. Folic acid deficiency has become uncommon in North America because of fortification of grains, but some people may still experience it. Adequate folic acid levels during early pregnancy are said to reduce the risk of birth defects such as spina bifida. If you are pregnant, speak to your doctor about proper supplementation.

If you are a vegetarian and you experience RLS, it is important to remember that red meat is the major source of iron in the western diet. Although some plant products contain considerable stores of iron, some people may simply not take in enough of the right foods (for example, bran flakes, chick peas, beans, and spinach) that contain significant amounts of iron. Vitamin B_{12} is found mainly in meat, eggs, and dairy products. Although some plant products may contain vitamin B_{12}, they are not as reliable sources of this important vitamin. Vegetarians should consider taking vitamin B_{12} supplements or eat fortified products so that the daily intake is 1.5 micrograms per day (or 2.0 micrograms during pregnancy).

If the RLS seems to be associated with a condition causing pain, such as arthritis, one approach to treatment is to make sure you are treated for the underlying medical condition. Your doctor might prescribe a medication such as a nonsteroidal anti-inflammatory (examples of such drugs include Celebrex or Vioxx), to treat the arthritis and/or the pain.

If the symptoms of RLS are clearly associated with the use of antidepressant medications, discuss this issue with your doctor. There may be an alternative treatment.

If the Cause of RLS Is Not Found

If your doctor can't determine an obvious cause for your RLS, which happens quite often, then drugs to reduce movements could be prescribed as a treatment option. It is expected that in 2004 or 2005 Requip will be the first drug specifically approved by the FDA to treat RLS. The drugs that doctors prescribed for the disorder are medications normally used for other conditions but have also been found to be effective in RLS.

Drugs that increase dopamine levels or attach to dopamine receptors in the nervous system have been found to be the most effective treatment yet for RLS. These are the same types of medications that are used in Parkinson's patients, but at a smaller dosage. Parkinson's disease, which has afflicted Pope John Paul II, actor Michael J. Fox, and the boxer Muhammad Ali, is also a movement disorder in which dopamine levels are reduced in parts of the brain. Mirapex, Sinemet, Permax, and Requip have been the most widely used. These drugs should never be used without a doctor's assessment. Rarely, these medications can cause a side effect of sleepiness.

An alternative treatment approach is to use drugs that reduce the brain's *response* to the excessive movements. In other words, these drugs permit the brain to ignore the movements. Such drugs are in the class of benzodiazepines (clonazepam is an example; also see Chapter 20). Sometimes these medications might still be working after the patient wakes up, which results in a hangover. Thus, in some patients, taking this type of medication one or two hours before bedtime might help counter this side effect. Some doctors have reported that a medication used for seizure disorders, Neurontin, may also be effective.

In the most severe cases, when other treatments have not proved effective, we might recommend low doses of codeine at bedtime, a treatment that has been known to be effective for many years. How codeine works is not clear, but this medication has an effect of decreasing activity in some parts of the nervous system. For example, it can suppress the cough center in the nervous system. Codeine is a narcotic and in most places is classified as a controlled substance. You should discuss this type of medication carefully with your doctor and review the possible side effects.

Lifestyle recommendations include decreasing caffeine and avoiding alcohol and nicotine. Moderate exercise may be helpful, as well as relaxation techniques, massage, and hot or cold compresses on the limbs. Some people find that cooling their legs or feet at night helps them; others find the exact opposite. RLS is truly a mystifying disorder.

Back to the Doctor's Wife Who Couldn't Stop Moving

She had iron-deficiency-related anemia. Her tests revealed a very low ferritin level, a low level of hemoglobin, and decreased red blood cells. She did not need a sleep test because her clinical history was so typical of RLS. What she needed was iron treatment. Her husband, who was a doctor, would not believe that taking an iron preparation would solve her problem. But it did! Three months later, her RLS symptoms, which had been present for thirty years, were completely resolved and her sleep was normal. This case illustrates that many doctors don't know enough and don't ask enough about women's sleep disorders, even when the patient is a relative.

Restless legs syndrome is a common disorder that causes insomnia. It is particularly problematic in women because it frequently comes on during pregnancy and may also be related to the blood loss of menstrual cycles, which lowers iron levels. The disorder is extremely common in elderly women.

Although the woman who can't sleep is in great distress, so is the woman who can't stay awake. The most common cause of daytime sleepiness is sleep apnea, a condition that can shorten a woman's life. It is discussed in the next chapter.

12

Sleep-Breathing Disorders: Snoring and Sleep Apnea

The Case of the Farmer's Daughter

One morning a fourteen-year-old and her father came to see me. She was a slightly overweight blonde with red cheeks; her sad and tired-looking blue eyes stared at the floor. She didn't say much. I noticed that her mouth was always a little bit open. She had grayish bags under her eyes, which is unusual in teenage girls. Her father, a farmer with overalls and calloused hands, did all the talking.

When I asked why they had come, the father said, "my daughter is a bit slow." I could only imagine the embarrassment and shame this poor child felt hearing those words. He continued to tell me that she had trouble learning and that she was being treated with pills for depression but was not getting any better.

I told the father that I wanted to ask his daughter some questions, and that I preferred that she answer. Quite slowly, the extent of her tragedy emerged. For several years, she had been doing very poorly in school, and in fact, about a year earlier had dropped out because of bad grades. She'd had a great deal of difficulty concentrating and had frequently nodded off in class.

I turned to the father and asked him whether his daughter snored. He said that she had been snoring loudly for several years. I then asked if he had ever noticed that she stopped breathing while she was asleep. The answer was yes.

As I started my physical examination, I knew that I would find the cause of her problem with that simplest of medical instruments, a flashlight.

Sleep-Breathing Disorders

Sleep-breathing problems are so common that almost everyone knows a person who has one. The most common ones are snoring and sleep apnea. Snoring, the less serious of the two can cause conflicts in the home because the noise can be disruptive. But sleep apnea, a disorder in which people stop breathing during sleep, can ruin a person's life as it did for my fourteen-year-old patient. It can also cause death. While snoring can be a symptom of sleep apnea, not everyone who snores has sleep apnea.

Snoring

All of us think we know what snoring is and most of us have observed it first-hand or in people we know. Snoring is the loud noise people make while they are breathing in during sleep. Although the butt of jokes and countless cartoons, snoring usually signifies that the person's upper breathing passage is obstructed. Snoring represents vibration in tissues as the person is trying to suck air in. It can be so loud and disruptive that couples may start to sleep in different rooms or on different floors of the house. Couples in my office often get into loud arguments about whether one of them snores.

Is There a Problem?

Fortunately, the vast majority of people who snore do not have a medical problem. If the person snores but has no daytime sleepiness and has never been observed to stop breathing, and if his or her blood pressure is normal, then the snoring is not a medical problem. (However, it may still represent a tremendous problem for the bed partner.)

A snorer who is without symptoms or any other medical problem probably does not need detailed sleep testing. But it's a good idea to have a medical assessment just to be on the safe side. If nothing else, a blood pressure check could be helpful. In addition to a routine check, the doctor might find out whether the person's nose is stuffy at night (perhaps the person is allergic to the feather pillow or the cat). The doctor will probably ask whether the person has ever broken his or her nose or whether the person wakes up with a sore throat (caused by mouth breathing). The breathing passage should be inspected by a doctor to make sure that there aren't any abnormalities such as a crooked or blocked nose, enlarged tonsils, or other lumps and bumps. The doctor should inspect the person's jaw to make sure it is not too small or set too far back. The tongue is attached to the lower jaw. If the jaw is too small or too far back, the tongue will also be too far back, and this can block the breathing passage behind the tongue. This is an important issue if you have children who snore. The doctor should also check the patient's dental hygiene and examine the teeth. Though this may sound like a lot of checking, there are treatments available for snoring—and the right treatment can make a snorer's bed partner forever grateful.

Women with no prior history of snoring may start snoring during pregnancy. Not all snoring that comes on during pregnancy is related to sleep apnea. In fact, few of the women who snore during pregnancy have sleep apnea. Snoring in pregnancy can be related to several factors. Increased hormonal levels during pregnancy are the more likely cause at this time. Progesterone, a breathing stimulant, may actually protect the pregnant woman from sleep apnea. In some women, the nose becomes stuffed up because they have put on too much weight and the upper breathing passage has decreased in size. It is also believed that some hormones that increase in pregnancy might relax certain tissues and make the breathing passage floppier. In either case, the airway may become partially blocked and snoring may occur. Most of the time, snoring in pregnancy is not a problem, but the woman might want to discuss the symptom with her doctor to make sure it is not an indication of sleep apnea or a marker of preeclampsia (see Chapter 4).

Treatment of Snoring

Snoring is not a disease, so I do not recommend any surgical procedures except as an absolute last resort, and only if there is something fixable, such as a deviated nasal septum. I don't believe surgery is necessary as a primary treatment when there is no medical problem. I have seen many patients over the years who have had failed surgical treatment of their snoring and sleep apnea. However, the type of surgery that is done usually involves removing tissue of the soft palate. This will not solve the problem if the obstruction is somewhere else—for example, behind the tongue—or because the person has a small jaw.

Weight Loss

This brings us to what is ultimately the most effective but the most difficult treatment in snorers and sleep apnea patients who are overweight: losing weight. We have seen some dramatic examples of people who lost weight and completely cured both their snoring and their apnea. Sometimes a relatively small weight loss results in a dramatic improvement. Sometimes a larger weight loss is required.

Most snorers and about three quarters of patients with sleep apnea are overweight. The Western world is in the middle of a major epidemic of obesity that is affecting all age groups. Currently, about two thirds of American adults are obese, compared to less than one quarter just forty years ago. The proportion of people with extreme obesity tripled between 1990 and 2000. Half of all people with such extreme obesity are likely to have sleep apnea. They are also much more likely to have cardiovascular disease and diabetes. Obesity is more common in women than men and females with sleep apnea are heavier than males with sleep apnea.

This is not a diet book, but I will mention a couple of things you might want to consider that are often not mentioned in diet books. A study published in the *Journal of the American Medical Association* in 2003 that studied women over six years reported that women who watch two hours of TV a day have a 23 percent increase in risk of becoming obese and a 14 percent increase in risk of developing diabetes. The more they watch, the greater is their risk. If they watch four hours of TV, the risk doubles to 46 percent for obesity and 28 percent for diabetes. How many hours of TV do you watch a day? What would you do with the extra time? The same study found that a brisk one-hour walk each day reduced the risk of obesity by 24 percent and the risk of diabetes by 34 percent.

A study published in 1999 reported that between 1991 and 1998 in the Mid-Atlantic States the percent of the population that was obese increased by 32 percent, while in the South Atlantic States the increase was 67 percent. The state with the smallest increase was Delaware with 11 percent, while the state with the largest increase was Georgia with an astonishing 102 percent!

Avoiding Alcohol and Other Stuff That Makes One Sleepy

One treatment that can be widely recommended is the avoidance of alcohol, especially before bedtime. Alcohol, by reducing the tone of the muscles that keep the upper breathing passage open, worsens snoring. If possible, avoid medications that might also have a similar effect. Such medications might include sleeping pills and other sleep inducers such as certain types of anti-histamines that are used for colds and allergies. If the label warns you about drowsiness, there will probably be an increase in the tendency toward snoring and apnea.

Dental Appliances

Some people, particularly those who are not very overweight or who might have a small jaw or an overbite, benefit from using an oral appliance. These appliances resemble a mouthpiece that a boxer or a football player might wear, except that it has to be custom made to exactly fit the patient's teeth and jaw, and it is only worn during sleep. If the cause of the problem is obesity, there is less chance the appliance will work. The purpose of the appliance is to bring the lower jaw up and forward. The tongue is attached to the jaw, so this will bring the tongue forward, enlarging the breathing passage behind the tongue.

Gadgets

There are many gadgets on the market to treat snoring and many snorers have tried them. Some gadgets and sprays work for some people. The most commonly used are adhesive strips placed on the nose to flare the nostrils. You have probably seen this type of thing on professional athletes. At this time, I am not aware of any gadgets or sprays that are effective enough to be used by all snorers. Some people realize that sleeping on their side reduces the snoring so sometimes a poke in the ribs by the bed partner may help.

Sleep Apnea

Sleep apnea is a sleep-breathing disorder. The symptoms can be a combination of snoring, pauses in breathing, and severe daytime sleepiness. It was believed until roughly a decade ago that obstructive sleep apnea was primarily a disorder of middle-aged overweight males and that it was nonexistent or rare in females, especially young women. Certainly it was not something we thought a fourteen-year-old girl, such as the one I described in the beginning of the chapter, would have.

The reality is that obstructive sleep apnea is an extremely common condition in both males and females—as prevalent as asthma. The percentage of males with the disorder is roughly double the percentage of females, but it is certainly not rare in females; it affects roughly 2 percent of adult women. It is much more common in postmenopausal women (about 10 percent). Based on year 2002 census data, this means that there are roughly 4.3 million men and 2.3 million women with sleep apnea in the United States. We now know that obstructive sleep apnea can strike children as young as four months and in people as old as ninety. Some of these people are normal weight.

The bottom line is that the stereotype of the male victim of sleep apnea has resulted in a failure to recognize the disorder in women. Not only were far fewer women with sleep apnea diagnosed and treated, but they also were frequently treated for the wrong condition. We found, for example, that women with sleep apnea were frequently treated for depression before the correct diagnosis was made. A busy family doctor, who may not realize that apnea is common in women, might conclude that sleepiness in a woman patient is depression or stress related. As a result of the stereotype of the male snorer and sleep apnea sufferer, the vast majority of research studies involving sleep apnea have been done primarily with male patients.

Research from Harvard University published in *JAMA* in 2003 shows that at age thirty, men are five times more likely to develop sleep apnea over a ten-year period than are women. By age fifty the tables have turned; at that point, women are two times more likely to develop sleep apnea over a ten-year period than are men. The main cause of this increase is menopause (see Chapter 5). Women are more likely to have a variant of sleep apnea called upper airway resistance syndrome (UARS), though the percentage of women who have UARS is currently not known. This condition will be discussed later in the chapter.

"I was having some health problems related to anxiety attacks, sleepiness, and depression. I spoke with my doctor and she suggested that I begin taking an antidepressant. My doctor and I tried another drug the year before, and I found that they were both not working for me. I started thinking that I was becoming overstressed at my job, and I wasn't able to cope on some days without becoming ridiculously irritable. I would start thinking that I was being overworked, etc. My doctor suggested that I take some time off work, which I did. I thought that all my problems would be solved if I could just get some sleep. I found I was in bed sleeping a lot and was never feeling refreshed. I was gaining weight and not feeling any better."

—LL, twenty-nine-year-old sleep apnea patient

Where were people with sleep-breathing disorders before the 1970s? Doctors will usually have some patients whose clinical history is permanently etched in their memory. I encountered one such patient when I was a medical intern at the Michael Reese Hospital in Chicago, Illinois, between July 1971 and 1972. I was on a rotation on one of the medical wards and one of the patients, a woman, had me completely stumped. The medical staff at the hospital was trying to determine the cause of her severe incapacitating sleepiness. Almost every time I went to see her, she was sound asleep and when she awakened, she seemed sleepy. Otherwise, she was normal. However, she was about one hundred pounds overweight, and this combined with the sleepiness indicated to me that she might have something I had learned about in medical school, the Pickwickian syndrome.

At the time, the Pickwickian syndrome was known to be a disorder in which people did not take in enough air. It was also widely believed that the reason people with this syndrome were sleepy during the day, was because their carbon dioxide levels were too high when they were awake. When tested, her carbon dioxide level was normal, as was every other blood test that checked for abnormal states of consciousness. Her results proved she didn't have Pickwickian syndrome. Furthermore, she did not fit any other syndrome based on what I knew or had read about. I was as stumped as the specialists at the hospital who had consulted on her case. I remember thinking that if I had been a bit smarter or if we had known more, I would have been able to help her.

Roughly two years later, while I was a medical resident at the Royal Victoria Hospital in Montreal, I had a case that was nearly identical to the patient in Chicago. However, this was a man who had one other symptom—he had seizures while he slept. One night I observed that this gentleman stopped breathing when he slept, and I wondered whether this was related to his problem. That quickly led to what I believe to be the first sleep-breathing study in Canada and the publication of the first paper I wrote in the sleep field. I had found a case of sleep apnea, a disorder thought to be extremely rare, which had only been described a few years before in obscure European medical journals. This was probably the disorder that should have been diagnosed in the Chicago patient. The lesson that I had learned is that what happens during sleep, which makes up roughly a third of one's life, can make one feel great the following day or, at the other extreme, it can put one's life in danger. The latter was the case for my Montreal patient. When his breathing stopped, so did his heart—sometimes for up to ten seconds—and that was what was causing his seizures.

If you were to search the National Library of Medicine Databases (www.ncbi.nlm.nih.gov/entrez/query.fcgi) on the Internet for all the articles written that contain the keywords *sleep apnea syndrome*, you would find that there are more than 2,500 articles; yet not one of them is listed before 1975.

What accounts for this dramatic emergence of a disorder that seems not to have existed before 1975? Has there been an epidemic? The answer of course is no. In reality, this is not a new disease; it was not recognized clinically until the 1970s, but it has probably existed for thousands of years. There are examples from history and literature demonstrating that sleep apnea has been around for at least two thousand years. In 360 B.C., the tyrant of Heracleia (now called Iraklion, on the island of Crete) was a man by the name of Dionysius. He was so overweight that during public appearances he allowed audiences to see only his head. Historical texts reveal that he had a tendency to fall into a very deep sleep and had hired people to poke him with long thin needles, presumably to keep him breathing. Even that did not help, because the same historical texts say that he eventually died, having "choked" on his own fat.

Another example comes from the great author Charles Dickens. His first novel, *The Posthumous Papers of the Pickwick Club*, was published when he was only twenty-one years old in 1836. Dickens, a wonderfully accurate observer of the human condition, described a character, Joe the Fat Boy, who clearly had sleep apnea syndrome. The boy had all the features we now know are present in sleep apnea. He snored, and he was sleepy and overweight. The medical profession did not start to understand nor did they observe this disorder until about 120 years after Dickens described it.

An American president, William H. Taft, who was elected in 1908, had sleep apnea while he was in office, but none of his doctors knew it. He was overweight, he snored, and he was sleepy during most of his presidency. He lost much of his excess weight after he left office, was apparently cured, and became a professor of law at Yale, and later the chief justice of the U.S. Supreme Court.

The Causes of Sleep Apnea

Two types of problems lead to sleep apnea. In the less common type, sometimes called central sleep apnea (the word *central* refers to the central nervous system), there is a reduction in the electrical impulses from the nervous system to the muscles used for breathing. This disorder sometimes occurs when there are abnormalities in the nervous system and may also occur in people with heart failure. The second type of apnea is called obstructive sleep apnea (OSA). In people with OSA, the breathing passage is open while they are awake but obstructs when they are asleep. Normally, the breathing passage is kept open by muscles of the upper airway, but several types of problems can overpower the muscles' ability to keep the passage open. Normally, air going into the lungs travels through the nose, then makes a turn and travels behind the soft palate, and down the throat (pharynx) before finally getting into the lungs. A condition that interferes with the flow of air to any of these locations can result in sleep apnea. Thus, anything from a blocked nose to enlarged tonsils to a narrowed breathing passage due to obesity can all lead to obstructive sleep apnea.

When people stop breathing, the level of oxygen in the blood goes down and the level of carbon dioxide goes up. The low blood oxygen level forces the cardiovascular system to work harder with changes in the heart rate and changes in the autonomic nervous system that may increase blood pressure.

The increases in carbon dioxide level also affect the circulation, particularly the circulation of the brain. As a result, patients may awaken with headaches. For breathing to resume, the brain needs to wake up a bit and open the breathing passage. People with sleep apnea awaken many hundreds of times per night. These disruptions result in a lack of quality sleep, which in turn causes severe daytime sleepiness.

In *upper airway resistance syndrome*, the variant of sleep apnea more common in women, breathing passages aren't actually completely blocked, but awakenings are caused by snoring or snorts.

When we study people with sleep apnea, we see that the worst episodes occur while dreaming (in REM sleep). One of the reasons for this is that people are paralyzed in REM and so the muscles that keep the airway open are paralyzed. Another reason is that the body's defense mechanisms are inhibited in REM. Normally, there are systems that protect us against low blood oxygen and high carbon dioxide levels. These are the systems that make us breathe more deeply and will actually wake us up if necessary. These alarm systems seem to be suppressed in REM so the defense mechanisms don't kick in until the oxygen level is very low and the carbon dioxide level very high. In some women with sleep apnea, the only time their breathing becomes abnormal is during REM.

Recognizing Sleep Apnea

When I was a medical student, I was taught that if one could understand everything there is to know about syphilis, one would know all there is to know in medicine. Of course, this statement was an exaggeration, but the point was that syphilis is a disease that can affect many different organ systems including the neurological system and the cardiovascular system. In addition, patients could have many different symptoms, so that by understanding syphilis, a medical trainee could learn about all of these systems and understand many aspects of internal medicine and microbiology.

I believe that the same thing is true of sleep apnea. If we knew everything about sleep apnea, we would know a great deal of medicine. Sleep apnea affects many organ systems. People with sleep apnea have a bewildering array of symptoms that take them to the doctor. Perhaps one of the reasons it took so long for medicine to recognize the disorder was because of its multitude of symptoms. Another reason that sleep apnea was missed is that sleepiness was never considered a symptom. It was not something that doctors asked patients about; people with sleepiness were simply dismissed as not getting enough sleep or being lazy.

The most important cluster of symptoms in sleep apnea is the combination of sleepiness, snoring, and cessation of breathing during sleep.

Sleepiness

People with sleep apnea have no trouble falling asleep in low-stimulus situations such as watching television, waiting at a doctor's office, and traveling as a passenger in an automobile. Additionally, even small amounts of alcohol may dramatically worsen their sleepiness. What is much more troubling for them is that they might fall asleep at times when they should not, such as when they are operating a motor vehicle or piloting an aircraft. This has really happened. The two most unusual circumstances in which patients of mine with apnea had fallen asleep were during their own wedding ceremony (the groom snoring while standing up) and during sexual intercourse. In both instances, the spouses insisted on immediate consultation!

Snoring

Many people with obstructive sleep apnea believe they sleep well. Because they cannot hear their own snoring, they cannot believe they snore or that their snoring is disruptive to others. In our sleep clinic, we have patients look at a digital video of themselves sleeping that is taken during the sleep test. They often remark, "My God, is that me? What have I put my family through?"

Alcohol worsens snoring, making it louder and more severe. Someone who normally only snores may actually stop breathing while sleeping after drinking even small amounts of alcohol. Thus, alcohol can turn snoring into apnea.

Apnea

The word *apnea* means "stopping breathing." Though you might think that any silence emanating from a snorer would be a good thing, nothing could be further from the truth. When a person who snores suddenly becomes silent, the listener waits with trepidation for breathing (and snoring) to resume. This happens again and again and again during the night. What is worse to the listener than the loud snoring is the repetitive cycles of noise, quiet, noise, quiet, which may happen several hundred times per night. Along with sleepiness and snoring, these apneic events make up the last of the three main features of sleep apnea. However, there are other symptoms.

More Symptoms of Sleep Apnea

Stopped breathing affects several organs of the body, which can cause many other symptoms and be even more of a problem than the main three symptoms discussed so far. People with sleep apnea may complain of awakening with choking or headaches either during the night or in the morning, loss of interest in sex, frequent trips to the bathroom at night, symptoms of cardiovascular disease due to high blood pressure, and heartburn. In some patients, the clinical findings mimic a psychiatric disorder; people might complain of symptoms that are similar to those found in depression or other conditions. Consequently, women are frequently treated for depression before their apnea is recognized. No wonder it took so long to recognize and understand sleep apnea patients.

The Devastating Effects of Sleep Apnea

As is true of most people who have sleep disorders, the average person finally diagnosed with sleep apnea will have seen many doctors before the correct diagnosis is made. One study showed that, before receiving a diagnosis, sleep apnea patients were seeing doctors more frequently than normal for as long as ten years in an effort to get the correct diagnosis. Most doctors do not question their patients about how they sleep, whether they snore, or whether they are sleepy in the daytime. Many doctors still believe the stereotype of apnea as a disease of obese middle-aged men and so they discount the symptoms of apnea in the women and children they see. The best data out there, based on studies done by the University of Wisconsin in 1993, is that sleep apnea occurs in 2 percent of women and 4 percent of men. This means that if a family doctor sees one hundred adult patients (50 women, 50 men) each week, three of them (two men and one woman) will have sleep apnea. Imagine how many patients a single doctor misses in a year!

In our sleep clinic, the average age of patients being diagnosed with sleep apnea is about fifty, but many have had symptoms for five to ten years before they are diagnosed. Some of our patients have lost their jobs and homes because of the disorder. Additionally, many patients with apnea are being treated for conditions that they may not have, such as depression, and receiving medication that is unnecessary and could have serious side effects. Many of my patients have fallen asleep driving. Not just cars, but tractor-trailers and even aircraft. Studies in several countries have shown apnea patients are at much greater risk of having car accidents. Doctors are not making the connection that patients who fall asleep while driving may indeed have a major sleep problem.

"I found that this was an especially challenging time in my life, as pregnancy leaves you tired, as you are creating another human being inside you, and to struggle breathing at night, not even knowing that you are actually not breathing is scary. I found many short rests during the day and night was all I could do. I don't think there was one night that I didn't get up about six or seven times to use the washroom or to get water or simply could not sleep while I was pregnant. I would sleep an hour, then wake every night during my whole pregnancy."

—Twenty-nine-year-old sleep apnea patient

Are You Overweight?

About 75 percent of sleep apnea patients at our clinic are overweight and the symptoms often started after a substantial weight gain. In the Body Mass Index chart on page 162, find where your weight (down in pounds) and height (across in feet and inches) intersect. The number you land on is the body mass index (BMI). Any number greater than 30 is considered obesity. The average sleep apnea patient in our clinic has a BMI of 33. You can also calculate your BMI on the Internet at nhlbisupport.com/bmi/bminojs.htm. Weight, rather than general health seems to be a factor. Often young, apparently healthy ath-

Body Mass Index (BMI) Chart

HEIGHT → / WEIGHT ↓	59 in (1.50 m)	60 in (1.52 m)	61 in (1.55 m)	62 in (1.57 m)	63 in (1.60 m)	64 in (1.63 m)	65 in (1.65 m)	66 in (1.68 m)	67 in (1.70 m)	68 in (1.73 m)	69 in (1.75 m)	70 in (1.78 m)	71 in (1.80 m)	72 in (1.83 m)	73 in (1.85 m)	74 in (1.88 m)	75 in (1.90 m)
90 lb (41 kg)	18	18	17	17	16	15	15	15	14	14	13	13	13	12	12	12	11
95 lb (43 kg)	19	19	18	17	17	16	16	15	15	14	14	14	13	13	13	12	12
100 lb (45 kg)	20	20	19	18	18	17	17	16	16	15	15	14	14	14	13	13	12
110 lb (50 kg)	22	21	21	20	19	19	18	18	17	17	16	16	15	15	15	14	14
120 lb (54 kg)	24	23	23	22	21	21	20	19	19	18	18	17	17	16	16	15	15
130 lb (59 kg)	26	25	25	24	23	22	22	21	20	20	19	19	18	18	17	17	16
140 lb (64 kg)	28	27	26	26	25	24	23	23	22	21	21	20	20	19	18	18	17
150 lb (68 kg)	30	29	28	27	27	26	25	24	23	23	22	22	21	20	20	19	19
160 lb (73 kg)	32	31	30	29	28	27	27	26	25	24	24	23	22	22	21	21	20
170 lb (77 kg)	34	33	32	31	30	29	28	27	27	26	25	24	24	23	22	22	21
180 lb (82 kg)	36	35	34	33	32	31	30	29	28	27	27	26	25	24	24	23	22
190 lb (86 kg)	38	37	36	35	34	33	32	31	30	29	28	27	26	26	25	24	24
200 lb (91 kg)	40	39	38	37	35	34	33	32	31	30	30	29	28	27	26	26	25
210 lb (95 kg)	42	41	40	38	37	36	35	34	33	32	31	30	29	28	28	27	26
220 lb (100 kg)	44	43	41	40	39	38	37	36	34	33	32	32	31	30	29	28	27
230 lb (104 kg)	46	45	43	42	41	39	38	37	36	35	34	33	32	31	30	30	29
240 lb (109 kg)	48	47	45	44	43	41	40	39	38	36	35	34	33	33	32	31	30
250 lb (113 kg)	50	49	47	46	45	43	42	40	39	38	37	36	35	34	33	32	31
260 lb (118 kg)	52	51	49	48	47	45	44	42	41	39	39	37	36	35	34	33	33
270 lb (122 kg)	54	53	50	50	49	47	46	44	43	41	40	38	38	36	36	34	34
280 lb (127 kg)	56	55	51	52	51	49	48	46	45	43	42	40	39	38	37	36	35
290 lb (132 kg)	58	57	53	54	53	51	50	48	47	45	44	42	41	39	39	37	37
300 lb (136 kg)	60	59	55	56	55	53	52	50	49	47	46	44	43	40	40	38	38

*Shaded area shows range for obesity. About one half of the people with a BMI more than 40 will have a sleep breathing problem (darkest shading).

letes who are overweight are subject to sleep apnea. For example, a study in 2003 reported that about one third of NFL linebackers have sleep apnea.

Is It Sleep Apnea?

Figure 12-1 is a modified version of a questionnaire that is widely used to assess a person's risk of sleep apnea. I have modified the questionnaire slightly to include not just overweight people, but also those who might have other abnormalities such as small jaws that may lead to a sleep-breathing disorder. Like any tool that estimates risk, it may overestimate or underestimate. If you think you have a sleep-breathing problem, you should describe the symptoms to your doctor as accurately as possible. Taking this completed questionnaire with you will demonstrate why you are concerned.

How Many Risk Factors Do You Have?

Copy the questionnaire in Figure 12-1 and fill in the information starting with box A, then B, then C. If the number of items checked in each box is two or

Figure 12-1 Modified Berlin Apnea Questionnaire

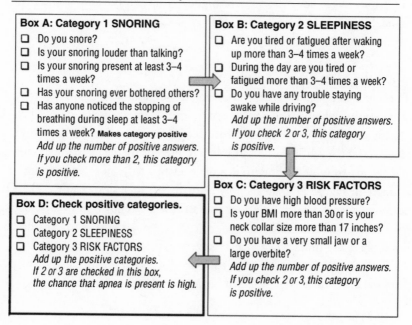

Box A: Category 1 SNORING
- ☐ Do you snore?
- ☐ Is your snoring louder than talking?
- ☐ Is your snoring present at least 3–4 times a week?
- ☐ Has your snoring ever bothered others?
- ☐ Has anyone noticed the stopping of breathing during sleep at least 3–4 times a week? **Makes category positive**
  Add up the number of positive answers. If you check more than 2, this category is positive.

Box B: Category 2 SLEEPINESS
- ☐ Are you tired or fatigued after waking up more than 3–4 times a week?
- ☐ During the day are you tired or fatigued more than 3–4 times a week?
- ☐ Do you have any trouble staying awake while driving?
  Add up the number of positive answers. If you check 2 or 3, this category is positive.

Box C: Category 3 RISK FACTORS
- ☐ Do you have high blood pressure?
- ☐ Is your BMI more than 30 or is your neck collar size more than 17 inches?
- ☐ Do you have a very small jaw or a large overbite?
  Add up the number of positive answers. If you check 2 or 3, this category is positive.

Box D: Check positive categories.
- ☐ Category 1 SNORING
- ☐ Category 2 SLEEPINESS
- ☐ Category 3 RISK FACTORS
  Add up the positive categories. If 2 or 3 are checked in this box, the chance that apnea is present is high.

more, that box is positive. Indicate which of boxes A to C are positive in box D. If box D has two positive categories, there is a high risk of apnea.

The questionnaire in Figure 12-1 indicates the statistical likelihood that a person has apnea. Like most tools, this one is far from perfect. Some people who score positive might turn out not to have apnea, while some who score negative might turn out to have it. To be on the safe side, the questionnaire is weighted to be sensitive so that it would miss the least number of people who *might* have sleep apnea.

Treatment of Sleep Apnea

If your doctor suspects you have sleep apnea, he or she will ask about sleep and sleepiness during the daytime. It is best if you bring your regular bed partner (if you have one) to the doctor with you, as you may not be aware of all that happens when you sleep. Expect the doctor to assess the person as we outlined in the section about snoring. The doctor may order blood tests and some other tests to make sure that your respiratory system and heart are normal. If the doctor strongly suspects you have sleep apnea, he or she will likely refer you to a sleep disorders clinic for overnight testing, which is described in Chapter 18. In some places, overnight testing can be done in the patient's home; however, the home testing is not usually as comprehensive as the testing done in a laboratory setting.

What the Sleep Test Shows in Sleep Apnea

To prove that apnea is present, the sleep test evaluates brainwaves (the EEG) to determine whether the person is sleeping; eye movements to see when the patient is in REM sleep; the electrocardiogram to examine the heart rhythm; blood oxygen levels; measures of effort to breathe by the chest and abdomen; and results from an airflow indicator in front of the nose and mouth. The example in Figure 12-2 shows only a small part of a sleep study. When the person is awake, breathing effort and airflow are regular and blood oxygen level is steady. When the person is asleep, although efforts to breathe continue, there are times when airflow is zero. The blood oxygen level drops to dangerously low levels with each episode of stopped breathing and the oxygen level is no longer steady, but it now goes up and down with each episode.

Figure 12-2 Detail of a Sleep Study

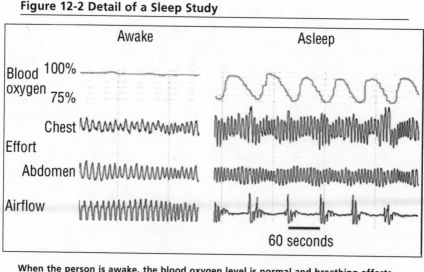

When the person is awake, the blood oxygen level is normal and breathing efforts result in regular flow of air in front of the nose and mouth. When the patient sleeps, the breathing efforts continue, but airflow stops (the airflow line goes flat) and the blood oxygen drops. The apnea episodes occur about once each minute.

Not included in the example is the EEG, which showed an awakening right before the patient started breathing again with each episode. The typical patient stops breathing usually between ten and one hundred times each hour. The average patient in our clinic stops breathing and wakes up about 45 times every hour or about 360 times each night. In our laboratory, we also digitally video record the entire night and show patients their record and video the following morning. When they see and hear the results of their sleep study, they often become frightened and are more aware of the dangers associated with these events. This is usually the time that they realize that they must get treatment.

Weight Loss and General Measures

Treatment of sleep apnea includes the measures used for all people who snore (weight loss and avoidance of alcohol and certain drugs), which were described earlier in this chapter, and specific treatments for apnea to open the airway that becomes blocked during sleep.

When I diagnose patients with sleep apnea, I also point out to them something that I have observed many times. The forty-five-year-old sleep apnea sufferer is still mobile and might be in reasonable health. The fifty-five-year-old sleep apnea sufferer who is overweight will likely have already had a major cardiovascular event such as a heart attack and frequently has developed diabetes. Arthritis in the knees or the hips may also be present. The hips and knees are particularly vulnerable because those joints are under the greatest amount of stress when a person is overweight. With knee and hip problems, the patient is no longer as mobile as he or she once was, exercise dwindles, and weight balloons upward. I often hear patients use the excuse, "I can't lose weight because I can't run or walk on the treadmill or use the bicycle. There is no exercise I can do." I tell them to go to their local public swimming pool. Exercise programs are available or can be designed for these patients. Walking in the water, which removes pressure from weight-bearing joints, is excellent exercise. Supervised exercises in water can be very beneficial. Along with regular exercise, once a person's food intake is normalized, the weight should come off. It is beyond the scope of this book to focus on dieting, but if a person cannot lose weight, there may be another medical condition underlying her obesity and she should seek professional help.

Opening the Blocked Breathing Passage

When obstructive sleep apnea has been confirmed by testing, the treatments mentioned earlier for snoring (weight loss, alcohol avoidance, oral appliances) are usually recommended. In cases that don't respond to these treatments, if severe obesity or apnea are present, or for very severe cases—we recommend more aggressive treatment, especially continuous positive airway pressure (CPAP).

CPAP. With this treatment, the patient wears a mask, usually over the nose, but sometimes over the nose and mouth. This is attached by a hose to a device the size of a small toaster oven, which generates pressure. This pressure acts a bit like putting air into a balloon; the walls spread apart. The pressure opens the breathing passage. This usually gets rid of the snoring, effectively reestablishing regular breathing. This type of treatment does not work for everyone because some patients have difficulty getting used to the pressure in the nose or they develop symptoms of a blocked or runny nose. Sometimes, humidification is added to the system, but some people still have difficulty. CPAP seems to be tolerated and effective in about 70 percent of severe sleep apnea cases. You might assume that the noise of the machine simply replaces the noise of the snoring patient. The noise of the machine is like an air conditioner, and believe it or not, most bed partners prefer by far the noise of the machine to the noise of the snoring bed partner.

Surgery. If apnea is caused by an obvious problem, such as enlarged tonsils, surgery might cure the problem. In very severe cases not responding to CPAP, the person might require an operation called a tracheostomy, which involves cutting a hole in the front of the neck into the windpipe. The person breathes in and out of the hole rather than the mouth or nose. Until the mid-1980s, this was the only treatment available and it was usually effective, although highly invasive. This is the treatment of last resort in people severely affected with sleep apnea.

Another type of operation that has been performed for snoring and apnea is to remove tissue from the back of the soft palate including the uvula, the tissue that hangs down when you look into the back of someone's throat. This type of surgery has been done using scalpels, lasers, and radio waves. As mentioned earlier, when looking at the results of such operations, many people do not respond well; thus most sleep specialists (myself included) do not recommend surgery as the first treatment.

Treating Sleepiness in Sleep Apnea

Because people with untreated sleep apnea stop breathing and then awaken repeatedly when they sleep, naps are not refreshing for them; they usually wake up groggy. Some people find that they sleep best when resting upright, and these people may benefit from naps.

The treatment for the sleepiness of sleep apnea is to open the blocked breathing passage as mentioned in the previous section. A patient with apnea who is on CPAP should use the CPAP every time he or she sleeps, including naps.

Stimulant and wake-promoting drugs (see Chapter 20) *are not* recommended for patients whose apnea is untreated. Some patients on CPAP may continue to have some sleepiness even though the apnea is controlled. The FDA has recently approved the use of the wake-promoting drug Modafinil (known as Provigil in the US, Alertec in Canada) for these patients.

What About Operating a Motor Vehicle?

In many parts of the world, someone diagnosed with sleep apnea may not be able to operate a motor vehicle until she or he has been treated. In most places, driving a car is considered not a right but a privilege—and that privilege can be withdrawn or suspended. This not only applies to people who have sleep disorders but to anyone with a medical problem that may endanger them or the public. This would include people with epilepsy and those who have had a heart attack and/or stroke. Since the regulations vary from place to place, you should check with your doctor to see what the regulations are in your state.

I am reminded of a patient who finally sought help, but not until he fell asleep driving and crashed his station wagon with three of his grandchildren in the backseat. Sometimes the symptoms come on so slowly—over a period of years—that the person is not as aware of them and believes that he or she is still normal.

I was once invited to give a lecture to a group of family physicians about sleep disorders. The room was small, and the doctor who invited me to speak, a thin young man, promptly fell asleep when my presentation began. I awakened him to demonstrate to the rest of the audience how to do an interview with a patient who might have a sleep disorder. When I asked him whether he fell asleep while driving, he said, "Doesn't everybody?" This gentlemen had been falling asleep while driving his entire life and believed that this was a normal state of affairs. To make a long story short, this doctor had a classic history of obstructive sleep apnea caused by a small jaw. His symptoms resolved entirely when he was fitted with an oral appliance, which he wears at night.

Sleep Apnea in Pregnancy

For some women apnea is present before the pregnancy occurs, while in other women it can come on with a massive weight gain during pregnancy. Pregnant women with apnea should be evaluated and treated because they might be prone to high blood pressure or a more serious problem, preeclampsia (see Chapter 4). There is medical evidence that suggests that babies born to these pregnant women may be smaller than usual. If the blood level of oxygen is too low in the mother when she sleeps, it will be too low for the baby. If the woman is untreated, the symptoms and the sleep quality will tend to worsen as the pregnancy progresses. If the pregnant woman is not on treatment for apnea, and if she is working and accommodations are not possible (reduced number of days or shortened workday), then she may need to consider taking a medical leave. It is best that pregnant women who have untreated sleep apnea do not drive a car.

"After a time, my husband started noticing that I would stop breathing and that he would actually count thirty to sixty seconds before I would start breathing again. I remember seeing and hearing about sleep apnea, but I still didn't think that maybe this could be the reason why I felt so crummy. Then I saw a television show on the topic, and thought that I would mention to my doctor that there may be a possibility that I have sleep apnea. By the time I mentioned it to my doctor, I was already pregnant. She explained that I should wait until after I had the baby to have it checked."

—LL, twenty-nine

Motherhood

Because a mother must be alert when taking care of a newborn and older children, it seems best for all that the mother be started on CPAP as soon as the diagnosis is made and to continue using it after the baby is born. The woman should continue using the CPAP until she has lost weight and the apnea is gone.

Menopause

Women are about three times more likely to have sleep apnea after menopause. There are several reasons for this. One is that the levels of the sex hormones that protect the women against apnea get very low during menopause. Another is that many women put on weight at this time. Research reported in mid-2003 showed that hormone replacement therapy seemed to improve sleep apnea in postmenopausal women. This is currently an area of active research.

Recognizing Sleep Apnea in Others

From the symptoms mentioned in this chapter, it will be quite easy to recognize when a sleep-breathing problem is present. Listening to the loud struggling snoring sounds—and the quiet periods when breathing is totally obstructed—is frightening. Strangely enough, the symptoms come on so slowly that their significance is missed entirely until something dramatic happens, which then becomes a wakeup call to the family. This could include falling asleep at the wheel, missing important appointments, or nodding off at unfortunate times. In general, if your bed partner snores, is observed to stop breathing while asleep, has had changes in personality (for example, irritability, inability to concentrate, etc.), or falls asleep at the wrong time and in the wrong place, there is a high probability that the problem is apnea. The questionnaire on page 163 can help predict risk of apnea.

Many people, even those with severe apnea, might believe that there is no problem and that they are champion sleepers. It is not until they see and hear themselves that the significance of their problem become apparent to them. The spouse or bed partner should persevere to make sure that the problem is evaluated.

Sleep apnea can occur in people of any age, including children. The symptoms and causes in children may be different than in adults. There are a few general rules for mothers to keep in mind. If a child snores loudly most nights and is observed to stop breathing, that may be a signal that he or she has apnea. If this symptom is associated with very restless sleep such as moving the neck or the jaw to open the breathing passage, then there may be a problem. If such a child has very large tonsils, is very overweight, or has a very small jaw, these factors may be the cause of the obstructed breathing passage. Children who are sleepy may appear to have attention deficit hyperactivity disorder; in other words, they may seem hyperactive rather than sleepy.

Back to the Case of the Farmer's Daughter

When I examined the girl's throat with my trusty flashlight, I saw a giant set of tonsils, each of them almost the size of a golf ball, meeting in the middle of her throat and virtually blocking her breathing passage. That was the cause of her apnea, and she was referred to an ear, nose, and throat surgeon. After removal of her tonsils and her adenoids, her breathing became normal. I wish every medical problem had such a happy ending, but I also wish that she hadn't had to suffer needlessly for so long.

Sleep-breathing disorders are very common; yet, they are an underdiagnosed problem for many women. These disorders can have a devastating impact. Also underdiagnosed are many unusual ailments that affect sleep. The next chapter reviews narcolepsy, a condition that is severe and has tremendous impact on the person's life. Because most doctors know so little about narcolepsy, many sufferers find that it takes more than ten years to attain a correct diagnosis.

13

Narcolepsy

The Case of the First-Year Med Student

Every year, I give a lecture on sleep and its disorders to the first-year medical school class. At the end of a recent class, seven or eight students rushed down to speak to me about their personal sleep problems. This was not unexpected as medical students often worry about having whatever illness they've just learned about. All but one had a problem with daytime sleepiness caused by not getting enough sleep due to the demanding schedule. After tiring lectures almost all day and a huge amount of studying each night, most students come to class toting a large cup of coffee, and several nod off during the class. One young student was sleepy, but she also had another symptom that I had mentioned during the lecture. Unfortunately, she had ignored this symptom for several years, assuming—incorrectly—that it was normal.

She told me that about twice a week, she awakened from sleep, almost always during a dream and was absolutely paralyzed. She could breathe, but she was unable to move her arms, legs, or head and could not speak. The problem had started about five or six years earlier and it had terrified her, especially when the dream involved a devil-like creature staring at her. The paralysis was not her only symptom. She also experienced a great deal of dream imagery as she was falling asleep and at times even before she was falling asleep. There were times when she had vivid dreams and she could not tell whether she was awake or asleep. Furthermore, because she had experienced these symptoms for so long and her sister had identical symptoms, she assumed everyone did. I assured her that these symptoms were definitely not normal and that, in fact, she and her sister very likely had a sleep disorder called narcolepsy. She then became concerned about whether this disease, which she had just learned about, would keep her from getting through medical school. It wouldn't.

Recognizing Narcolepsy

Narcolepsy is a chronic neurological disorder caused by abnormal brain chemistry, which leads to a perplexing constellation of symptoms that may include one or more of the following: severe sleepiness, vivid dream imagery upon falling asleep or waking up (hypnagogic hallucinations), waking up paralyzed (sleep paralysis), and sudden-onset temporary muscle weakness (cataplexy). The most common symptom is falling asleep at inappropriate times and places. If that is not enough, in spite of being extremely sleepy most of the time, these patients frequently have difficulty in falling and staying asleep the entire night. Narcolepsy most often comes on in the mid-teenage years and affects women and men equally.

"As I became more conscious of how tired I was, I also became more aware of how this was affecting my day-to-day life. I would promise my son a trip to the zoo or the children's museum or a movie, or a friend over to play, but after lunch I would fall asleep. When I woke up, I would hope he had forgotten because usually I still felt too tired to take on a long and active afternoon."
—A twenty-seven-year-old single mom with narcolepsy

The Devastating Effects of Narcolepsy

One study of a large group of patients (63 percent were women, 37 percent were men) in 1997 reported that people had symptoms for roughly fifteen years before their narcolepsy was correctly diagnosed. People with narcolepsy are often treated for some other condition, often depression, which they may not have. Children may be misdiagnosed with attention deficit disorder when they are actually just too tired to pay attention. Some doctors assume that a woman who is sleepy probably has depression. Not only does the incorrect diagnosis delay the correct treatment, some of the drugs used to treat the depression can make the narcoleptic's sleepiness even worse. Because the disorder comes on often during the middle teenage years, people with narcolepsy are left untreated at precisely the time when they are going to school and developing the skills that will carry them through the rest of their lives. Patients with narcolepsy may feel unable to cope; they may drop out of school because the problem was not recognized. Narcoleptics are at much greater risk of having automobile accidents. Narcolepsy can be especially devastating for women. Keeping a job is difficult when you can't stay awake. Maintaining a relationship is a challenge. Raising children and keeping up with their busy schedules is even more exhausting. Simply put, narcolepsy can ruin people's lives. A correct diagnosis as soon as possible is essential.

"Recently I was diagnosed with narcolepsy and cataplexy. To finally have an explanation for all the time I spent tired or sleeping was a relief. I found myself more aware of exactly how much time I was spending asleep during the day. My regular family doctor would test my iron levels or my thyroid but these always came back normal."

—The twenty-seven-year-old, diagnosed fourteen years
after onset of symptoms

How Common Is Narcolepsy?

Scientists around the world have been trying to determine how common narcolepsy is, and the answer seems to vary from country to country. It seems to be very common in Japan. In North America it is estimated that it affects approximately 1 out of every 2,000 people. In the United States there are between 100,000 and 150,000 people with the disorder. Most of them have not been diagnosed.

Causes of Narcolepsy

We do not know for sure the causes of narcolepsy, but many clues are coming in from unexpected sources, such as research on Doberman pinschers and mice. Science made a huge leap forward about five years ago when a new chemical culprit was discovered—one that might play a major role in narcolepsy. This chemical is known by two names, *orexin* and *hypocretin*. Different research groups discovered the chemical at about the same time and each gave it a different name. Research suggests that patients with narcolepsy do not produce sufficient quantities of this chemical, or receptors in the nervous system may have ceased to respond to it adequately. Experiments have been done in which the genes responsible for the production of this chemical are knocked out in experimental animals, and the experimental animals develop the features of narcolepsy, sleep attacks, and cataplexy. The discovery of this chemical was a big step forward in the understanding and treatment of this debilitating sleep disorder.

Narcolepsy seems to be due to the brain's abnormal regulation of REM (rapid eye movement) sleep. Normally, during REM sleep or dreaming sleep, humans are paralyzed as are virtually all higher life forms including birds and mammals. During REM sleep, most of the muscles of the body are paralyzed except the ones necessary to sustain life, such as the breathing muscles (diaphragm); muscles such as the heart, which are controlled within themselves; and some of the muscles at the top and bottom of the gastrointestinal system.

It's not known why we are paralyzed during REM sleep—it may be so that we cannot physically react to what we are dreaming. Normally, adults do not have the first episode of REM sleep until they have been asleep for ninety minutes. Thereafter, they will have an episode of rapid eye movement sleep about every ninety minutes. Most people will dream three to five times each night and during each dream, they are paralyzed. This is normal sleep.

Patients with narcolepsy fall into REM sleep at the wrong time and in the wrong place. The dreamlike imagery that they see at the onset of sleep or even

"I have seen a man at the window with a pointed face and when he sees that I have seen him he turns around to leave and the entire back of his head is a metal plate that is actually screwed into his head. This is one dream that I had when I was very young and still have recurring dreams with him in them. At the time of this dream I had difficulty believing that this man was not real because I thought I was awake.

"The recurring dreams with him have been my brother, my cousin, and myself being chased in a forest by "the pointed-face man" as I call him, and in the middle of the forest is a couch that we all hide behind, and when the pointed-face man reaches us he pulls each of us out one by one and cuts our feet off with an axe then I wake up.

"Another dream with pointed-face man: It is winter and my brother and myself are outside. My bother is younger than me in the dream but he is actually older than me. We are playing outside and my brother is wearing his favorite gray snowsuit and the pointed-face man comes up from behind him in front of me and pulls back my brother's head and cuts his throat. I am unable to stop him or run to get help then the pointed-face man drops my brother and cuts off my feet so I cannot run and leaves me to bleed to death with my brother."

—Hypnagogic hallucinations in an eighteen-year-old narcoleptic

while they are still awake is called a hypnagogic hallucination. Sometimes when a patient with narcolepsy awakens from a dream, the paralysis of REM persists.

One other symptom of narcolepsy, which can be very upsetting to the sufferer, is the experience of a sudden loss of muscle control. This sometimes happens when patients are awake and they become excited. For example, after hearing a joke, a person might feel some of the manifestations of REM sleep come on leading to a form of temporary paralysis called cataplexy. This paralysis might cause the individual to collapse in a heap. One patient had felt like a puppet with all the strings cut off whenever she heard a joke. Women with cataplexy might not have orgasms during sexual intercourse because they try to avoid arousal that might lead to a cataplexy attack. At other times, the loss of muscle tone is more limited and may involve the muscles of the face or the neck. These episodes are sometimes misinterpreted as an epileptic seizure and others may not realize that the person with narcolepsy who has just collapsed is actually conscious of what is going on around her.

Animals with narcolepsy (the Doberman pinscher is a breed with this problem) collapse in a heap when they are excited—for example, when they see food or when they see a cat! However, to the thousands of women who are plagued with it, narcolepsy is anything but a joke.

Diagnosis

One reason that narcolepsy is underdiagnosed is that most doctors do not question patients about how they sleep. Another reason is that many doctors know little if anything about narcolepsy. In most medical schools, they might receive just two to four hours of sleep medicine training during their entire educational process. Most of the patients with narcolepsy that I have seen have a classical clinical history. Many doctors are embarrassed when they finally realize that their patient's condition could have been diagnosed in a few minutes by asking three or four specific questions. The next section will help you discuss narcolepsy symptoms with your doctor.

Clinical Interview and Examination

When was the last time a doctor asked you whether you dream while falling asleep? As discussed earlier, many doctors do not ask women about their sleep, and certainly not about symptoms of narcolepsy. Thus many women remain undiagnosed or misdiagnosed and are treated for conditions such as depression, which they might not have. We have reported in a medical article in 2002 that family doctors diagnose narcolepsy only about 20 percent of the time even when people have classic symptoms. So if the symptoms that are the hallmarks of this disorder (mentioned earlier in the chapter) lead you to suspect you have narcolepsy, consult with your family doctor. Tell the doctor that takes your clinical history about all your symptoms and suspicions. It might be helpful to take educational materials or this book with you to share with your doctor who may not have any training in the diagnosis and treatment of narcolepsy. Because narcolepsy is a lifelong illness that will require lifelong treatment and because sometimes narcolepsy patients have another sleep disorder, most sleep specialists will order a sleep test to confirm the diagnosis.

Sleep Study

Before you embark on lifelong drug treatment, you will need sleep testing (see Chapter 18). At the sleep lab, we perform two sleep studies, one at night and one during the day. The night sleep study may show the early onset of REM upon falling asleep and sleep may be disrupted with many awakenings. Ironically, these people who fall asleep so easily during the day often have trouble falling asleep and staying asleep at night. This study should also make sure that other disorders such as sleep apnea are not present. The daytime study is called the multiple sleep latency test. In this test, the patient is given four or five opportunities to fall asleep every two hours. If it takes five minutes or less to fall asleep, on average, sleep scientists or technologists can tell that the person has severe sleepiness; if the person has REM sleep during two or more of the naps then this supports a narcolepsy diagnosis. Figure 13-1 shows data taken from a sleep recording. The left side shows the brain waves seen during non-REM sleep. The right side shows the waves and eye activity in REM sleep. Notice the big sharp movements of the eyes in the lowest two channels on the right. This data is from an eighteen-year-old student. On average, she fell asleep in about 4.5 minutes and had REM three times during the four opportunities to nap. These findings are characteristic of narcolepsy.

Figure 13-1 The Eighteen-Year-Old's Data from Sleep Recording

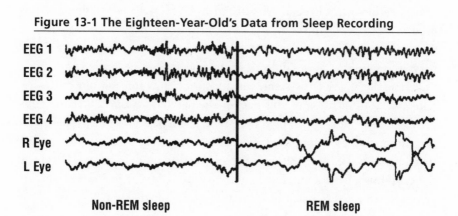

Treating Narcolepsy

Medical science can't cure narcolepsy; thus, we treat the symptoms and recognize that this is a disease that is not going to resolve on its own. Though the individuals will likely have to use some medication for the rest of their lives, they will be able to live a fairly normal life on treatment. It will certainly be a better life than before treatment.

Medication

Sleepiness, which is the most common and debilitating symptom of people with narcolepsy, is treated with medications that make one more alert and help prevent the irresistible urge to fall asleep.

Modafinil (Alertec in Canada, Provigil in the United States)

Modafinil is the most commonly prescribed medication, promoting wakefulness by working on the part of the brain that helps maintain alertness. In contrast to the stimulant medications described below, it has little effect on the remainder of the body. Additionally, patients with narcolepsy have different degrees of daytime sleepiness in response to medications; so the dosage needs to be customized to the individual. At this time, modafinil is the only medication developed and approved specifically for excessive daytime sleepiness associated with narcolepsy.

Methylphenidate (Ritalin)

Methylphenidate is widely known as the medication prescribed to children with attention deficit hyperactivity disorder (ADHD). Paradoxically, this drug used to wake people up is also used to calm down people with ADHD; it allows them to focus on their tasks. Besides having an effect on the central nervous system that makes individuals more alert, this medication also affects the sympathetic nervous system, which controls how some of our organ systems work. Stimulation of this part of the nervous system can result in an increased heart rate, rise in blood pressure, and a jittery feeling in some people. Although these symptoms may decrease with time, there is some concern that long-term use by people with narcolepsy may result in adverse effects on the cardiovascular system. This might be especially true in women who are generally protected from cardiovascular disease compared to males, but whose risk increases with the onset of menopause. Thus, most sleep experts no longer consider methylphenidate the first drug of choice in increasing alertness in narcolepsy patients.

Amphetamines

Many people think of amphetamine as an illegal street drug known as speed. They don't realize that it has also been a medication prescribed by doctors for many years and has been used to treat narcolepsy since the 1930s. See page 279 for a description of the amphetamine medications.

Amphetamines have a very powerful stimulant effect on the brain and the sympathetic nervous system. Amphetamines can also cause increases in heart rate and blood pressure, and they may cause sweating and jitteriness as well. Although amphetamines present the potential for abuse, I have seen this only rarely in my clinical practice. Because of the potential for abuse, many countries have removed these drugs from the market—although not the United States or Canada. As a result, crossing borders with containers of these medications may cause hassles or even confiscation. In some locations, the prescription regulations for amphetamines (and other drugs that may be abused) are so strict that doctors do not prescribe them. For example, I'm required to fill in a triple-copy prescription form. One copy of the prescription stays in the doctor's file, one goes to the pharmacy, and a third goes to the medical licensing authorities, who monitor the usage of such medications. Prescriptions cannot be refilled over the telephone, and only short-term prescriptions are allowed. In spite of these difficulties, some doctors are not familiar with modafinil and still prescribe amphetamines as the first treatment of narcolepsy. I rarely prescribe amphetamines as the first treatment for narcolepsy.

Other Drugs Used in Narcolepsy

Another medication, called pemoline (brand name Cylert) has been used for many years in the treatment for narcolepsy. This medication was effective, but there has been some concern about it possibly causing liver problems. It has been discontinued in some countries including Canada. In the USA, people are usually regularly tested to make sure that their liver is functioning normally when they are taking this medication.

These medications improve sleepiness, but they may not improve cataplexy, hallucinations, and sleep paralysis, which are REM-related symptoms. A new drug (sodium oxybate, Xyrem) was introduced in the United States in 2002 (not yet in Canada). This medication, when taken at night, reduces cataplexy the following day. The chemical in this drug is gammahydroxybutyrate, which has been used as a date rape drug. There are tight controls on the use of Xyrem. Some antidepressants have also been given at bedtime to reduce REM-related symptoms.

Napping

Imagine the patient's surprise when I prescribe naps. Naps can be extremely therapeutic for people with narcolepsy. A short nap, fifteen to thirty minutes can sometimes result in several hours of markedly improved alertness. On the other hand, long naps can leave a person feeling drugged or dopey. Often a nap around lunchtime is sufficient for several hours; some people may require a second nap later in the afternoon around 4:00 or 5:00 p.m. for a second wind.

Dealing with Others

Hollywood has not been kind to people with narcolepsy. In the movie *Deuce Bigalow: Male Gigolo* (released in December 1999) one of the characters is a woman with narcolepsy who is shown with her face falling into a bowl of soup. In *Bandits* (released in October 2001), one of the characters is a bank manager who falls into a heap with the excitement of being taken hostage and being forced to open a vault.

Whether it is because of the jokes about narcolepsy in popular culture or simply because the condition is so misunderstood and stereotyped, people with narcolepsy may feel ashamed of their condition or worried that they won't be taken seriously by coworkers, bosses, and associates. A very important aspect of narcolepsy management is for the patient to tell her circle of family and friends about the problem. "No, I am not stupid. No, I am not lazy. No, I am not disinterested in what you are saying." Also, at school, teachers and others should be notified. Then they will understand that at times the affected person may fall asleep and that this is not a sign of disrespect or laziness, but the result of a neurological disorder. In my experience, when a person with narcolepsy informs the right people about the problem (school principal, teachers, employer, etc.), and educates them about the disease, very often those people will try to make proper accommodations. For example, for one of my child patients, the school set up a room where she could nap right after lunch, which resulted in improvement in her academic performance.

A very important function of daily life affected by narcolepsy is driving a car. Specifically, driving regulations vary substantially from place to place; in some areas people with narcolepsy cannot drive unless they are undergoing treatment. So, when a child with narcolepsy is about fourteen or fifteen years old, the implications of their disorder as it relates to operating a motor vehicle must be discussed. Even while on treatment, the narcoleptic must be taught about the importance of napping, and the importance of not driving late at night, when the medications might have worn off. Obviously, ignoring these lessons can have tragic consequences.

Narcolepsy in Pregnancy

Because narcolepsy usually comes on during the teenage years, it is likely that women will have to face the problem of what to do about it during pregnancy. In my experience, narcolepsy does not affect fertility. The big question becomes how to treat symptoms during pregnancy. The safest approach is for the pregnant woman to stop using medications during pregnancy as she would most prescription and over-the-counter drugs. If the alternative treatments, such as daytime naps and other accommodations are not possible, then the pregnant woman may have to take a medical or other leave from employment. Further, it is dangerous and in many places illegal for the untreated woman to drive a car. Pregnant narcoleptics must make sure they do not become deficient in iron and folic acid as that may cause them to develop restless legs syndrome, which would worsen their already severe sleep problem.

Motherhood

Because a mother must be alert when taking care of a newborn and older children, it is best that she resume her medications after the baby is born. However, because the long-term implications of these medications on breastfeeding babies are not known, the woman should discuss this with her doctor before giving birth. Additionally, narcoleptic mothers may find that extra help with a newborn at home is invaluable, and even necessary to cope—especially at night. New motherhood can be a trying and tiring time for any woman, but it's significantly more so for a new mother who is narcoleptic.

Narcolepsy in Other People

By this point, you could probably recognize narcolepsy in yourself if you had it. But what about recognizing the disorder in others?

Children

Recognizing narcolepsy in young children is difficult, but there are clues to watch out for. A child over the age of five who starts to take naps again might have narcolepsy. Falling asleep at the wrong time and the wrong place, for example at school, or having to take a nap when coming home from school are clues that the sleepiness is not normal. Some children may complain of frightening nightmares that are actually hypnagogic hallucinations. Teachers may tell parents that their child is very sleepy in the classroom. The child's sleepiness may appear as or be diagnosed as attention deficit hyperactivity disorder, which may be treated with methylphenidate (Ritalin), a central-nervous-system stimulant. The child who falls asleep easily in the car, watching TV, or at school may have narcolepsy or one of the other disorders that cause sleepiness, such as apnea or a movement disorder.

"When she was much younger, she used to come into our bedroom afraid after a dream; we would make her a bed beside ours to sleep there the rest of the night. One particular dream was of a pointed-face man looking into her bedroom window. She was so scared that we actually investigated the window and outside to make sure someone hadn't been there. We found that it was not physically possible for anyone to be looking in. This was still not enough for her and we never completely convinced her it wasn't real. She had many more dreams that unsettled her over the years and some she just could not bring herself to relate to us."

—Mother of an eighteen-year-old narcoleptic

In Adolescents and Teenagers

Most often the narcolepsy first appears during the teenage years. The teenager may start to sleep in and have to be dragged out of bed, even though she has gone to sleep at a normal time. She might fall asleep in school. Her school performance may suddenly plummet along with her grades. Narcoleptics are almost always sleepy. They differ from normal sleep-deprived teenagers, who become alert as soon as they have a few normal nights of sleep. They also differ from teenagers with circadian clock problems (see Chapter 8), who might fall asleep late and wake up late, but who have no trouble staying awake in the afternoon. A research study published in 2002 found that pediatricians seldom diagnose narcolepsy. Unfortunately, the symptoms of these young patients are often interpreted as depression and the narcolepsy goes undiagnosed and, therefore, untreated for years. Sometimes children might become so discouraged by the constellation of problems facing them that they start to avoid school. This can also be a warning sign for parents. When children simply do not want to go to school—because they fall asleep in class and their friends make fun of them—there is more going on than just laziness. At this time in any adolescent's life, when so many hormonal and growth changes are occurring, the addition of the symptoms of narcolepsy can be extremely difficult, which means it's even more important that she be diagnosed correctly.

"She complained at age twelve of not having slept. We knew she had gone to bed at a good time and seemed to be asleep, but she woke tired and often in a bad mood or very emotional—more than just hormones. She came home from school and would take a nap. We took her to one doctor and asked if we could have her tested just to find out if she was actually sleeping. He felt that she was just a teenager and had not been making the effort to make sure she had regular sleep patterns. He suggested that she should try all of the other so-called ways of getting a better sleep, i.e., no cola, no caffeine, more exercise. The problem was that we had already exhausted all of those solutions with no improvement."

—Mother of an eighteen-year-old narcoleptic

Back to the Case of the First-Year Med Student

The medical student with narcolepsy had legitimate concerns about how this disorder was going to affect her life, and whether she would be able to complete her medical education. Although her sleep had been a problem for years, she now knew that it was a medical condition that could be treated but not cured. I encouraged her to go to her doctor to get diagnosed and treated. I also told her about another medical student I had diagnosed with narcolepsy a few years before. This student was referred to me when he was in his last year of medical school. He had been falling asleep at rounds and he was functioning at a low level. His instructors believed he was lazy; they wanted me to confirm that there was nothing medically wrong with him before they could fail him out of medical school. Such decisions after someone has already spent more than three years in medical school are not taken lightly and are only discussed when there are severe performance issues. I found that instead of being lazy, he had a classic case of narcolepsy that had been totally missed by his professors and doctors. Had they asked him a few simple questions they would have been able to diagnose him. He was started on treatment, graduated from medical school, finished his postgraduate specialty training, and is now quite successful. After hearing this, the medical student was reassured that there was hope for her. She had just attended a lecture that probably saved her career.

The lesson here is that even medical professors don't know everything about medicine, so why should the average overworked doctor? In the next chapter I will review several unusual sleep disorders that range from innocuous to dangerous. These sometimes also take years to diagnose because patients who have them sometimes don't want to talk about their symptoms with anybody, fearing they might be labeled crazy. Consequently they may remain untreated for years.

14

Afraid to Sleep and
Other Unusual Ailments

The Woman Who Was Afraid She Would Be Killed in Her Dream

In the specialized field of sleep medicine, the best way to discover what is really going on with a patient's disturbed sleep seems to be to interview both the patient and the bed partner. The forty-six-year-old woman in my office was a perfect example of this approach; she was accompanied by her husband who provided useful information on his wife's sleep patterns. She had been referred to the sleep clinic because she was afraid to fall asleep. When she started to describe her problem, she was almost smiling, as though she was somewhat embarrassed about wasting my time and telling me such a silly story. Her husband looked on; he seemed extremely concerned and upset. Her problem was that she had "lots of dreams and bad dreams" and that they had begun as far back as she could remember. Even as a young child, her parents would have to come into her room to calm her down after one of these events.

Now, as an adult, she dreaded going to sleep each night because she knew she was likely to have a bad dream. In most of her dreams, she was trying to protect herself from being attacked by a masked man who was trying to kill her with a knife. Her husband had been awakened by her dreams, and he was able to observe her reactions. She yelled, made her hands into fists, and tried to strike out many times. These episodes usually began at about 1:00 in the morning. Besides making fists, she would move her head from side to side as though she was frightened and being hit. Sometimes her husband would awaken her during the more severe episodes. She would wake up in a panic, and he would hug her until she settled down. Then she would drift off to sleep. Because of all this, traveling and staying with other people in their homes was out of the question. Unfortunately, this woman and her husband had experienced this trauma for most of their twenty-eight years together.

Often during her dreams, she hit her husband "pretty hard," and at times he had the bruises to show for it. When she woke up at night, she was afraid to go back to sleep for fear the dream would simply continue. Though she tried to think pleasant thoughts and was sometimes able to drift off into a dreamless sleep, often she would go right back into the dream. She was desperately seeking relief—for herself and for her husband.

When she had finished telling her story, I asked her some questions about what medications she was taking, whether she'd ever had any brain injury, infection, or loss of consciousness. The answer to all these questions was no. She had absolutely no history or symptoms of psychiatric disorders. For about forty years, this woman's sleep had been a painful experience with none of the refreshing qualities that most people associate with a night's rest. Instead, the thought of going to sleep every night was terrifying. The good news was that I could identify the problem quickly and knew of a treatment that would solve her problem virtually overnight.

The Many Faces of Sleep

Although sleep is normally considered a peaceful time, distressing events and behaviors can occur during sleep. Called parasomnias, these abnormalities occur when the mechanisms that control behavior, such as yelling, screaming, walking, talking, urinating, and so forth don't function normally during sleep. In some people these mechanisms break down and have disturbing consequences.

Chapter 1 described the three states of our brains. One state is being awake, a second state is non-REM sleep, and the third state is REM sleep, which is the time when we dream. There might be many other states not yet discovered, but we have learned that in some people the boundaries between these three main states can collapse.

When you are awake both your brain and muscles are active so that you think and your senses are actively giving you information about your environment. Your body automatically maintains muscle tone, controls breathing rate, heart rate, blood pressure, and needs such as urinating, eating, and drinking.

During non-REM sleep, you continue to receive sensory data from your environment, but your body and brain filter out irrelevant environmental information. For example, after a few nights, you no longer respond to the plane flying overhead at 4:00 a.m., but you continue to respond to the noises from the baby's room down the hall. Your brain is still controlling all the automatic functions such as breathing, heart rate, and blood pressure. Sphincters in your body are working to keep various fluids where they belong. During this stage of sleep, you do not eat or drink. Some mental activity and some dreaming may occur during this state. Muscle tone is still maintained during non-REM sleep.

During REM sleep you are dreaming, and your body is almost entirely paralyzed. The muscles of the arms and legs can't move. The main breathing muscle, the diaphragm, continues to work, as do sphincters in the intestinal tract. Control of some of the automatic functions such as blood pressure and heart rate may become erratic.

A breakdown in the boundaries between these states (awake, REM, and non-REM) is believed to be the cause of several disorders, such as sleepwalking, sleep terrors, and reacting to the content of violent dreams, all of which will be discussed in this chapter.

Sleepwalking

Sleepwalking is equally common in males and females. Perhaps as many as 10 to 15 percent of people have experienced sleepwalking, particularly when they were children. Sleepwalking becomes much less common as people leave the teenage years, although I frequently have had adult sleepwalking patients.

While sleepwalking, the person gets up and starts to walk or may demonstrate what is best described as robot-like behavior. This may seem purposeful—for example, the sleepwalker may go to the kitchen—but usually it is not. One of my sleepwalking patients, a child, would walk into the laundry room and urinate into the laundry hamper.

Most of the time, sleepwalking is not dangerous unless the walker ventures outside or turns on appliances (such as a stove). Usually, he or she just ends up back in bed asleep. It's a mystery to me (and very fortunate) that people do not hurt themselves more often when they are in this state.

Sleepwalking occurs when parts of the brain are asleep, and other parts of the brain—those that control walking and other physical activities—are in some way awake. The part of the brain that deals with thinking and alertness is asleep, and the following day, sleepwalkers usually have no recollection of their sleepwalking.

Having the brain awake and asleep at the same time is not as far-fetched as it seems. Some marine mammals—for example, dolphins—may swim around while one side of their brain is asleep and resting and the other side of their brain is wide awake and controlling many functions. That may be what allows marine mammals to spend their whole lives in the water.

What Causes Sleepwalking?

Sleepwalking seems to occur most often during very deep sleep. Children spend more of the night in deep sleep than adults do, so it follows that they sleepwalk more often than adults. Deep sleep is more common in the first third of the night, so that is when sleepwalking is most likely to occur. Adults and children who are sleep deprived also fall into a deep sleep more quickly and tend to sleepwalk more often. Sleepwalking seems to run in some families and is also found more often in people who are under stress or who have been drinking alcohol. Violent crimes have occurred when the defendant claimed he or she was sleepwalking. The accused has sometimes even been acquitted using this defense, though it is difficult to prove what state the person was really in when the crime actually occurred.

Dealing with Sleepwalking

If sleepwalking is not associated with anything dangerous, nothing really needs to be done. If you encounter a family member sleepwalking, it is best not to waken the person, but simply to lead the person back to bed. Sleepwalkers who are awakened too abruptly may be upset and have trouble falling asleep; they also may become overly concerned about what their sleepwalking signifies. If the sleepwalker has been discovered in a dangerous situation, then the chance of harm must be reduced. For example, one may need to set up alarms for a sleepwalker who has stumbled down the stairs.

Sleepwalking in combination with sleep deprivation, stress, or alcohol abuse, can be addressed. If sleep deprivation is the culprit, proper amounts of sleep usually solve the sleepwalking problem. In severe cases of sleepwalking, the problem may be resolved by teaching the sleepwalker how to get the right amount of sleep. If the sleepwalking occurs on nights when the person has been drinking, the problem may be solved by eliminating alcohol consumption. Finally, when the sleepwalking seems to be related to stress, it's helpful to find and eliminate the cause of the stress. Sometimes this might involve referring the patient to a psychologist to learn how to cope with the stress.

Because these treatments are usually effective, I seldom recommend medications for sleepwalking unless they are used to suppress sleepwalking in situations when the person has had dangerous episodes. I had one patient, for example, who found herself walking in a cemetery several blocks from her house, wearing her bed clothes and no shoes. It was many degrees below zero, and there was snow on the ground! I will also sometimes recommend medications when the patient is traveling; sleepwalking in a strange environment can be dangerous. The medication I recommend most often is clonazepam, but you should discuss this medication with your doctor to determine if it is right for you.

Sleep Talking

Sleep talking is quite common among adults and children. Most of the noises that come out are actually gibberish, although one might be able to make out individual words. I have not heard of people blurting out secrets during sleep talking episodes. This might be considered an embarrassing condition, but it is not one that requires treatment.

Sleep Terrors

This disorder, which can occur in children and in adults is also called "night terrors." Sufferers get out of bed abruptly, sometimes screaming with their eyes wide open, and sometimes sweating. They appear to be terrified; sometimes they seem as though they are about to commit a violent act. The person may let out a bloodcurdling scream and display other bizarre behavior.

Although it would seem that the person might be reacting to a dream, usually he or she is not. Sleep terrors are a form of sleepwalking and the treatment is the same. There is no need to awaken people who are having these episodes; it is best to calmly walk them back to bed. The following morning, they have no recollection of the distress that they caused for the other people in the house or of the actual event. Sleep terrors can be bizarre, but are not usually dangerous enough to require further treatment.

Sleep Paralysis

In this disorder, which usually affects adults, the sleeper usually wakes up from a dream, and finds that he or she cannot move. It can be quite frightening, especially the first few times it happens. Sometimes the sensation of paralysis occurs while the active dream is continuing, and the content of the dream might be extremely frightening. A person might dream that there is someone in the room or that something unpleasant is happening in the house, such as a robbery. Women might dream that there is a devil-like creature that is about to sexually violate them. Men might dream that they are about to be raped by a creature resembling an old woman. These sexually disturbing images have been described in several countries around the world. Episodes of sleep paralysis may last only a few seconds or perhaps a few minutes. What sometimes snaps the person out of the paralysis is simply being touched. There is nothing that the person can do to stop the paralysis. It goes away on its own.

The reason why people have sleep paralysis is because the boundary between wakefulness and REM sleep has been blurred. The person's brain is awake, but one of the manifestations of dreaming, the paralysis, remains.

Sleep paralysis is a feature of narcolepsy, a disorder described in Chapter 13. Sleep paralysis can also occur in people who don't have narcolepsy; for example, in severe sleep deprivation. We have seen some cases of sleep paralysis that run in families. Sometimes, when the sleep paralysis is quite distressing, I treat it in the same way I treat sleepwalking. I reassure the patient that the condition is not dangerous; in more severe cases, I may prescribe a drug such as clonazepam or one of the antidepressants that suppresses REM sleep. If you experience sleep paralysis, check with your doctor.

Terrifying Nightmares

Nightmares are dreams that are frightening and vivid. Women report having nightmares more often than men. It is surprising that people do not have this symptom more often, as most people dream three to five times a night. Most of the time nightmares are of no consequence. Some people don't remember any of their dreams; others seem to remember one or more per night. Most people eventually learn to ignore these dreams, and they become less concerned about them. However, nightmares can present a distressing problem in children who may begin to fear going to sleep. The best approach for the parent is to reassure the child after demonstrating that their fear is unfounded. This might involve making a tour of the bedroom with the child and demonstrating that there is nothing under the bed or in the closet. In rare cases this problem may require help from a doctor or a psychologist.

Dreaming, but Not Quite Asleep

People who are extremely sleep deprived or who have narcolepsy sometimes dream even before they are asleep. This isn't normal. People do not usually dream until they've been asleep for roughly ninety minutes.

The dreams that people have as they are falling asleep or while they are awake are called *hypnagogic hallucinations*. Sometimes these hallucinations are mundane and fleeting thoughts; sometimes, however, they can be quite vivid and sometimes even frightening. The people who have these hallucinations generally know that they are "not real." They may not appreciate, however, that they are dreams. The strangest example I ever saw of a person experiencing hypnagogic hallucinations was a young woman who was in an intensive care unit. She had a severe form of sleep apnea associated with a neurological condition. She was extremely sleepy during the daytime, and as I approached her, I could see that she was talking to an invisible object that seemed to be about fifteen yards away from her. She told me that she was talking to the giant Cheshire cat over there. She then turned to me and smiled and said, "Of course I know there is no Cheshire cat over there, this is just some sort of dream."

This is quite different from what happens in a patient with schizophrenia who has hallucinations. The schizophrenic believes that the hallucinations are real. The inability to differentiate reality from hallucination is one of the hallmarks of schizophrenia (see Chapter 16).

Dreamlike hallucinations might also occur in people when they wake up, during the day, or even while they are participating in some activity. I've even had patients who had hypnagogic hallucinations as they were driving their automobile and knew that the images that they were seeing were not real!

We tend not to treat the hypnagogic hallucinations. Instead we focus on the conditions that cause them. The hallucinations themselves are not particularly distressing to adults, but they can be distressing to children. If you have this type of hallucination, sleep deprivation caused by your lifestyle is the most likely cause, and you should consider taking steps to remedy the situation. Usually this means lifestyle changes. If sleep deprivation is not the cause and daytime sleepiness is not present, reassurance usually suffices. I may suggest REM-suppressing drugs (usually antidepressants) if the hypnagogic hallucinations are frequent (more than once a week) and distressing to narcolepsy patients.

Reacting to Dreams

The woman I described at the beginning of the chapter was reacting to her dreams. The boundary between awakening and dreaming was blurred. While she was actively dreaming, she was able to move some muscles; she was not paralyzed, the normal state during REM sleep. This is called REM behavior disorder (RBD). People with this problem have been known to inflict severe injuries on their bed partners. It is a disorder that is more common in men. Bed partners should encourage the person to seek help if they observe such behavior. Most of the time, the violent activity is related to a dream that includes being attacked by an unknown but terrifying person or animal. The patient I discussed in the beginning of the chapter dreamed most often that she was being attacked by a masked figure. Other patients dream they are being attacked by one or more animals. One patient of mine had a dream that he was being attacked on the beaches of Normandy during World War II.

The dreamer's physical reaction to the dream is what injures the bed partner. For example, a patient dreaming about being chased by a moose and a bear (go figure) is running away from the animals toward a building. He arrives at the building, but the animals are coming closer and closer. The door of the building is closed. He starts to bang his fists on the building only to be awakened by his wife's screams, and he slowly becomes aware that he has been pounding her. People who react so strongly to their dreams have also been known to injure themselves and damage their homes. I have had patients report that they have banged their fists through glass, broken lamps, and damaged furniture. In one case, a patient lunged out of bed, fell on the floor, broke his neck, and died.

Though 90 percent of the people who have RBD are men, it's important that women be aware of the disorder because two thirds of men who suffer from it have assaulted and often injured their spouses. The reason why this condition is so much more common in men is not known. The disorder is common in people who have had head trauma or an infection of the brain much earlier in their lives, and it is more common in alcoholics. It has also been reported as a rare complication of certain antidepressants. Some people with this condition may go on to develop Parkinson's disease or other neurological conditions years or decades later.

The identification of this disorder is fairly recent in that it was first described about fifteen years ago. People who have RBD are often embarrassed to talk about it, or are inhibited by fears that they might be diagnosed with a psychiatric condition. Although RBD bears some similarities to posttraumatic stress disorder, the two are actually quite different. PTSD patients have terrible recurrent nightmares, but they don't physically react to what they are dreaming while they are asleep. The tragedy of not recognizing RBD—some patients have suffered with it for forty or fifty years!—is that it can be treated quite effectively with clonazepam. No one knows why this medication is effective for this condition. People who react physically to violent dreams, especially if they have injured themselves or others, should seek medical help.

Urinating in Bed

Enuresis, or urinating in bed, occurs because the mechanisms that normally keep the sphincters of the urinary system working are not effective. This is a problem in children and the elderly. In children, the problem is caused by slow development of bladder control. In the elderly, it is generally related to changes in anatomy brought on by the aging process.

Childhood enuresis can be very troubling for both the child and the parents. This problem is twice as common in boys. Children might develop a fear of going to sleep because they are afraid that they will wet the bed. They become afraid to sleep over at a friend's house. To make sure that there is no medical reason for this symptom, children who have this problem should be evaluated by their pediatrician. The pediatrician can then advise the family about what to expect and how to handle the problem. In many cities, there are specialized clinics that deal with this situation.

There are alarm systems available that are triggered when the bed has been dampened. Such an alarm awakens the child, who eventually gains bladder control during sleep. If this treatment is not effective, the doctor might recommend one of several medications. Desmopressin acetate (DDAVP) is a medication that imitates the effect of a chemical produced by the pituitary gland that reduces the amount of urine. This drug, which is immediately effective, can be taken just before bedtime either in a nose spray or in pill form. A low dose of the antidepressant imipramine taken one to two hours before bedtime has been used for many years to treat children who wet the bed. It is successful in less than half the time. These treatments do not cure the problem, though. Thankfully, nearly all children eventually gain bladder control.

Urinary incontinence can become a major problem in women as they age. About one in twenty older women wet the bed at night. If it is not possible to deal with the medical problem causing the incontinence, then the only solution may be to use an incontinence pad. Check with the doctor to see what resources or social services might be available to help. Some older people might be entitled to home care or to have the pads donated by an agency.

Teeth Grinding, or Bruxism

Bruxism is an increase in the activity of the jaw muscles while sleeping. This condition occurs in children and adults and is equally common in females and males. We don't know much about it except that it is more common in people under stress and can occur as a reaction to certain drugs. The grinding can be extremely disruptive, and it can literally wear down a person's teeth.

In some people, stress reduction alone is an effective treatment for bruxism. If the teeth are wearing down or if there is pain in the jaw, this should be checked out with a dentist, who may recommend a mouth guard to be worn at night.

Head Banging and Body Rolling

One of the most unusual problems we see in the sleep clinic is a disorder in which a person repeatedly bangs her head against a mattress, a crib, or a wall. Some people rock their bodies the entire night and move around a great deal. As painful as it is to watch these patients, it turns out that this is not a serious problem. They are quite normal in the daytime. Though it is scary for parents, most children who have this disorder grow out of it, although sometimes it continues into adulthood. The disorder is found in about 8 percent of four-year-olds, and the number decreases even further with older children. For reasons that are not known, this condition is four times more common in males than in females. Some people with neurological problems might display similar movements. This is a disorder that we do not normally treat unless the person is injuring herself.

Back to the Woman with the Killer Dreams

The woman who had dreamed almost nightly for forty years that she was going to be stabbed by a masked man and had to defend herself against the killer had RBD. I could not determine the cause of her problem because she had no history or evidence of brain damage, had never been in a coma or lost consciousness as far as she knew, was not an alcoholic, and was not on any medication that might lead to this problem. I recommended to her family doctor that she be started on clonazepam. This drug is also used to treat some forms of epilepsy and panic disorder. It is sometimes prescribed to help a person fall asleep. It seems to make the brain less likely to respond to stimuli including the stimuli from dreams. We do not know why, but this medication works for most people with this disorder. When I spoke to my RBD patient several months after she began taking the medication, she was dramatically improved. She no longer had recollections of having dreamed about the killer. Her husband told me that she sometimes still moved a great deal during sleep, but the hitting had stopped.

The disorders mentioned in this chapter are not usually dangerous to the sleeper. REM sleep behavior disorder is more common in males, and women are frequently the victims of the physical assaults and violence that can happen when the bed partner has this problem. These patients often go undiagnosed for many years. People with medical problems often have sleep problems that are undiagnosed because doctors seldom ask patients about their sleep. In the next chapter I will cover sleep problems caused by medical conditions.

15

Medical Conditions

The Case of the Woman with a Black Curtain

The woman sitting in front of me was in her seventies, quite articulate, and obviously in distress. She had just walked perhaps ten yards from the waiting room to my office and she was breathless, almost panting. I let her settle down and when she had composed herself, I started to interview her, expecting her to focus on her breathing problem or her sleep. After all she was at a sleep disorders clinic! Instead, she told me about a black curtain that had descended over her mind, and that because of it, she could no longer continue her work as a well-known visual artist. Consequently, she couldn't prepare for an art show that she was putting together. She insisted that her main problem was that her creativity had been totally blocked by this black curtain.

Her family doctor, on the other hand, believed that her main problem was insomnia and had referred her to the sleep clinic. I examined the woman and found that she had swollen ankles and noises in her lungs, which suggested the presence of excess fluid in them. I instantly realized that an entirely different organ system was causing her insomnia, and I knew I would be able to help her and hopefully lift the black curtain.

Chronic Medical Problems Can Lead to Sleep Problems

Insomnia, difficulty in falling asleep and staying asleep, is a symptom and not a disease. When a person has a problematic symptom such as insomnia, it is up to that person to go to the doctor. It becomes the job of the doctor to determine the cause of the symptom and then to treat the cause. The symptom of insomnia can be caused by many different medical problems—a disturbance in sleep often indicates that there is something else wrong in the body, and it might be serious. Disorders involving almost every single organ system can cause problems with sleep, which makes it all the more amazing that doctors have only been asking about their patients' sleep for the past few years.

You name a chronic disease and it is probably associated with a sleep problem. Diabetes, kidney failure, arthritis, Parkinson's disease, heart failure, and cancer are some of the commonly occurring medical conditions that can affect sleep and lead to sleep complaints.

The Nervous System

The nervous system is made up of the brain, spinal cord, and nerves going to all parts of the body including to the organs, muscles, and skin. Not surprisingly, several disorders of the nervous system may result in disturbed sleep since the system that controls sleep is in the brain.

Alzheimer's Disease

Sleep problems and wandering at night are extremely common in Alzheimer's disease, which is a chronic neurological disorder that affects the brain resulting in progressive deterioration of mental functions. This source of great stress for the family is covered in Chapter 7.

Headaches

Headaches can be associated with sleep and other medical disorders. Some people with sleep-breathing problems awaken with headaches. For example, this is common in people with sleep apnea (see Chapter 12). The reason for this symptom is that when you don't breathe enough it causes an increase in the carbon dioxide level in the blood, which leads to increases in blood flow to the brain, which then increases pressure in the brain. This problem also occurs in some people with chronic lung diseases.

Headaches are much more common in women than men. The only exception is cluster headache, a less common type of headache, which is diagnosed more often in men. People with severe headaches from whatever cause may have difficulty in falling and staying asleep. Two types of severe headaches that typically have an effect on sleep are migraines and cluster.

Migraine Headaches

Migraine headaches are about three times more common in women than men. In many cases, they can incapacitate the sufferer. These headaches are throbbing and often affect one side of the head. They are sometimes accompanied by nausea and vomiting. Additionally, the sufferer may have increased sensitivity to light, sounds, and smells. In many people, migraine attacks are recurrent but tend to become less severe as the person ages. Many people begin to see shimmering lights around objects, zigzag lines, and wavy images about ten to thirty minutes before the onset of a migraine. Some people experience hallucinations or even lose their vision temporarily. Not only do these headaches interfere with sleep, but also the ensuing sleep loss may cause the migraines to become more frequent.

Cluster Headaches

The cluster headache is perhaps the most severe form of headache. It is roughly twice as common in men. Because some doctors consider cluster headache a male phenomenon, they often miss it in women. Consequently the diagnosis in women can be delayed. The word *cluster* is used to describe the disorder because the headache episodes occur in clusters or one after another within a short period of time, often lasting two to four months. During one of these clusters, the person might have two to ten headaches each day. The headaches often occur at the same time each day like clockwork until the cluster ends. Then there may be no headaches for several months or even years. The headache is on one side of the head and face and often begins with a drooping of the eyelid, tearing, and dilation of the pupil of the eye on the affected side. The pain becomes unbearable after five to ten minutes. The headache usually lasts about thirty to forty-five minutes (although some last up to two hours). Once the headache starts to subside, the pain may dissipate within five to ten minutes. The headaches are so severe that people pace, rock their bodies, and sometimes bang their heads against a wall to try to stop the pain. These headaches commonly start during sleep, particularly dreaming (REM) sleep, and frequently the pain awakens the sufferer. People with this problem should seek medical help.

Parkinson's Disease

Parkinson's disease is a common neurological problem, which affects the parts of the brain that produce the chemical dopamine. The disease causes involuntary movements including tremors, masklike facial expressions, and an abnormal gait. Parkinson's disease is more common in older people. It is also more common in men than women.

About 70 percent of people with Parkinson's disease have trouble falling asleep and staying asleep. They may awaken during the night and be unable to fall asleep again. This might happen as their medication wears off and is eliminated from the body. Sometimes days and nights become reversed. About 25 percent of patients have REM behavior disorder (RBD), a condition in which the person physically reacts to the content of his or her dreams (see Chapter 14). Patients with this condition may harm themselves or their bed partners. Many patients may also have very frightening hallucinations while they are awake. As a result of RBD, sleep apnea (Chapter 12), a movement disorder (Chapter 11), or medications, patients may experience severe daytime sleepiness. Some doctors have begun to treat severe daytime sleepiness with the wakefulness-promoting medication modafinil. When taken in the morning, this medication does not interfere with a patient's ability to sleep at night (see Chapter 20).

Lung Problems

Any lung problem, most commonly asthma and chronic obstructive pulmonary disease (COPD) that causes excessive coughing, wheezing, or shortness of breath at night can lead to insomnia.

Asthma

Asthma, which is the constriction of the bronchial tubes causing excessive coughing and shortness of breath, affects roughly 5 percent of the population. Up to about thirty years of age, asthma is more common in men than women. After age thirty, it is about twice as common in women than men. This is important because when the disease starts at a younger age it tends to improve, while in the older age groups in which women predominate, the disease is much less likely to remit or improve. Female asthmatics have a 70 percent higher risk of being admitted to hospital for asthma than their male counterparts.

Medication usually relieves symptoms. However, in some people, the first sign that their asthma is not under control is when they develop a wheeze at night that awakens them. Sometimes when awakened by coughing, a person doesn't know what is happening. Some patients who are referred to me because of insomnia are only able to discover the extent to which the coughing disturbed their sleep through sleep studies.

Chronic Lung Disease Caused by Smoking

Chronic obstructive pumonary disease occurs in long-time cigarette smokers. It is most often irreversible and can be fatal. Research suggests that tobacco has a greater adverse effect on lung function in women than men, and women are more likely to be hospitalized for COPD. As in asthma, coughing and shortness of breath are common symptoms of COPD. In addition, because many COPD sufferers are cigarette smokers, they often awaken during the night craving nicotine. Some people awaken in the morning with their lungs filled with sputum, which they have to cough up in order to breathe normally. The combination of waking up coughing and shortness of breath makes restful sleep difficult in these patients.

Sinus Disease

Over the years, I have seen many people who have a cough only when they lie down. Frequently they might have a cold or a sinus infection before the cough begins. Coughing may not occur during the daytime, but as soon as they lie down, they start to cough. Most likely, lying down causes their sinuses to drain and some of the secretions may make contact with the vocal cords, which leads to the coughing. In some people, this problem may go on for months before it is discovered. In the meantime, their coughing causes them to wake up in the night, which affects the quantity and the quality of their sleep.

Cardiovascular Diseases

Although there is a widespread belief that diseases of the heart and blood vessels are mainly male problems, this is simply not true. In fact, about sixty thousand more women than men die each year of cardiovascular disease in the United States. About sixty million Americans are estimated to have cardiovascular diseases. Recent research has shown that cardiovascular diseases can cause sleep problems. It also shows that sleep disorders can cause cardiovascular disease.

Heart Attack

Women having a heart attack may have different symptoms from men. Although chest pain is considered the classic symptom of a heart attack, research reported in late 2003 found that 43 per cent of women having a heart attack did not have chest pain. Seventy percent of women who had a heart attack had fatigue and about half had trouble sleeping in the weeks before the episode. Fatigue was the most common symptom.

Heart Failure

About five million Americans have heart failure. Statistics indicate that heart failure is a bigger problem in women than previously thought. For example, a 2000 study reported that almost twice as many women as men were being treated for heart failure by family doctors. Twice as many women as men die of heart failure. Because of the belief that heart problems are less common in women, once women are admitted to hospital for heart attacks, they tend to receive slower and less detailed testing than men. In one study, 21 percent of women admitted to hospital for heart attack died compared to 11 percent of men who died.

Some people with heart failure develop a sleep-breathing pattern that at times becomes progressively deeper, then progressively shallower. Sometimes it stops completely for short periods of time. To restart breathing the brain has to go through a mini awakening. The pattern of breathing too much followed by breathing too little repeats itself about once a minute. This is a form of sleep apnea (see Chapter 12), which results in insomnia. People with heart failure frequently have trouble falling asleep, and when they awaken during the night they are frequently extremely short of breath and feel as though they must sit up. Some of the medications used to treat heart failure, such as water pills or diuretics, may result in frequent trips to the bathroom at night.

People with heart failure might face the unfortunate combination of extreme sleepiness (because their sleep is so disrupted), and an inability to fall asleep. Recent research has shown that treatment of the sleep-breathing abnormality, for example with oxygen or a CPAP machine (which is used in apnea, see Chapter 12), may result in dramatic improvement.

Palpitations

Some people awaken during the night and are aware of an abnormal heart rhythm. They might notice that the rhythm seems very fast or very slow, or they may feel an irregularity, such as an extra or missed beat. In some people, these awakenings can come from frightening dreams; in these cases, palpitations are not a medical problem. In other cases, however, the symptom may represent an important cardiac rhythm problem that should be evaluated by a doctor.

Some people awaken from sleep with a rapid heartbeat, sweating, and a feeling they are about to die. This feeling of impending doom is found in some people who have a panic disorder, which for some occurs mostly at night (see Chapter 16). This type of reaction can also be a symptom of posttraumatic stress disorder (see Chapter 16). The episodes can be so alarming that the sufferer may develop a fear of falling asleep.

Chest pain, caused by an inadequate amount of oxygen going to the heart at night, might also cause awakening from sleep.

High Blood Pressure

It is now known that sleep apnea (see Chapter 12) can cause high blood pressure or may make control of blood pressure with medications more difficult.

Gastrointestinal Diseases

There are several common diseases of the gastrointestinal tract that commonly disturb sleep.

Gastroesophageal Reflux (GER)

At the bottom of the esophagus, the tube that carries food from the mouth into the stomach, is a sphincter that keeps stomach acid from entering the esophagus. In some people, this sphincter does not work properly and acid backs up into the esophagus (reflux) and causes heartburn. In the most severe situations gastroesophageal reflux disease (GERD) can actually injure the esophagus. This very common condition affects men and women equally; it's estimated that perhaps 30 to 40 percent of the adult population suffers from a reflux disorder. Overweight women and pregnant women have a higher risk.

When gastroesophageal reflux occurs at night, it can keep the person from falling and/or staying asleep. First, the acid might make its way all the way up to the mouth and awaken the sleeper with a bitter taste or with severe coughing and choking. If the acid touches the vocal cords, they can sometimes go into spasm, and she will feel unable to breathe and feel as though she is going to die. Second, the acid reflux may cause heartburn that awakens the sleeper. Research has shown that acid can sometimes enter the esophagus without causing any pain, but still awaken the sleeper.

Twenty years ago, there were no effective medications for gastroesophageal reflux. Today doctors can prescribe excellent medications that shut down the stomach's production of acid.

Peptic Ulcer Disease

When a person's stomach produces too much acid or cannot properly deal with the normal acids it produces, an ulcer may form in the stomach or in a tube called the duodenum. The disease in many people is caused by an infection from bacteria called *Helicobacter pylori*. Some medications, such as aspirin or certain nonsteroidal anti-inflammatory drugs, even when used as prescribed, can cause ulcers. People with peptic ulcer disease frequently awaken one or two hours after going to sleep with either pain or the sensation of hunger. Eating food or taking antacids often relieves the pain temporarily. There can be serious complications from ulcer disease, such as bleeding in the intestinal tract. People with this symptom should see medical help. There is excellent treatment for peptic ulcer disease, which can also help the sufferer regain a normal sleep pattern.

Diseases Causing Diarrhea

Crohn's disease, ulcerative colitis, and any other disease causing diarrhea will disturb sleep.

Common Disorders of Hormone Production

Most diseases involving hormone production can cause disturbed sleep. Some of these diseases are very common, and some are much more common in women than men.

Diabetes

In diabetes, a very common medical problem, the body doesn't produce enough of the hormone insulin, or there is a resistance to insulin's effect on cells of the body, resulting in high blood sugar levels. In 2000, there were 5.9 million men and 6.2 million women with diabetes in the United States. The rate of diabetes is similar in non-Hispanic white men and women, but is much higher in women than men in African-American and Hispanic populations.

Research has shown that about 50 percent of people with diabetes experience sleep problems. There are many reasons why diabetics develop this symptom. First, when blood sugar is too high, the kidney filters the sugar into the urine, which forms more urine than normal and results in an increased need to get up to go to the bathroom.

Second, diabetics might develop blood sugar levels during the night that are too low and they might awaken with sweating and a rapid heart rate. This symptom usually occurs when they have taken too much insulin or have eaten too little food before bedtime.

Patients with the most severe forms of diabetes develop nerve damage called neuropathy. This may cause excessive movements, unpleasant sensations in the legs such as restless legs syndrome (see Chapter 11), which keep the person from falling asleep. In addition, the neuropathy might affect the nerves of the gastrointestinal tract, and some patients with diabetes end up with diarrhea at night.

Diseases of the Thyroid Gland

The thyroid gland is located in the neck in front of the trachea (the breathing passage) right below the Adam's apple. This crucial and sensitive gland produces thyroid hormone, which is involved in the regulation of metabolism in most of the body's cells. All thyroid disorders are five times more common in women than men.

Goiter

In some people, the thyroid gland enlarges to such an extent that it starts to block the breathing passage behind it. Most of the time, this is due to enlargement of the cells, which is sometimes caused by a deficiency of iodine. This condition is called a goiter. When the gland becomes large enough, and the breathing passage becomes too small, the person may develop sleep apnea, which is described in more detail in Chapter 12.

Hypothyroidism

The second problem caused by disease of the thyroid is when the gland does not produce enough hormone. This condition, called hypothyroidism, is at least twice as common in women as men. The symptoms of hypothyroidism come on over many months or sometimes even years. The woman's skin becomes coarse and dry and her hair may start to fall out. Weight may actually increase to the point of obesity. The weight gain is caused by a drop in the metabolic rate due to lack of thyroid hormone. With this condition, a woman can continue to eat the same amount of food she usually does, but because fewer calories are burned, her weight increases.

Important symptoms of thyroid deficiency include feelings of fatigue (muscle weakness) and sleepiness, which can be debilitating. When the disease is severe enough, patients might actually lose consciousness and develop breathing failure that requires immediate treatment. One of the reasons patients who are deficient in thyroid hormone suffer from sleepiness may be sleep apnea. This form of apnea usually develops because the thyroid patient's tongue becomes so enlarged that it blocks the breathing passage during sleep.

The ideal treatment for these patients is to take thyroid hormone to replace the hormone their bodies fail to produce. This hormone replacement medication is usually very effective. Most women are prescribed a very low dose of hormone to start because their metabolic rate is so low that a normal dose of thyroid might bring on symptoms of hyperthyroidism. Often the dosage is slowly increased over a matter of weeks or months. It is vital that the patient go to see a doctor regularly to monitor the dosage. I have seen many women at the sleep clinic who have low or deficient thyroid levels because they have not had their doses increased. Without the correct dosage they continued to have symptoms of low thyroid levels.

Hyperthyroidism

Hyperthyroidism is the third major malfunction of the thyroid gland. Like the other thyroid conditions, it is far more common (five to ten times) in women than men. In this disorder, too much hormone is produced and the person becomes hypermetabolic—meaning she actually burns ups more calories than she takes in. These people sweat, tremble, and lose a great deal of weight in a short period of time. Sometimes the disease will cause their eyeballs to bulge outward. This latter condition is called Graves' disease. Patients with excessive thyroid hormone may find it very hard to fall and/or stay asleep. They frequently sweat at night and have nightmares that wake them. These patients are sleepy during the daytime and they become physically very tired because the excess thyroid hormone may reduce muscle strength. Furthermore, hyperthyroidism may cause an extremely rapid heart rate, which can cause symptoms such as dizziness and fainting. The rapid heart rate may awaken the person during sleep. Hyperthyroidism is a serious medical condition that should be treated and monitored by a medical professional.

Diseases of Pituitary Gland

The pituitary gland is a pea-sized gland that is in the brain. This gland produces some hormones and regulates others that are produced in glands in other parts of the body. There are two abnormalities of the pituitary gland that can affect sleep.

Acromegaly

In this condition the pituitary gland produces too much growth hormone. The effect of this overproduction varies depending on whether or not the patient has already stopped growing. For example, overproduction of growth hormone might turn a child into a giant. People with this condition have a characteristic look. Besides being extremely tall, the excess growth hormone makes the jaw and forehead grow to a much larger size than normal. On the other hand, when someone who has stopped growing begins to produce excess growth hormone, some parts of the body may begin to grow again—for example, the jaw and other parts of the face and even the hands and feet. If the disease is not controlled, it can have devastating effects on the body. The heart can become too large and fail. Severe arthritis may follow. Sleep problems can develop. Acromegaly patients have enlarged tongues, which can obstruct their breathing passage when they sleep and lead to severe sleep apnea. I recently had a patient that had been successfully treated for acromegaly with surgical removal of the part of her pituitary gland producing the growth hormone. She had been excessively sleepy for years before it dawned on her doctor that the acromegaly had caused sleep apnea that now needed treatment. This disorder can also lead to diabetes and might also cause other hormonal problems, especially if the cause of the excess hormone production is a tumor.

Tumors of the Pituitary Gland

When tumors of the pituitary become too large, they may squeeze the normal parts of the gland and compress another important area of the brain called the hypothalamus. When this happens, the system responsible for regulating sleep and wakefulness may not work properly, and the person may have severe sleepiness or may develop a random sleep pattern of falling asleep at inappropriate times. However, if the tumor is still growing, it is often difficult to diagnose the problem. It may become large enough to compress some of the nerves involved in vision. The person's peripheral vision may be impaired causing her to bump into things. Pituitary tumors can compress the normal tissue in this gland, which can in turn reduce the secretion of other hormones including the sex hormones. Another sign that doctors look for in diagnosing and treating pituitary diseases is a reduction in the amount of hair in the pubic area and the armpits. A tumor growing in the pituitary can affect sleep directly, or cause other medical problems that affect sleep.

Diseases of the Urinary System

When you reduce your fluid intake, the kidneys try to keep water in the body and urine becomes concentrated. In people with some kidney diseases, urine doesn't become concentrated. These people consequently produce too much urine and they have to go to the bathroom multiple times per night. If kidney function fails and the person has to go on dialysis, she frequently will experience very severe movements and restless legs syndrome (see Chapter 11) that inhibits sleep.

Arthritis and Fibromyalgia

Many types of arthritis are caused by painful chronic inflammation (or destruction) of the joints. Some affect the larger joints (for example the hips and the knees), while others affect smaller joints of the fingers, hands, toes, and feet. These conditions can lead to serious insomnia. Diseases of joints such as rheumatoid arthritis are about three times more common in women than men.

Women are often affected by a condition called fibromyalgia, which is also associated with excessive sensitivity and perception of pain in the muscles and elsewhere. This condition is about nine times more common in women than men. People with fibromyalgia report more pain following a poor night of sleep. Any painful sensation can lead to trouble sleeping, daytime sleepiness, fatigue, or tiredness (see Chapter 6).

Cancer

Cancer may result in sleep problems for many reasons. First, the diagnosis itself can cause a great deal of stress, and stress can lead to insomnia. Second, depending upon what organ is affected by the cancer, there may be symptoms from that organ. Unfortunately, some of the treatments for cancer, such as chemotherapy, may result in severe symptoms such as nausea and vomiting, which also may result in difficulty sleeping.

One 2002 study reported that the most common problems in cancer patients were fatigue (44 percent of patients), restlessness in the legs (41 percent), insomnia (31 percent), and excessive sleepiness (28 percent). Sleep problems were most prevalent in those with lung cancer. Women should note that since 1987, more women have died from lung cancer than from breast cancer. Insomnia and fatigue were more common in those with breast cancer.

Some treatments for breast cancer or ovarian cancer may lead to the immediate onset of menopause, which can interfere with sleep. For example, tamoxifen, a widely used anti-estrogen drug for the treatment of breast cancer, may cause menopausal symptoms including hot flashes and night sweats that might lead to insomnia. Some cancer patients who have been treated with chemotherapy or radiotherapy may experience severe daytime sleepiness or overwhelming tiredness. Some patients even develop neuropathy (nerve damage) and other symptoms suggesting restless legs syndrome due to chemotherapy drugs.

Many doctors do not ask about sleep problems in cancer patients. In cases in which the cancer is not cured, there are treatments available for the relief of the pain and help for those patients who have trouble sleeping. For instance, restless legs syndrome can usually be successfully treated. If the cause of the sleep problem can't be solved, then the patient might need a sleeping pill— or a wakefulness-promoting medication such as modafinil (Provigil in United States, Alertec in Canada) to make her more alert in the daytime.

Pain

Pain from any condition can lead to insomnia. With joint disease, unless there is relief of the pain either with a medication or joint replacement surgery, sleep might be severely affected on an ongoing basis. Research has shown that people with painful joint diseases or disc problems of the lower back may develop restless legs syndrome. Sleep is one of the first functions that suffers when people injure their back or sustain other injuries that cause ongoing discomfort. The first line of defense is to treat the problem causing the pain. If that doesn't work, the patient might need pain relief via medication, massage, or even referral to a pain clinic. Such clinics are available in many large medical centers.

Back to the Woman with the Black Curtain

Let's go back to the woman described at the beginning of the chapter, whose "black curtain" had blocked her ability to be creative. An overnight sleep test confirmed that her breathing pattern was consistent with heart failure. In the sleep lab, she was tested while breathing oxygen supplied by small tubes ending near her nostrils. This improved her breathing pattern and she slept more deeply. She was sent home on oxygen.

The "black curtain" lifted for the patient. She was able to muster enough creative energy to put her art show together. Although her sleep was markedly improved, she still had an abnormal heart. This woman taught her family doctor an important lesson. Insomnia has many faces, many symptoms, and many causes. In some cases, the last thing a woman with insomnia needs is a sleeping pill. In nearly every case, the first thing she needs is a diagnosis.

Many medical problems cause sleep difficulties. Some medical problems are more common in women. Others, because of doctors' belief that they are found primarily in males, go largely undiagnosed in women. In the following chapter, you will see that sleep problems are also very common in psychiatric conditions. The most common psychiatric condition, depression, is much more common in women than men and is closely associated with sleep problems.

16

Psychiatric Disorders

The Case of the Woman on Stress Leave

When I first see certain patients, I notice that they look intensely sad, and I know that no matter what tests I do and what medical problems I find, a lot more is going on than meets the eye. Sadly, I may never get to the root of their problems. Such was the case with a woman in her sixties who had been referred to me because she had severe sleepiness. I noted her appearance for clues that might shed light on the cause of her problem. She was roughly fifty pounds overweight and was not groomed; her hair was uncombed and her clothes were ill fitting and old. The expression on her face was sad and withdrawn.

Her doctor suspected sleep apnea as a possible cause of her daytime sleepiness, and it was therefore appropriate for him to send her to me for evaluation. She did have the common symptoms of sleep apnea. She snored, stopped breathing during sleep, and was overweight. But there was more. Many nights she experienced severe restlessness and difficulty falling asleep.

I asked her about her work. She explained that she was on medical disability. When I asked why, she replied that she was on stress leave. She had been a senior executive at a bank, in charge of a loan department, but was now unable to work at all. She blamed her current situation on a nervous breakdown, and she told me her doctor was treating her for depression. She was also convinced that if her poor nighttime sleep and daytime sleepiness were treated, all her problems would go away. It turned out that her treatment for severe depression involved several medications that could both disrupt her nighttime sleep and make her sleepy during the day. It was possible as well that she had a sleep disorder that could worsen her depression. I knew that this was going to be a tough case.

Her sleep test showed that she moved a great deal during sleep and she also stopped breathing about six times per hour. Although her breathing pattern improved when she was tested while being treated with nasal continuous positive airway pressure (CPAP), her sleep was still unstable partly because of excessive movements. I knew the cause of her sleep-breathing disorder, but the solution for the movements would be more difficult.

Mental Disorders and Sleep

Symptoms of a mental disorder and sleep problems are often interwoven. Sleep disturbance is a common occurrence in mental illnesses, and the disturbed sleep, in turn, can cause daytime sleepiness and other symptoms, which can then worsen the mental disorder. In fact, disturbed sleep itself can cause a mental disorder. Furthermore, some of the symptoms of sleep disorders are similar to the symptoms seen in psychiatric conditions, and many people are misdiagnosed with a mental condition.

To confuse matters even further, the drugs used to treat psychiatric conditions frequently cause sleep disturbance. Often it is very difficult to figure out just what is responsible for these symptoms.

The category of psychiatric illness or mental illness lumps together many conditions in which patients experience changes in mood, perception of reality, thought processes, or behavior. Traditionally, these were not thought of as medical disorders, but were considered disorders of the mind. We now know that several of these conditions are caused by biochemical abnormalities involving the brain, and treatment often involves attempts to correct the biochemical abnormalities.

The mental disorders we most often see at the sleep clinic in association with sleep problems are depression, bipolar disorder, schizophrenia, and anxiety disorders (which include panic disorder and posttraumatic stress disorder).

Mood Disorders

Mood disorders are broken into two general types, depression and bipolar disorder. People with depression feel sad most of the time even when there is no apparent reason. In children and in teenagers, depression sometimes manifests as irritability instead of sadness. Some people have a condition called dysthymia in which there is a chronic depressed mood that is not severe enough to be classified as a major depression.

Depression

Depression is very common in female patients who come to a sleep clinic. In my practice, about 21 percent of women referred for sleep apnea are being treated for depression compared to only 7 percent of men referred for sleep apnea. About 8 percent of North American adults can expect to have severe depression at some time in their lives. Most of those affected will be women.

Depression is much more common in women than men; twice as many women as men receive this diagnosis. It has been estimated that 12.4 million women and 6.4 million men are suffering from depression in the United States at any given time. Roughly one in seven people with this mood disorder commit suicide and about two-thirds of all suicides occur in people who have depression. Women are two to three times more likely than men to attempt suicide, although because of methods used (for example, firearms) men are four times more likely than women to die by suicide.

The bottom line is that depression is a very serious condition, and most depressed people have sleep problems.

Depression in Adolescence

In my clinic I have seen many children with sleep problems who were being treated for depression. Before puberty, boys and girls experience about the same rates of depression. Between the ages of eleven and thirteen, however, there is a dramatic rise in the rate of depression in girls. By age fifteen, girls are twice as likely as boys to have been depressed. The stresses of adolescence, including physical, emotional, and hormonal changes, seem to affect girls more. Female high school students have higher rates of depression, anxiety disorders, and eating disorders than their male counterparts. The reason for this difference is, at least in part, hormones.

Depression in Women

Sexual hormones can cause fluctuations in mood that can lead to depression in some women. These hormonally related fluctuations occur during the menstrual cycle (Chapter 3); pregnancy and the time following childbirth (Chapter 4); and infertility and the time immediately before, during, and after menopause (Chapter 5). Some women experience severe mood and physical changes associated with the menstrual cycle. Symptoms include irritability; depressed feelings; and physical changes such as bloating, tender or painful breasts, and cramps. This is premenstrual syndrome (PMS). The symptoms are worse during the days before menstruation starts. When the mood changes are severe, the disorder is called premenstrual dysphoric disorder (PMDD; see Chapter 3).

Mood swings are common in pregnancy and some pregnant women may become depressed. Women who are trying to become pregnant or who are infertile may be under great stress, but there is no evidence that this alone leads to depression. Nor is there evidence that having an abortion leads to depression.

The days and weeks that follow giving birth are a high-risk time for women who have had a major psychiatric illness. Some women experience postpartum depression, an extreme mood disorder that requires medical intervention (see Chapter 4). Such women often have had symptoms or history of depression before they became pregnant.

Motherhood, with all its demands and stresses, may increase the risk of depression in some women (see Chapter 4).

Finally, in most women, menopause does not lead to depression, although for many menopausal women sleep may become very abnormal because of symptoms such as hot flashes (see Chapter 5).

While hormonal differences may partially explain why depression is so much more common in women than men, some scientists also believe that the greater stresses that many women face make them more likely to become depressed. These stresses include having major responsibilities both at home and at work, being a single parent, trying to make ends meet financially, and being the main caregiver for children and/or aging or sick parents.

Many of my women patients who have had sleep problems related to depression were in the process of divorce or were in a poor relationship. Others had children who had marital or other problems. Rates of depression are highest among men and women who are separated or divorced and lowest in those who are married. The quality and stability of a marriage may play a role in depression. Sometimes depression in women is related to a lack of intimacy and confiding relationships; sometimes it is linked to frequent or severe marital disputes. Unhappily married women have very high rates of depression.

Depression is not a part of normal aging. Most older people lead satisfying lives and are not depressed. Though there is a perception that they suffer from empty-nest syndrome when their children leave home, research has not confirmed that this situation is a likely indicator of depression.

Being single (either never married, divorced, or widowed) increases the risk of depression. About a third of widows and widowers (there are about 800,000 more every year in the United States) have depression in the first month following the death of their spouse; in half of those with depression, the symptoms are still present a year later.

Sexual abuse and harassment is an acknowledged cause of depression. Among children, girls are much more likely to be sexually abused than boys. Adult women who were sexually abused as children are more likely to suffer from depression than other women. Adolescent girls and adult women who have been raped are also more likely to become depressed.

I have seen many cases in which stress in the workplace was the cause of severe insomnia. One was an air traffic controller who was no longer able to deal with the stress of her job. She became clinically depressed, could not sleep, and nodded off while working. She had to go on disability.

Sleep Problems in Depression

About one in five adults who complain of insomnia are diagnosed with depression. In some people depression manifests as oversleeping. About one-third of all people who experience insomnia will have depression sometime in their lives, as will a quarter of those who have daytime sleepiness. Half of patients with both symptoms will have depression at some point in their lives. Thus, there is a very strong correlation between depression and poor sleep. In fact, one of the symptoms that are used in the diagnosis of depression is having insomnia or being excessively sleepy.

Symptoms of Depression

If three to five or more of the following symptoms are present for more than two weeks, depression may be present.

- Persistent sad, anxious, or empty mood
- Loss of interest or pleasure in activities, including sex
- Restlessness, irritability, or excessive crying
- Feelings of guilt, worthlessness, helplessness, hopelessness, pessimism
- Sleeping too much or too little; early-morning awakening
- Loss of appetite and/or weight loss or overeating and weight gain
- Decreased energy, fatigue, feeling "slowed down"
- Thoughts of death or suicide; suicide attempts
- Difficulty concentrating, remembering, or making decisions
- Persistent physical symptoms that do not respond to treatment, such as headaches, digestive disorders, and chronic pain

—From the National Institute of Mental Health

People with depression have a variety of sleep problems. About 90 percent of people with depression have insomnia. People with depression might have trouble falling asleep or staying asleep, or they wake up early in the morning and have trouble falling back to sleep. Later that day, they might take a long nap, making it more difficult to fall asleep that night. Because they may be very sleepy during the day, they often drink excessive amounts of caffeinated beverages, which could inhibit their nighttime sleep.

Treatment of Sleep Problems in Depression

I am not a psychiatrist. I see hundreds of people a year who are depressed, and if I believe that their sleep problems are caused by depression I recommend they see a psychiatrist or a psychologist. Most medical practitioners use medications to treat depression. More than twenty-five different types of antidepressants are available and between 60 and 80 percent of people with depression respond favorably to one or more of these medications. It may take several weeks or months of treatment before progress becomes apparent. Sometimes the sleep problem will resolve itself before the mood improves and sometimes after. Doctors treat depressive patients with antidepressants but they may add a hypnotic medication in the form of a sleeping pill (see Chapter 20). Some antidepressants produce side effects that affect sleep, such as insomnia, excessive sleepiness, or difficulty falling asleep due to symptoms of restless legs syndrome (see Chapter 11). A patient who is prescribed an antidepressant that keeps her awake might be advised to take the medication in the morning. Similarly, if a person is given an antidepressant whose side effect makes her sleepy, she might be told to take the medication at night. After evaluating a patient who has been referred to me for insomnia, I sometimes simply make a recommendation that the family doctor reconsider the drugs being prescribed or change the timing of when the patient takes the medication.

Traditional Medications

The older antidepressant medications are the tricyclics (examples include amitryptyline and imipramine) and monoamine oxidase inhibitors (MAOIs; examples include phenyelzine). Newer medications that primarily affect serotonin levels in the brain are selective serotonin reuptake inhibitors (SSRIs). These include fluoxetine (Prozac), paroxetine (Paxil), sertraline (Zoloft), fluvoxamine (Luvox), and citalopram (Celexa). Other newer drugs that affect levels of brain chemicals are bupropion (Wellbutrin), trazadone (Deseryl), nefazodone (Serzone), venlafaxin (Effexor), and mitrazipine (Remeron). A reversible MAOI medication, meclobamide (Manerix) is available in Canada but not in the United States. Generally speaking, the newer medications have different—but fewer—side effects than the older medications. For example, drugs that affect serotonin levels may cause sexual dysfunction (decreased interest in sex, decreased bodily response during sex, and decreased ability to orgasm).

It's important to remember that several of the antidepressants I have listed (especially the newer ones) may have insomnia as a side effect. Others (especially the older ones) might have sleepiness as a side effect. If a person being treated for depression continues to have major sleep problems, she should review with her doctor the benefits of the medications she is taking.

Herbal Products

Though doctors don't usually prescribe them, recently there has been great public interest in treating both depression and anxiety with natural products. One plant that is widely used in some European countries to treat depression is St. John's Wort (*Hypericum perforatum*). In the United States, the National

Institutes of Health conducted a large study that compared the effects of this herb in treating depression to traditional medications and a placebo. Although the herbal treatment did have a positive effect on mild depression, people functioned better overall taking the traditional antidepressant rather than either the herb or placebo. In 2000 the FDA advised the public that St. John's Wort appears to affect the way the body handles certain drugs, including some used to treat AIDS. Remember that alternative treatments are not always safe. Tell your doctor if you are using herbal treatment for depression.

Other Types of Therapy

Many patients do not want to see a psychiatrist, or they prefer an approach without pills. There are several types of psychotherapy used to treat depression. In these treatments, talking with a therapist helps people understand and solve (or at least cope with) problems that might have an impact on their depression. Behavioral therapists, often psychologists, help people to unlearn the behavioral and thought patterns that may be causing or aggravating their depression. Such treatment can also prevent insomnia from becoming chronic (see Chapter 19). With cognitive/behavioral therapy, patients learn to change negative attitudes and behaviors that contribute to or maintain depression. Doctors may also combine psychotherapy with medications.

While most depression responds to medication, electro-convulsive treatment is highly effective when the patient's depression is unresponsive to medications.

Because depression is so common in women, and along with its treatment so frequently causes sleep problems, a woman being treated for depression should make sure her doctor is aware of her sleep difficulties.

Bipolar Disorder

People with bipolar disorder, also called manic depressive disorder, have features of both depression and mania. When the patient is in a depressive phase, the symptoms are similar to those of depression. During a manic phase, however, the patient might feel inappropriately elated and appear to have boundless energy. A person with this disorder may also do inappropriate things such as spending huge amounts of money. Some studies have reported that bipolar disorder is 50 percent to 100 percent more common in women than men. There are important differences between women and men with this diagnosis: women switch more often between the manic and depressive phases, but they have more depressive episodes and fewer manic episodes than men with bipolar disorder. Women with bipolar disorder are at high risk for having increased episodes after childbirth. Bipolar disorder is far less common than depression. I see only five cases or so each year in which bipolar disorder causes a sleep problem.

Bipolar disorder can also cause severe sleep problems particularly when people are in their manic phase. They sometimes have a great deal of difficulty falling asleep at night and their days and nights might switch. People may report that they do not need as much sleep as before, and will say that they feel excellent after only two or three hours of sleep. When people switch from the depressed phase to the manic phase, and sometimes before the switch, there are several days of very poor sleep. Some patients might claim they do not sleep at all during this time. Additionally, in what has been called a mixed state of bipolar disorder, patients have mania and depression simultaneously. Such patients may become worse when they are treated with antidepressants. Almost all these people have a sleep problem, because it is likely that the chemical changes that are affecting their mood are also affecting the parts of the brain controlling sleep.

Symptoms of Mania

Mania might be present if three to five or more of the following symptoms are present for more than one week.

- Abnormally elevated mood
- Irritability
- Decreased need for sleep
- Grandiose notions
- Increased talking
- Racing thoughts
- Increased activity, including sexual activity
- Markedly increased energy
- Poor judgment that leads to risk-taking behavior
- Inappropriate social behavior

—From National Institute of Mental Health

Treatment of Sleep Problems in Bipolar Disorder

Doctors often prescribe medications called mood stabilizers to treat people with bipolar disorder. These medications may also make the person very sleepy. The most widely used medication is called lithium carbonate, although other mood stabilizers have been used in the last decade. If depression is also a major problem, the doctor might decide to also prescribe an antidepressant. Treatment with lithium has two important effects on sleep that women need to keep in mind. First, lithium may lead to an underactive thyroid gland, which could cause sleepiness, weight gain, and even sleep apnea (see Chapter 12). Second, some studies have suggested that lithium may slow the body clock and result in people falling asleep and waking later.

Schizophrenia

Schizophrenia is a devastating illness affecting roughly 1 percent of the population. Research suggests that estrogen may protect women from schizophrenia. Although schizophrenia is equally common in men and women, in males it usually starts in the teens or early twenties; in females it's usually later, in the twenties or thirties or, frequently, after menopause. Schizophrenia is associated with a very high suicide rate, and in spite of marked improvements in treatment, about 20 percent of affected people are incapacitated by the illness. Those who do not require intensive treatment often require many visits to their health-care providers and might require some hospitalization.

People with schizophrenia have problems in how their brain deals with thoughts, problems with the content of the thoughts themselves (delusions), and the belief that their delusions are real. In other words, the schizophrenic's thinking process becomes illogical, disorganized, and sometimes repetitive. She may experience either delusions (false, unchangeable, and irrational beliefs) or hallucinations (sensations, sounds, sights, touches, tastes, and smells that are not really present). Hearing voices that other people do not hear is the most common type of hallucination in schizophrenia, as was depicted in the movie *A Beautiful Mind*. For example, schizophrenics may start to believe that they are being followed, persecuted, robbed, or poisoned. They might develop bizarre behavior and start to ignore personal hygiene.

Not surprisingly, people with schizophrenia have extremely abnormal sleep patterns. Their dreams can be terrifying, and falling asleep sometimes takes hours. The patients also have nightmares. I will always remember the video-tape of one patient that we saw who had awakened during the night with a terrible hallucination, delusion, or nightmare who started hitting his own head to try to stop the terrible thoughts. Several of the patients I have seen have become nocturnal; that is, they are awake at night and asleep during the day-time and they come complaining of insomnia. Though the sleep problems in people with schizophrenia are severe, they can often be treated.

Treatment of Sleep Problems in Schizophrenia

Again, as with the other mental disorders, treatment begins for the underlying schizophrenia problem. There are excellent medications specific for this condition now available that help control the disease. Almost all schizophrenic patients I've seen in the sleep disorders center were already being treated for their schizophrenia but still had sleep problems. They were absolutely sure that if their sleep problem was solved the schizophrenia would go away. Unfortunately, that's not the case. Though some medications used to treat schizophrenics also help to improve their sleep, the sleep does not usually become completely normal. However, because of this improvement in sleep, doctors sometimes prescribe the medication to be taken at bedtime. It also turns out that a large number of schizophrenic patients (roughly 10 percent) have other sleep problems such as obstructive sleep apnea syndrome (see Chapter 12) or a movement disorder (see Chapter 11). These are treated as in other patients with these conditions.

Sadly, we have had patients at the sleep clinic that had narcolepsy, but were misdiagnosed with schizophrenia and were incorrectly treated for this condition. One young teenager was even hospitalized in a psychiatric ward. Narcolepsy is a disorder in which people have vivid dreams at sleep onset and generally know and will tell you that the images they have are dreams and are not real (see Chapter 13). On the other hand, the schizophrenic patient, at least when untreated, believes the hallucinations to be real.

Anxiety Disorders

Tomorrow's the big day. You are about to propose a toast at your best friend's wedding. You are about to be interviewed for a job. You are about to take a final exam. You are about to go onstage for a musical performance. You are trying to fall asleep but can't because the next morning you will be going on your first overseas flight. You have butterflies in your stomach and your heart is pounding. It is normal to feel nervous or anxious in such stressful situations and the feeling usually goes away quite quickly when you actually start the activity. However, in some people, these feelings of fear and dread come on at the wrong time and place. Feelings of anxiety take over people's lives and prevent them from performing these tasks or activities. These feelings are brought on by an anxiety disorder.

It has been estimated that nineteen million American adults may have one of several types of anxiety disorders that include: panic disorder, generalized anxiety disorder, social phobia, obsessive-compulsive disorder, and posttraumatic stress disorder. These disorders are more common in women than men. All of the disorders can be treated, and they can worsen if they are left untreated. Medications (most often antidepressants, or sometimes antianxiety drugs), psychotherapy, and cognitive behavioral treatment are the most common treatments.

Panic Disorder

Your heart is beating fast, you are sweating and shaking, time seems to be standing still, and you feel dizzy. You might have chest pain or trouble breathing. You feel as if you are about to die. You have these episodes over and over again, yet the doctor never finds anything abnormal during your checkups. When people have these symptoms for more than a month, they are usually diagnosed with a panic disorder.

Sufferers of panic attacks usually connect them with the situations in which they occur. This can lead to a fear of a particular situation, which the person then tries to avoid. More than half of people with panic disorders awaken with nighttime panic attacks and many develop a fear of falling asleep. I see perhaps five women a year with nighttime panic attacks. Waking up at night afraid of dying is a terrifying symptom.

Generalized Anxiety Disorder

You are always worried about your job, family, or health even when you have nothing to worry about. You have trouble controlling the worrying. This problem is as common in women as in men, and it usually begins to affect people in their early twenties. Not surprisingly, most people with generalized anxiety disorder have trouble sleeping because they can't stop worrying at bedtime, can't turn their minds off, and consequently worry about not falling asleep. We frequently see women who worry about their sleep and complain of insomnia.

Social Phobia

This problem can be called extreme shyness that interferes with a person's life. People with this disorder are afraid of being embarrassed or humiliated and are uncomfortable in situations that involve social interactions or that might draw attention to them. That would include meetings, parties, classroom activity, or even eating in public. Students might start to miss classes. This problem is also as common in women as men. Some of these patients may develop panic attacks. Some might start depending on alcohol to relax, which would result in a whole new set of problems. Patients do not usually complain of trouble sleeping unless they start to think about someone or something they might have to face the following day.

Obsessive-Compulsive Disorder (OCD)

This disorder, which affects about 2.5 percent of the population during their lifetime, has two types of symptoms. *Obsessions* are thoughts or ideas that even the patient will admit are "crazy," "silly," "pointless," "stupid," or make no sense. In spite of knowing that the thoughts are irrational, the person cannot seem to keep from thinking the thoughts. *Compulsions* are behaviors that occur in response to the obsessions. For example, the person might believe (have the obsession) that the gas burner has been left on and will keep checking the burner (the compulsion) over and over again. The compulsions are usually repeated each time in exactly the same way. People with OCD don't tend to have sleep problems unless they are worrying at night or their obsession leads them to compulsive behavior at night. This might include repeated checking to make sure the doors are locked, the windows closed, the baby is breathing, or the water faucets are turned off. There are medications that can treat OCD. Drugs that affect brain levels of serotonin have been shown to improve symptoms in some patients. Medications approved by the FDA for use in the treatment of OCD include the following antidepressants: clomipramine (Anafranil), flouxetine (Prozac), fluvoxamine (Luvox), paroxetine (Paxil), and sertraline (Zoloft).

Post-Traumatic Stress Disorder (PTSD)

Almost sixty years after being liberated from a concentration camp, a Holocaust survivor still wakes up almost every night with nightmares. A woman is brutally raped and she relives the horror every night in her dreams. This disorder, now called post-traumatic stress disorder, has had other names over the years including shell shock and battle fatigue. People develop PTSD after being exposed to or having witnessed something horrible and had a reaction of intense fear, helplessness, or horror. PTSD sufferers reconstruct the terrible events frequently, often awakening from nightmares in a sweat with their hearts thumping and sometimes screaming. PTSD is more common in women than men. When a patient is referred to the sleep clinic for insomnia, sometimes the assessment identifies the cause as a very traumatic event. These patients need psychiatric care.

Alcoholism and Drug Abuse

Alcoholism and drug abuse, which are covered in Chapter 17, are commonly known to cause sleep problems.

Back to the Case of the Woman on Stress Leave

The woman told me that she had put on a great deal of weight, a side effect of one of the antidepressant medications, which she was taking because she was severely depressed and had considered suicide. Unfortunately, some antidepressants cause restlessness during sleep and increase movements during sleep, which is exactly what we found in her sleep test. To top it off, one of the medications that she was using for anxiety had the side effect of making her sleepy during the day. We were between a rock and a hard place. I suggested that we treat the sleep apnea with nasal CPAP. I also recommended that the psychiatrist consider adjusting her medications. I knew deep down that it wasn't a sleep disorder that was causing her psychiatric disorder. The reality was that she had a psychiatric disorder and was on medications for this disorder that were having profound effects on her sleep. I knew that her sleep would not improve until the darkness of her depression lifted.

Psychiatric conditions often result in sleep problems. The psychiatric conditions are generally more common in women, so it is not surprising that sleep disorders are so common in women with these conditions. As with the patient discussed in this chapter, many patients' sleep problems are caused by the drugs they are taking to alleviate other problems. It can be very frustrating when medications used to treat a problem actually make the problem not better but worse, a topic covered in the next chapter.

17

Drugs and Products That Contribute to Sleep Disorders

The Truck Driver with Insomnia

Doctors always remember the cases that were easily solved just because the right questions were asked. One such case involved a woman in her mid-thirties who'd had severe insomnia for several years before she came to see me. She was concerned because she drove a truck for a living, delivering soft drinks for a major bottling company, and she was having trouble staying alert in the daytime. She told me it took her several hours to fall asleep and that she frequently awakened from sleep and then had trouble falling asleep again. Though she estimated that she probably only slept two to four hours each night, she did not want to take sleeping pills or any other medications. She was at her wit's end about what to do.

We went through her medical history but I couldn't find anything obviously wrong. She was a nonsmoker and she didn't drink alcohol or coffee. She had never had any medical problems and didn't use any medications. I was stumped. However, the solution to her problem became clearer when I asked her how the sleepiness was affecting her job. She told me that she was very sleepy during the day but that she perked up when she drank the soda she delivered—and she drank about ten liters a day. Instantly, I knew what caused her insomnia.

This chapter reviews what women consume or take into their bodies that may make them sleepy or keep them from sleeping. The chapter covers the medications people take to help them fall asleep or to keep them awake, as well as other products people take that can have unwanted effects on sleep.

Products That Can Cause Unwanted Effects on Sleep

A side effect of many medications is sleep disturbance. There are literally hundreds of widely used medications and products likely to cause sleep problems, so only the most commonly used ones will be discussed here. As in other places in this book, when drugs are mentioned, their chemical or generic name will be lowercase while the brand name will be capitalized.

If you are taking a medication that you believe may be causing problems with your sleep, discuss the issue with your doctor. You can also look the product up on the Internet or use some of the websites listed at the end of this book. Product inserts can usually be found on the manufacturer's website. Sometimes they are hard to read and understand, but look for the keywords *insomnia, restlessness,* and *somnolence* as you search.

Many medications can lead to sleep problems. Two-thirds of the population use prescription medications each year. In general, women are more likely than men to be using medications; consequently women are more likely to experience side effects from these medications. For example, research done by a Canadian health research group showed that from age fifteen on, women use about 25 percent more prescription drugs than men; 1.5 times the use of antianxiety drugs; and twice the antidepressants.

Antidepressants

Antidepressants are the number one drug taken by people referred to a sleep disorders clinic. There are several reasons for this. Depression is a common cause of sleep disorders. The antidepressants themselves may cause sleep symptoms, and some patients who have sleep disorders that cause sleepiness are incorrectly diagnosed as being depressed, and may be on antidepressants.

It is understandable that antidepressants can have an effect on sleep. First, their main action affects certain chemicals in the brain, which is where sleep is controlled. However, not all antidepressants have unwanted side effects on sleep. It is sometimes a challenge for the doctor and the patient to figure out which problems are related to the medication, and which are related to the underlying depression.

In some people, certain antidepressants can cause sleepiness as a side effect. Some doctors consider this a benefit. Unfortunately, this side effect can be inconsistent from person to person. For instance, the same antidepressant can cause sleepiness in one patient and insomnia in others. Some patients might even have both side effects simultaneously—in other words, they might become very sleepy yet have difficulty falling asleep. These unwanted effects often become less of a problem as treatment continues. Changing the timing of when drugs are taken may lessen the impact of the side effects. For example, if an antidepressant causes sleepiness in a patient, it might be more effective if the patient takes the drug at bedtime. On the other hand, if a medication is stimulating, the patient will probably be better off to avoid taking it at bedtime.

Other drugs used to treat psychological and psychiatric conditions can also affect sleep, so it is always safest to check with your doctor.

Drugs Used for Cardiovascular Disease

Because cardiovascular diseases are so common, medications used to treat these conditions are among the most widely used.

Drugs Used to Treat High Blood Pressure

Beta blockers (for example, propanolol or Inderal), which are used to treat diseases of the heart and hypertension, may cause nightmares and insomnia. Not all of the drugs in this category have these effects. Check with your doctor. Alpha-2 agonists (clonidine, methyldopa) may cause nightmares, insomnia, and daytime sleepiness. Calcium antagonists and angiotensin converting enzyme inhibitors are used to treat high blood pressure; they very rarely cause problems with sleep.

Cholesterol-Lowering Drugs

These drugs called statins (such as Crestor, Lipitor, Pravachol, and Zocor) are widely used to lower blood cholesterol levels. These are among the most widely used medications and have very few effects on sleep. However, some patients have reported insomnia when taking these medications.

Drugs Used to Treat Abnormal Heart Rhythms

A small percentage of people may experience fatigue during the day when taking these medications. Some might also have insomnia. There are many such drugs on the market; it is always safest to check with your doctor.

Antihistamines

Histamine is a chemical found in some specialized cells of the body. It is released from these cells during an allergic reaction. Histamine itself then interacts with receptors on other cells. There are two main types of histamine receptors (called histamine-1 and histamine-2) in the body. Histamine-1 receptors are found in the nervous system as well as in cells that are activated in an allergic reaction. The antihistamines that you probably took until the last few years blocked these receptors and their major side effect was to cause sleepiness. Diphenhydramine is used in several over-the-counter sleep medications. Some medications include the ingredient triprolidine and azatadine and are usually available in North America in combination with pseudoephedrine. People taking these combined medications may find that they have daytime sleepiness and insomnia. The second generation antihistamines do not have this side effect.

The most widely used second-generation histamine-1 antagonists, cetirizine (Reactine in Canada and Zyrtec in the United States), fexofenadine (Allegra), and loratadine (Claritin), cause few symptoms related to sleep. The lack of these side effects perhaps explains why these types of antihistamines have become much more popular in recent years.

Drugs Used to Reduce Stomach Acid

Histamine-2 receptors are found in cells of the stomach lining. When activated they can cause overproduction of stomach acid. Histamine-2 receptor antagonists (for example ranitidine, or Zantac) block this receptor directly and thus reduce the production of acid. Proton pump inhibitors (e.g., omeprazole or Losec in Canada, Prilosec in the United States) have a different effect on the same cells to reduce the production of acid. These widely used medications have little effect on sleep.

Nasal Decongestants

Pseudoephedrine and phenylpropanolamine are ingredients in medications that treat nasal congestion. These medications can cause insomnia. Phenylpropanolamine has been withdrawn from the market in both Canada and the

United States because of concern that the product may cause stroke in rare instances.

Asthma Medications

Asthma itself can cause problems with insomnia, particularly if the person wheezes or coughs at night, which causes sleep disruption. Most of the treatments currently available that involve puffers (bronchodilators or steroid medications) have very little effect on sleep. However, patients who overuse over-the-counter bronchial dilator puffers that contain older medications such as epinephrine may experience difficulty in falling asleep, particularly as these medications are stimulants. Medications containing theophylline may cause insomnia in asthmatics because this medication is chemically related to caffeine.

Drugs Used to Treat Pain and Joint Diseases

Nonsteroidal anti-inflammatory medications (NSAIDs), which are used in joint diseases to relieve pain, have no known effects on sleep. Examples include ibuprofen (Motrin or Advil), celecoxib (Celebrex), and rofecoxib (Vioxx).

Narcotic painkillers including codeine and morphine lead to drowsiness, but typically what ensues will be a light sleep with many awakenings. Morphine and drugs with morphine-like effects can suppress breathing. I have seen several patients with sleep apnea brought on by the use of morphine or methadone.

Drugs Used to Treat Neurological Conditions

Since the brain controls sleep, one can expect drugs used to treat diseases of the nervous system to affect sleep. People receiving such medications should be warned about sleepiness as a possible side effect, and they should not drive if they have this side effect.

Drugs Used to Treat Parkinson's Disease
Parkinson's disease itself can cause sleep problems. The drugs used to treat the condition usually improve sleep. However, sometimes the same drugs

(those that imitate the effects of a chemical called dopamine) might cause the patient to become very sleepy in the daytime.

Anti-Epilepsy Medications
There are a very large number of drugs available to treat epilepsy. Most cause sleepiness in the daytime.

Drugs Used to Treat Cancer

There are many chemotherapy medications used for different types of cancer. We cannot review them all here but a few points are worth mentioning. Many chemotherapy medications have nausea and vomiting as side effects that can impact sleep. Some of the drugs can also affect the nervous system and some people develop restlessness and restless legs syndrome. Many people on chemotherapy experience overwhelming fatigue. Tamoxifen (Nolvadex in the United States; Apo-Tamox, Gen-Tamoxifen, Nolvadex, Nolvadex-D, Novo-Tamoxifen, Tamofen, and Tamone in Canada) is widely used as additional treatment for breast cancer after surgery and currently is being studied as a breast cancer preventative. Estrogen stimulates breast cancer cells to grow. Tamoxifen is an anti-estrogen drug, which counteracts this effect of estrogen on the cancer cells. Unfortunately, the anti-estrogen effect frequently causes menopause symptoms including hot flashes and night sweats, which can result in sleeplessness (see Chapter 5). Sleep problems are very common in women with cancer and not just those with reproductive cancers.

Alcohol

Many people use alcohol as a sleep aid. This is ill advised. Although alcohol does make one drowsy, when the blood alcohol level drops, it activates the sympathetic nervous system that wakes one up, speeds up the heart, and might cause sweating and headaches. Ironically, it is probably best that people go to sleep after the alcohol has disappeared from the body to avoid this type of awakening. It takes the body roughly one hour to clear the alcohol from each drink containing a single ounce of alcohol. After three such drinks, the wait should be roughly three hours.

Another negative side effect of alcohol is that it can make some people snore. In some people, for example those with sleep apnea (see Chapter 12), the sleep breathing problem becomes much worse after alcohol consumption. Hundreds of women have told me their husband's snoring is worse after alcohol. When the snorer wakes up with a hangover or severe headache, it might be because of apnea. Alcohol makes you sleepy and the combination of the alcohol and sleep deprivation or some medication that normally makes you sleepy might cause you to pass out. Alcohol use increases sleepwalking in those who have a tendency toward this type of nocturnal wandering. Alcohol is a nervous system depressant, and it can worsen the symptoms of depression.

Drug and Alcohol Abuse

Obviously, not all the possible drug abuse problems that a woman might encounter can be covered here. This section will address the most common ones. The basic rule to keep in mind is that all drugs that affect the brain can affect sleep. This includes alcohol, caffeine (see Chapter 20), prescribed drugs, illegal drugs such as cocaine, amphetamines, and many others.

Abuse of Prescribed Drugs

Some prescription drugs can be addictive. This is certainly true of narcotic painkillers and is sometimes the case with pills used to treat anxiety and insomnia. Often a person is not truly addicted but is psychologically dependent on a drug. A discussion of coming off sleeping pills is in Chapter 19.

Alcohol Abuse

Alcoholics have many problems with sleep. They may have trouble falling asleep, staying asleep, have episodes of sleepwalking, and be very sleepy in the daytime. When binge drinking, they might drink, then have a short sleep, then drink again, and so forth. Many recovering or recovered alcoholics find that their sleep does not return to normal. They may continue to have severe difficulty in falling and staying asleep.

Illegal Drugs

Almost all illegal drugs have an effect on the nervous system and can lead to sleeplessness or sleepiness. A big change in personality and sleep pattern often signifies either a psychiatric problem or a drug problem. Either of these is beyond the scope of this book and should definitely be discussed with a doctor.

Club Drugs

Just as alcohol was widely available during prohibition, drugs that affect the nervous system are widely available and are used illegally, mostly by teenagers and young adults. These compounds, often categorized as club drugs, are taken at bars and dance parties such as raves, which might last all night. Parents should be aware of the dangers of drugs to their children. A website listed in the resources at the end of this book tells you about current club drugs.

Stimulants (Uppers)

MDMA (also called ecstasy) is a commonly used drug among students. For example, in the United States about one in ten high school seniors admit to having used it. More than 3 percent admit to having used it at some point in the previous month. This is one of the drugs available at many bars, nightclubs, and parties; it is used to increase stamina. MDMA in high doses can cause body temperature to become so high that it can cause muscle breakdown as well as kidney and cardiovascular system failure. It can lead to heart attacks, strokes, seizures, and death. MDMA can permanently damage brain cells. Insomnia, which can be severe, is common with this drug, and may continue after the person stops using it. Amphetamines, cocaine, and illegally prescribed Ritalin can all cause insomnia.

Depressants (Downers)

Rohypnol, GHB (gamma hydroxybutyrate), opiates (for example, heroin), and ketamine (an anesthetic) are other drugs some people use, sometimes to counter the stimulant effects of uppers. They are often available at raves and are also categorized as club drugs. Some of these drugs make people pass out and have been used as so-called date-rape drugs.

Back to the Truck Driver with Insomnia

The truck driver was drinking about ten liters each day of a cola containing caffeine. Her insomnia was caused by the huge amounts of caffeine she was unknowingly taking into her body. Though she got the soft drinks for free, she had paid a big price over several years. She had never considered caffeine to be a stimulating drug. After she weaned herself down to a reasonable amount of caffeine, her problem was solved.

Drugs can have good, bad, and ugly effects on sleep. People planning to use medications, whether produced by pharmaceutical companies or available in health food stores, should inform themselves about what they are taking before making any decisions. What problem are they treating? Is it a disease, and do they know the diagnosis? Are they receiving the right treatment for the problem? What are the side effects of the medication?

Drugs can have severe negative effects on sleep and can cause both insomnia and daytime sleepiness. Women are much more likely to use prescribed medications than men and are more likely to experience symptoms similar to sleep disorders. If you do have a sleep disorder what should you do? The next section of the book offers help and suggestions for these problems.

PART IV

YOU HAVE A SLEEP DISORDER, NOW WHAT?

18

Getting Help from Your Doctor and the Sleep Clinic

The Case of Obvious Sleep Apnea

I was on my way to work at the sleep disorders clinic one morning and was waiting for the elevator in the lobby when I noticed an obese young woman fast asleep in a chair.

Two hours later I saw her again. Again she was fast asleep, but this time she was in the waiting room. When I finally saw her in my examining room, she was still sleepy. She could barely stay awake as we spoke.

The doctor who had referred this patient was sure she had sleep apnea. After all, she was sleepy and would nod off whenever she was inactive, no matter what she was doing. She weighed about 350 pounds. She snored. Her father had sleep apnea and was on a CPAP machine. This patient's doctor believed she didn't even need a sleep test and that she should be started on CPAP.

I would never start someone on CPAP without confirming the diagnosis. Part of the diagnostic process is a detailed interview, and when the patient told me that she had been sexually abused as a child and how she was being treated currently, I knew that a sleep test was absolutely necessary.

The First Step When a Sleep Problem Is Suspected

If you believe you have a sleep problem, go to your doctor. Make sure that you communicate your symptoms clearly (see Chapter 6). Don't assume your doctor will ask you about symptoms of a sleep problem during a routine visit for something else. It's a good idea to write down your concerns and questions before the appointment so you don't forget. This is important because your doctor might check you for one of the many medical and psychiatric conditions that cause sleep problems. Bring a list of all of the prescriptions (including the dosages) and over-the-counter medications you are taking, as these might be the problem (see Chapter 17). Bring your bed partner who will be able to add information about snoring, stopped breathing, movements, and behaviors you may exhibit while you sleep. Your doctor might not be comfortable evaluating or treating these problems and might refer you to a sleep specialist. The reason for this is that many doctors have had little or no training in the treatment of sleep disorders because this is such a new field of medicine.

Birth of a New Field of Medicine

In 1970, if you had a sleep disorder, neither you nor your doctor would have recognized it. This is because back then there was no awareness of sleep disorders and so there were no specialized centers or specialists to address the problem. Some medical centers had research labs that were part of medical schools because a few researchers were interested in what happened to the brain during dreaming, or in the relationship between dreaming and mental illness.

Sleep apnea put sleep medicine on the map in the mid-1970s when it became apparent that sleep could represent a danger to the sleeper. Between the 1970s and mid-1990s, a huge amount of research about sleep disorders was carried out, and in many universities the research labs became the nucleus for sleep clinics. Scientists studying sleep formed groups to exchange information, the first medical journal to focus on sleep problems was published, and standards for sleep clinics were established to protect patients. The effect of all this research was that it became obvious to the medical community that sleep disorders were very common—even more so than conditions such as asthma. In 1990, the first textbook about sleep disorders targeted toward doctors, *Principles and Practice of Sleep Medicine* (edited by myself and doctors

Bill Dement and Tom Roth), was published. The editors represented the diversity in the field: Dr. Dement, a psychiatrist and one of the pioneers in sleep research; Dr. Roth, a psychologist; and myself, a specialist in internal medicine and lung diseases. I was the only lung specialist at the first sleep meeting I attended in the 1970s. I went because I was doing research in breathing during sleep. I knew a lot about breathing but almost nothing about sleep. At that time most of the sleep experts were psychiatrists. Now there are thousands of lung disease specialists involved in treating sleep disorders. In response to research, growing awareness of sleep problems, and patient demand, sleep clinics began to spring up and government agencies and insurance companies all over North America started to fund tests and treatments for sleep disorders. A new field was born.

The diagnosis and treatment of sleep disorders are now part of mainstream medicine. Thousands of sleep laboratories are operating all over the world. Your doctor can now refer you to a sleep specialist for a sleep study evaluation. There are an estimated three thousand labs in the United States and Canada. Only about six hundred, however, meet the rigorous guidelines of the American Academy of Sleep Medicine and are fully accredited.

Accreditation

Within North America, the quality and the types of sleep medicine laboratory services vary widely. The American Academy of Sleep Medicine has been accrediting sleep disorders centers in the United States since 1977. There is no accrediting organization in Canada. Sleep laboratory accreditation in the United States reassures the consumer that the sleep laboratory has been inspected, and that the equipment and staff meet appropriate standards. To be accredited, the staff must include a board-certified sleep medicine specialist (also see Resources). Accredited centers ensure that the staff is trained and competent to examine patients, utilize the equipment, and conduct tests and analyze the results for the sleep evaluation. In addition to the American Academy of Sleep Medicine, in recent years some sleep clinics and sleep labs in the United States have chosen to be accredited by the Joint Commission of Accreditation of Healthcare Organizations (JCAHO). JCAHO is the largest U.S. standard-setting and accrediting body for health care. This organization does not specialize in sleep; it accredits facilities (hospitals, laboratories, home-care programs, etc.) for most types of medical procedures and tests. At this point, only a small fraction of U.S. sleep centers are accredited by JCAHO.

In the United States, the Board of Registered Polysomnographic Technol-ogists (BRPT), an independent nonprofit organization certifies, sleep tech-nologists who work in sleep labs. Technicians have an important role in a sleep laboratory because they are frequently the only people there while the patient is being tested overnight. If a medical emergency occurs, the technician must be able to recognize and manage it. For example, a patient might develop an abnormal heart rhythm during the night, and the technician must recognize the danger and seek appropriate action. A technician who has been registered has passed rigorous testing to ensure that he or she possesses the knowledge and skills to conduct overnight sleep studies and to work with patients who have sleep and medical disorders. In some parts of the United States, people who work as technicians must be registered respiratory therapists.

You Get What You Pay For and Sometimes Not Even That

In the United States, besides the accredited centers, there are literally thou-sands of labs that offer sleep studies. These vary widely in terms of the type, quality, and cost of the testing. However, be aware that an expensive study is no guarantee of quality. About fifteen years ago, I taught a course for doctors on how to evaluate people with sleep problems. A doctor in the audience asked why we had to measure so many things to make a diagnosis. He was meas-uring the level of blood oxygen only, and he billed patients and insurance companies $1,200 for the test. The equipment that he used for the test was worth roughly $2,000—and it wasn't even an accurate device. He had no training in sleep disorders (which is why he had enrolled in the course). He more than paid off the cost of the equipment in just two days of use, and he was charging double what some of the best labs in the United States charged for a very comprehensive study typically conducted by a trained sleep medi-cine specialist. I was ashamed that this doctor would cheat people in this way and I was even more ashamed when several other members of the audience expressed an interest in his methods.

Types of Sleep Studies

What is available throughout the United States depends completely on what the local insurance environment will cover. In parts of California, for example, some managed care companies do not pay for comprehensive evaluations, but often will pay for stripped down tests. Some companies do not provide the coverage that will allow patients to see a sleep expert who is qualified and therefore best able to determine the most appropriate treatment based on a comprehensive evaluation of the patient.

Screening Studies

The word *screening* usually means a test—often an initial test that attempts to identify or catch a potential problem but may not lead to a definitive diagnosis. Screenings are usually inexpensive and very sensitive. Thus, a problem may be identified that, on further examination, may not exist. Examples of screening include mammography to detect breast cancer and measurement of prostatic surface antigen (PSA), for prostate cancer in men. Both of these tests can come up with false positives, as some people who are screened positive do not actually have a problem. On the flipside, there are relatively few false-negative tests.

This is not true for sleep disorders, especially sleep-breathing disorders, which have a high false-negative rate when screening studies are used. In 10 to 30 percent of negative tests it turns out the patient actually has a problem. Since these tests are not conclusive, when they come out negative, they may give the patient a false sense of security. Since the tests usually only screen for sleep apnea, they will not provide a diagnosis for people who are sleepy from one of the many other sleep disorders. These tests generally collect information about the blood oxygen level, the breathing pattern, snoring, and sometimes an electrocardiogram. Such tests can be done in a laboratory setting or in a patient's home.

If a screening test is positive, the patient will usually have a second test to determine the best way to treat the sleep-breathing disorder. If the screening test is negative, in a patient strongly suspected of having a sleep-breathing disorder, the test is usually repeated in a sleep laboratory to make sure that no serious problem is present. You may wonder about the point of having a screening test at all if additional comprehensive testing is usually needed. Why not simply do the comprehensive testing and be done with it?

Comprehensive Sleep Studies

Comprehensive testing done in sleep laboratories measures all the information that is required to make a diagnosis. It also checks to see how the person responds to treatment. In addition, sleep disorders often affect several organ systems, and it is sometimes vital to see whether some of the measurements indicate that the patient is in dangerous territory. A technician usually monitors the test in case something dangerous happens.

Getting Ready

Some people going to a sleep lab might be concerned about sleeping in a strange environment. If you have special needs or are very modest, let the people in the lab know about your concerns and they will try to accommodate you. The technicians are professionals and have seen it all: four hundred pound men with teddy bears, people sleeping in nightshirts, people insisting on sleeping in the nude, teenagers sleeping with headphones on, and people fanning their feet or pouring water on their legs. If you are nervous, bring a friend or spouse for moral support while the technicians are getting you ready for the test. If one of your young children is having a sleep study, the staff will probably find you a place to stay or let you sleep in the lab.

Many people say things like: "There is no way I will sleep at all in the lab" or "What will you use to put me to sleep?" It is very unusual for a patient not to fall asleep in the sleep lab—even people who complain of severe insomnia. No sleeping gas or sleeping pills are used to help people fall asleep. Sometimes, patients will ask, "How do you measure all that without using needles?" No needles are used. The technicians help the patients relax and are trained to explain what will happen during the night. While the technician is applying the sensors to the patient, there will be a detailed explanation of procedures and the fact that during the night, the patient may be started on nasal CPAP, a treatment for sleep apnea. The patient will often be shown a videotape about the condition and about the treatment.

Brainwaves, Eye Movements, and Muscle Tone

It is important to measure brainwaves (EEG) so that the person analyzing the record knows when the patient is asleep. Remember that during REM or dreaming sleep, there are rapid eye movements and the sleeper is paralyzed. Thus, measures of eye movements and muscle tone are required in order to know whether the person is in REM or non-REM sleep. It is during REM sleep when the most severe sleep-breathing abnormalities occur. In some women, sleep-breathing abnormalities occur only in REM.

Is the Person Breathing?

It is important to determine whether the person is actually breathing efficiently and to find out the level of effort the patient requires to breathe. These measurements will help determine what type of sleep-breathing problem is present and what treatment will be the most appropriate.

Blood Oxygen Level

If you have a sleep-breathing problem, when breathing stops, the blood oxygen level drops. Measurement of the blood oxygen level is critical because, with severe drops in blood oxygen level, there is increased risk of cardiovascular problems such as abnormal heart rhythms.

Recording the Information

Ten years ago, most laboratories collected the information on paper. A full night's recording used between six hundred and a thousand sheets of continuous paper. Thankfully, almost all laboratories have switched to computerized systems (and thereby saved tens of thousands of trees annually).

In electronics, most systems have become smaller and smaller, and the equipment used in the sleep laboratory has shrunk from many hundreds or thousands of pounds to a mechanism about three times the size of a typical CD box. This equipment is used for gathering information about what stage of sleep the person is in, breathing and the efforts to breathe, the electrocardiogram, and the blood oxygen level. Sometimes other measures are included that look at specific problems such as acid reflux into the esophagus, or whether or not a male patient has erections during rapid eye movement sleep. These measures may be indicative of other medical problems. For example, in an impotent male who does not have any evidence of erections during sleep, it is likely that impotence has a medical, rather than a psychological, basis.

What to Expect in the Sleep Laboratory

The sleep center will give you detailed instructions about the test, what to expect and what to bring with you (pajamas, toothpaste and other hygiene items, etc.). Many labs have showers available in the morning. If you are going to a comprehensive sleep laboratory, you can expect to have electrodes on your scalp, chin, chest, and legs. You can also expect sensors that measure oxygen to be placed on your earlobe or on your finger and some sensors placed in front of your nose and mouth to measure when you stop breathing or when you snore. At this point, most patients resemble an alien from outer space. While the technician is applying the sensors, he or she will usually tell you what is likely to happen during the study, particularly if you are to be treated

Figure 18-1 Recording Equipment for a Sleep Study

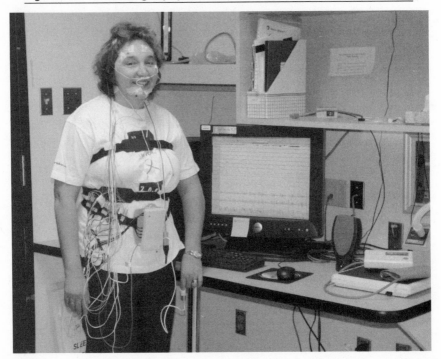

with a CPAP system. The entire recording system is in a computer on the woman's belt in the photo in Figure 18-1.

The typical sleep apnea patient falls asleep within five to ten minutes; she starts to snore and stops breathing fairly quickly while being observed and monitored by the technician. While the patient is sleeping, the technician will operate the recording instruments, which are usually either great big paper recorders with lots of channels or computerized systems that measure the information. In either case, these are very complex instruments that require a technician/operator who has received a great deal of training. The technician watches and videotapes the patient's sleep throughout the study.

Testing on CPAP

During the night, if the technician finds that you have a significant sleep-breathing problem, he or she may start you on nasal CPAP treatment to see if the treatment solves the problem (also see Chapter 12). This involves placing a mask that is connected to a blower over your nose, as shown in Figure 18-2. This type of study is called a split night study in which the first half is considered the diagnostic part and the second half adjusts the CPAP to determine how much CPAP pressure you will need.

Sometimes the lab may do a diagnostic study for an entire night, and study you again with treatment on a second night. Although there are advantages to such an approach, it is more expensive. Some labs have automatic CPAP machines that determine the correct CPAP pressure while the patient is sleeping instead of having a technician make the adjustments. Sometimes this testing takes place in the patient's home without a technician. This latter approach may not be as effective as having a person there doing the adjusting. The technician can deal with problems that may come up, such as the patient opening her mouth during sleep, which makes CPAP ineffective, or if the patient begins to panic with the CPAP mask on. Sometimes CPAP turns out to be the wrong treatment. In that case, nothing can compare with having an experienced technician at the patient's bedside.

Measuring Sleepiness

Another type of test carried out in the sleep lab is called the multiple sleep latency test. This test is a measure of sleepiness during the day and is used to

Figure 18-2 Face Mask for CPAP Treatment

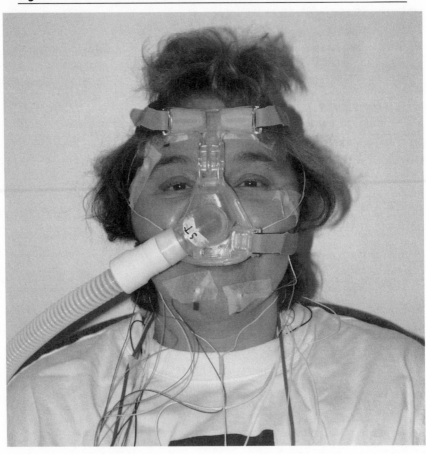

confirm the onset of REM sleep during naps in people with narcolepsy (see Chapter 13). In this test, people are given the opportunity to nap for twenty minutes every two hours during the day. They nap while wearing the same paraphernalia they wear in a night study. The opportunity to nap takes place in a quiet, darkened room. Sleepiness is measured by the amount of time it takes a person to fall asleep during these napping opportunities; shorter times indicate higher levels of sleepiness. On average, a person with extreme sleepiness will fall asleep in less than five minutes during the naps. People with narcolepsy will usually have episodes of REM sleep during two or more of the naps. People without narcolepsy seldom dream during naps.

Figure 18-3 Author Analyzing a Sleep Test

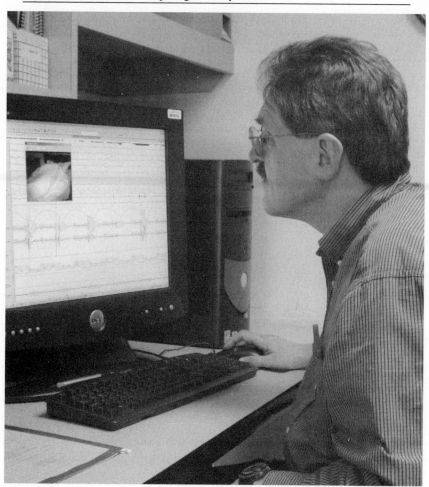

How a Sleep Test Can Help

There are more than eighty sleep disorders and some can only be documented by a comprehensive sleep test. Besides being useful in diagnosing sleep apnea and the required CPAP pressure, the lab is useful in confirming narcolepsy, movement disorders, and seizures during sleep. In the end, it may help improve the sleep of medical patients, such as those with heart failure who may benefit from the treatment of specific problems found in the sleep test.

Back to the Case of Obvious Sleep Apnea

The sleep test did not confirm sleep apnea or even the mild form of apnea called upper airway resistance syndrome that is common in women. My patient fell asleep quickly during the test and although she snored, her breathing pattern was absolutely normal. She had no REM sleep and very little stages 3 and 4 sleep, and her EEG frequently showed a type of wave that is common in people using certain types of medications. The sleep test did not show a sleep-breathing problem.

What was causing her sleepiness? Medications. She was on four drugs to treat post-traumatic stress disorder that had come on as a result of the sexual abuse. One of the drugs often causes weight gain. Three of them cause sleepiness. No wonder she was barely able to stay awake. My recommendation to the family doctor was to refer her to a psychiatrist so that her drugs could be modified. Although it did not confirm sleep apnea, her sleep test led to an accurate diagnosis. Sleep tests are as vital to the practice of sleep medicine as interviewing and examining the patient.

Once your sleep problem is diagnosed it must be treated. Some of the chapters of the book reviewed specific treatments for disorders such as sleep apnea, narcolepsy, and restless legs syndrome. The next chapter will cover a no-pill approach to insomnia. It will be followed by a chapter on medications used to treat sleep problems.

19

Treating Insomnia Without Pills

The Woman Who Was Afraid to Make a Fool of Herself

After a referral from her family doctor, a twenty-five-year-old woman came to my office and described her insomnia. She was very concerned—she even worried that her embarrassing sleep problem might break up her relationship with her boyfriend. When I asked her how insomnia could possibly embarrass her, she told me that it wasn't exactly the insomnia. It was the getting up and screaming that was the cause of her embarrassment. She thought her sleepwalking and screaming would make her boyfriend leave her. She worried so much about this that she now had great difficulty falling asleep. She also made it quite clear that she did not want to use pills. She was uncomfortable using any medications for anything. I believed that cognitive behavioral treatment (CBT) would work for her.

Cognitive Behavioral Treatment

Fortunately for this patient as well as many others, people with insomnia can often be effectively treated without medication. Before trying a medication-free approach, however, it is very important that other causes of insomnia, including medical disorders, psychiatric disorders, and the effects of drugs (including caffeine), have been evaluated by a doctor or sleep specialist.

Check to see if a clinical psychologist is available in your community and whether or not your health insurance covers such treatment. Psychologists treat people either individually or in a group setting. Many of these practitioners have told me that 70 percent of their patients are able to resolve their sleep problems with approximately six or seven therapy sessions. However, because individuals have different needs, some people require more sessions than others. Whereas many women can learn cognitive behavioral therapy techniques on their own and are successful at improving their sleep, others might require help from a health-care professional.

What Is Cognitive Behavioral Therapy?

Cognitive behavioral therapy is a psychological approach that includes techniques to treat people with insomnia as well as those with serious depression and anxiety problems (see Chapter 16). It is provided by many clinical psychologists and by other types of health professionals who have had training in this area.

Because it seeks to resolve the problem with behavioral change, cognitive behavioral therapy can help to reduce sleeping pill use. With this approach, the patient receives information about normal or average sleep, learns how to self-monitor her sleep, and is encouraged to practice good sleep hygiene (see the Thirteen Commandments on page 127). Typically the patient learns to identify and remove cues that may be promoting sleeplessness and to develop new habits that promote better sleep. Patients become more aware of their thoughts and expectations about sleep and are then able to modify them. They learn several different relaxation techniques that allow them to fall asleep more easily and to have more restful sleep.

Cognitive behavioral therapy is provided by many clinical psychologists and by other types of health professionals who have had specialized training in this area. Although some people are initially skeptical about the effectiveness of cognitive behavioral therapy for insomnia, many people become strong advocates of this approach once they have followed a course of such treatment (and even begin helping others around them with their sleep problems!). On average, 70 to 80 percent of individuals experience a significant improvement in their sleep after receiving cognitive behavioral therapy. The degree of improvement usually depends on how much effort individuals have put forth, so I must stress the importance of being committed to practicing at home.

It is important to keep in mind that to see an effect, you must apply these strategies every night for at least three to four weeks. Practicing these techniques just once or twice, or every now and then, is very unlikely to give you sustained sleep improvement. You have to be committed to doing the work.

Learning About Sleep

As discussed in Chapter 10, a significant problem for many people who experience insomnia is a tendency to become worried and apprehensive about sleep loss. It may help to know that research shows that each person has different sleep needs. This is not really surprising given that people have different shoe sizes, blood pressures, and weights—why would sleep be any less variable and unique? Some of us are by nature short sleepers and require only five to six hours per night to feel rested. Other people are long sleepers and require nine to twelve hours. Most people fall in between these extremes. Some of the people that sleep specialists see feel confident that they need eight hours of sleep per night to function well and to be healthy. These same people are often very surprised (and relieved) to learn that they can sleep for six or seven hours per night and feel well the following day. Many people have pressured themselves to obtain an amount of sleep that their body resists. In short, if you feel rested and alert upon waking with less than eight hours of sleep, that doesn't mean something is wrong with you—you just don't require the eight hours of sleep that some people need. In addition, some real negatives are associated with trying to sleep longer than you need. For example, some people who oversleep report morning headaches, grogginess, and sleepiness (ironically) the following day. Cognitive behavioral therapists suggest that patients conduct individual experiments to determine how much sleep they need to feel rested.

Self-Monitoring of Sleep

Cognitive behavioral therapists encourage patients to use a sleep diary to keep track of their sleep problems. See Figure 19-1 for an example. Completing these diaries before getting out of bed each morning—and spending no more than three to four minutes doing so—seems efficient for most women. The diary allows you to collect information about how regular your bedtime is, how long it takes you to fall asleep, how many times you awaken in the night, and the time you awaken in the morning. When you're working with a sleep diary, it's important not to look at the bedroom clock during the night. Instead you should guess or estimate how long it took you to fall asleep and how many times you awoke during the night. The sleep diary is an essential part of the therapy because it shows you the associations between your behavior and your sleep pattern. For example, if you note that you are involved in a lot of pre-bedtime activity (for example, doing chores) and are experiencing a delayed sleep onset, it might help to schedule a period of time before sleep when you do nothing but relax. You may find that your bedtime varies widely from day to day; in this case, you can make efforts to establish a more regular bedtime. By opening your eyes to your sleep behavior, this self-monitoring may help you close them.

Sleep Hygiene

Sleep hygiene refers to healthy habits that promote or prevent sleep. Some of these habits relate to diet, exercise, alcohol and substance use, noise, light, and temperature. In cognitive behavioral therapy, you will learn to assess your personal level of sleep hygiene and determine whether modifications are necessary. Some sleep hygiene areas were covered in the Thirteen Commandments on page 127. One area of sleep hygiene that women with insomnia often need to improve is sleeplessness caused by a snoring and/or restless bed partner. Cognitive behavioral therapists often encourage couples to consider sleeping in separate beds to evaluate the impact of this change on their sleep. Though they may be concerned about the effect this will have on their relationship, couples usually find that their sleep improves, and they discover other ways to have intimate moments without sleeping in the same bed.

Another problematic area of sleep hygiene is sleeping in the same room as the family pet. Frequently, dogs and cats disturb sleep by yawning, snorting, gasping, or moving around. You may feel guilty about limiting the movement of your pets at night, but preparing a special place for your pet with a nice

Figure 19-1 Cognitive Behavioral Therapy Sleep Diary

Name _____

Date _____ Weekday _____ or Weekend _____

Time you turned off the lights to go to sleep _____

Time you think you fell asleep _____

I awakened _____ times last night

Time you awakened   *Minutes to fall back asleep again*

_____ a.m.   _____ minutes

_____ a.m.   _____ minutes

_____ a.m.   _____ minutes

I woke up for the last time at _____ a.m. and slept a total of _____ hours

Circle your level of physical arousal when you went to bed:

Extremely calm/relaxed   *Extremely tense/aroused*

1   2   3   4   5   6   7   8

What were you thinking about as you were in bed? _____

_____

What did you do between dinner and bedtime? _____

_____

What did you do once you were in bed?   _____

_____

Time you napped   *Length of nap*

_____   _____

_____   _____

Time of medication/alcohol   *Type*

_____   _____

_____   _____

blanket and favorite toy outside of your bedroom is well worth the effort. For your own health, it is important to avoid sleeping in the same room as the family pet.

Cognitive behavioral therapists will ask you about your typical exercise pattern because it is related to your adherence to good sleep hygiene. As many women are juggling multiple roles of caring for family and working outside the home, they are left with little or no time for exercise during the day. However, coping with this by exercising at night or within three hours of bedtime can lead to sleep problems. Although exercise may leave you feeling quite tired and relaxed immediately afterward, many women experience an energy burst later on, which interferes with sleep. If you work outside the home, it may be worth your while to join a health club near your workplace where you can work out during your lunch hour.

Of course, no discussion of sleep hygiene is complete without mentioning the negative effects of caffeine (typically found in coffee, tea, colas, chocolate), alcohol, and nicotine (see Chapter 20). Although many people are aware of the unsettling impact of caffeine on sleep, some are surprised to learn that even one alcoholic beverage can interfere with sleep. Similarly, although some people tolerate caffeine well, many people notice an improvement in their sleep when they stop consuming caffeine even if they have been in the habit of drinking only one or two cups of coffee/tea/cola per day. Certain individuals appear to be very sensitive to the effect of caffeine. Additionally, nicotine can worsen sleep. If you are unable to quit smoking completely, one of the best strategies for reducing the impact of nicotine on sleep is to establish regular times during the day for smoking, and then have the last cigarette of the day several hours before bedtime.

Cognitive Therapy

Cognitive therapy is based on the idea that our thoughts about various events, activities, and people in our lives can affect our feelings and our behavior. Some people are surprised to learn that their thoughts about sleep can affect their sleeping behavior. In the context of insomnia treatment, cognitive therapy is used to help individuals become aware of what they are saying to themselves about sleep (their assumptions/beliefs) and to evaluate whether these are realistic and reassuring ways of viewing their insomnia.

Check to see if any of these automatic thoughts are familiar to you, and if so, how you can use coping thoughts to replace them and promote better sleep.

Automatic thought: "If I don't sleep well tonight, I won't be able to function tomorrow."
Coping thought: "If I don't sleep well tonight, I'll probably be grouchy tomorrow, but I'll manage."

Automatic thought: "My sleep is a hopeless situation and is never going to get better."
Coping thought: "My sleep needs work now but if I do the treatment techniques regularly, I will see a change in my sleep."

Automatic thought: "I have no control over my sleep."
Coping thought: "My body will tell me when it needs sleep."

Automatic thought: "If I sleep poorly tonight, it will disturb my sleep for the next week."
Coping thought: "If I sleep poorly tonight, the best thing for me to do is to remind myself that I'll sleep eventually."

Automatic thought: "If I don't fall asleep soon, I'm going to be up all night."
Coping thought: "I may not fall asleep soon, but I'll fall asleep eventually. The best thing for me to do is to get out of bed and wait until I become drowsy before returning to bed."

Automatic thought: "If I don't sleep well tonight, I'm not going to be able to go out after work, spend time with my family, or do my hobbies."
Coping thought: "If I don't sleep well tonight, I'll probably be more tired tomorrow, but I can still do those activities even if I am tired."

Automatic thought: "When I can't sleep, resting in bed is better than nothing."
Coping thought: "Resting in bed is likely to worsen or at least maintain my insomnia. Removing myself from bed when I am not sleeping is likely to improve my insomnia."

In cognitive behavioral therapy, you are asked to develop your own list of automatic thoughts regarding sleep and to develop reassuring but realistic ways of thinking about sleep. Many women find this to be well worth the effort.

Stimulus Control

Stimulus control is not a technique, but a term that refers to situations when a particular behavior (for example, insomnia) is likely to occur in the presence of a particular stimulus. In other words, certain activities can produce arousal or wakefulness when you are in your bedroom whereas others can promote sleep. Some activities that can enhance wakefulness include watching television in bed, using the computer in the bedroom, and reading in bed. Although many find that these activities help them to unwind and relax, most people with insomnia are unaware that these activities may actually be maintaining the problem. How could this be? Simply put, these activities require attention or alertness and stimulate the brain. The association of these activities with insomnia is reinforced and can become a habit. In addition, many people become dependent on these activities and feel that they won't sleep if they are prevented from engaging in them. If reading and watching television before bed are an important part of the patient's wind-down period, therapists usually suggest doing these activities outside of the bedroom. This will reduce the likelihood that these behaviors, and the concentration and attention they demand, will become associated with being in bed.

Another cue or activity that enhances wakefulness is remaining in bed even though you are awake. Staying in bed tends to strengthen the association between being in bed and being awake and struggling to fall asleep. This is something you don't want if you're trying to restore a normal sleep pattern. The therapist will encourage you to get out of bed if you have been lying awake for more than twenty or thirty minutes. Upon removing yourself from bed, you should engage in a nonstimulating activity until you feel drowsy. Then you should immediately return to bed and repeat this as many times as is necessary. Some women find that reading a book is a good choice of activity in this instance. However, others find that it is too difficult to put a good book down before finishing a chapter, and decide to choose a less engrossing activity (for example, reading the want-ads). Don't get started on prolonged activities that are harder to walk away from, such as paying your bills and doing household chores. On a personal note, I find it helpful to get up and write down what I need to do the next day. All the thoughts keeping me awake are, in a sense, taken out of my head and put on paper. Be reassured that a less stimulating, duller activity choice will help you feel drowsy eventually. Just be sure not to return to bed before you feel drowsy.

Therapists will help you learn about the cues that promote sleep. Establishing a bedtime routine and a regular sleep schedule (or bedtime and wakeup time) are two important cues that help your body transition from wakefulness to sleep. If you have children, you may be used to preparing your preschoolers for bed with a bath followed by a bedtime story. There is a very good reason why parents do this. You are placing cues in your children's environment to help signal that sleep is coming. In the midst of getting children ready for bed and other activities found in their extremely busy lives, women often forget or don't realize the need to schedule a similar type of bedtime routine for themselves. This is so important.

In addition to following a routine, scheduling a regular bedtime and wakeup time are also very important. Many people fall into the habit of sleeping in on weekends to make up for lost sleep. Although this feels good temporarily, it sets the stage for insomnia. Sunday night is the worst night of sleep for most people. This is partly due to apprehension about returning to work and responsibilities as well as a response to the increase in sleep during the weekend. Retiring for bed later than usual from time to time is not overly disturbing to sleep, provided that you continue to rise at a regular time. Therapists will help you to identify and review the types of cues that may be interfering with your sleep. They may ask you to conduct experiments to determine whether your sleep improves after removing or adding such cues. Typically, several weeks of applying these strategies are required to see a sustained improvement in sleep.

Sleep Restriction

Another component of cognitive behavioral therapy for insomnia is sleep restriction, a strategy of limiting the amount of time spent in bed to the time you are actually asleep. For example, let's say that a woman retires at 10:00 p.m. and gets out of bed at 7:00 a.m. (nine hours), but she only sleeps from 2:00 a.m. to 7:00 a.m. (five hours). Sleep specialists would say that her sleep efficiency is terrible! The patient is asleep for only 56 percent of the time she is in bed. So how can this situation be improved?

There are two basic approaches your therapist may use. He or she will put you on either a *strict* or *lenient* sleep restriction strategy. A *strict* strategy would involve calculating your current sleep efficiency, as was done in the previous example, and limiting your bedtime to your actual sleep time. So the woman in the example should go to bed no earlier than 2:00 a.m. for the next three nights and continue to remove herself from bed at 7:00 a.m. After three consecutive nights of likely near perfect (100 percent) sleep efficiency, she can begin to go to bed progressively earlier (increasing by thirty minute increments) until she reaches a sleep efficiency of 85 percent or until she is satisfied with her sleep.

Beginning this strategy on a weekend when you do not have many work commitments or other daytime demands is probably best. Expect to feel tired during the day, but be reassured that usually two weeks of practice with this strategy will bring about the desired effect.

The *lenient* approach to sleep restriction involves gradually restricting your time in bed over a number of weeks rather than immediately reducing time in bed to match your actual sleep time. Using the example above, the patient might postpone bedtime until 12:00 a.m. on the first week while continuing to arise at 7:00 a.m. During week two, the person would postpone her bedtime to 1:00 a.m., while continuing to arise at 7:00 a.m. This lenient sleep restriction process would continue until she achieved near-perfect sleep efficiency. At that point, bedtime could be scheduled progressively earlier as long as sleep efficiency could be maintained. Like the strict version of sleep restriction, most people will find that this strategy will not require them to be up late at night for months in a row. However, they can expect to follow the lenient approach longer.

Whichever sleep restriction strategy you choose, you should know that of all the components of cognitive behavioral therapy, sleep restriction has been found to be the single most effective treatment for insomnia.

Relaxation Training

Relaxation training refers to the practice of relaxation strategies to enhance the quality of sleep. Being relaxed helps you reduce bodily tension, but it can also distract you from overfocusing on your sleeplessness. Although there are many relaxation techniques available (and described in various self-help books), the strategies that follow have been extensively researched and found to be effective. These relaxation techniques include progressive or deep muscle relaxation, paced breathing, imagery-induced relaxation, and self-hypnosis. Each requires several weeks of daily practice before it can produce results.

Progressive or Deep Muscle Relaxation*

This is an exercise based on the idea that when your muscles are tense, you feel unsettled and anxious, and when your muscles are relaxed, you feel calm and peaceful. The purpose of the exercise is to train you to identify when your muscles are tense and to learn how to relax them in these situations. To do so, you will need to practice tensing each muscle group below for about five seconds, and then relax that same muscle group for about 10 seconds. When you are tensing, it is not necessary to create high levels of tension— simply tense the muscles firmly but not enough so that you feel pain, cramping, or trembling. You can do this exercise sitting up or lying down, whichever is more comfortable for you.

As you release the tension in each muscle group, say the word *relax* slowly to yourself. Focus on the word and on the feeling of relaxation as the tension flows out of your muscles. Tense and relax each group of muscles twice before moving on to the next group.

When you are first learning progressive muscle relaxation, following the instructions on an audiotape might be useful to help you focus. You can make your own tape by reading the instructions into a tape recorder.

To begin: Tense for five seconds then relax for ten seconds each muscle group. Remember to tense and relax each group twice before moving on to the next group.

1. Clench your right fist.
2. Clench your left fist.

---

*These instructions were adapted from *Clinical Behavior Therapy, Expanded Edition,* by Marvin Goldried and Gerald C. Davison, 1994. Published by Interscience.

3. Tighten the biceps muscles in your right arm.
4. Tighten the biceps muscles in your left arm.
5. Bring your right shoulder up toward your ear.
6. Bring your left shoulder up toward your ear.
7. Tighten the muscles of your forehead.
8. Tighten your jaw and grit your teeth.
9. Tighten the muscles in your stomach.
10. Stretch both legs out in front of you, and point your toes toward the ceiling.

After you have tensed and relaxed each muscle group twice, sit quietly for several minutes with your eyes closed. Enjoy the relaxation.

Paced Breathing

Shallow rapid breathing causes a reduction in blood carbon dioxide levels. It can result in an unsettled, nervous, or even light-headed feeling, caused by mild hyperventilation. This technique teaches you how to breathe slowly and deeply so that you can achieve a deeper state of relaxation. This slow, deep breathing also helps to release stress, a major culprit in insomnia.

Place one hand on your chest and the other on your abdomen. Inhale slowly through your nose, and as you do so, push your abdomen out about one inch. As you exhale, let your abdomen fall back in. Inhale slowly and exhale slowly. Imagine your stomach inflating like a balloon. Allow the hand on your abdomen to rise higher than the hand on your chest (which should move only slightly). Repeat this cycle as many times as needed; make sure you breathe slowly. If you begin to feel dizzy or light-headed, simply breathe through your nose and close your mouth.

After you have finished your breathing exercise, sit quietly for several minutes with your eyes closed. Enjoy the relaxation.

Imagery-Induced Relaxation

Imagery-induced relaxation is based on the idea that imagining a relaxing scene can lead us to feel more relaxed, breathe more slowly, and feel calmer. To use this strategy, think of a time or place in your life when you felt truly relaxed. You might be sitting on the edge of a dock at the lake, on the beach, in your backyard on a hammock, or out walking on a mild winter day. You might be at a vacation spot. If a particular memory doesn't come to mind, feel free to develop a new image to relax you.

Find a comfortable place, close your eyes, and imagine yourself in your relaxing scene. Try to think of the smells, sights, and sounds of your image. Let yourself become involved in the image as you get in touch with your senses. Feel free to change any aspect of the image at any time should it cease to be relaxing. After approximately ten to fifteen minutes, open your eyes. Sit quietly and enjoy the relaxation.

Hypnosis and Self-Hypnosis

The principle behind self-hypnosis is that we respond to information that comes from both our conscious and our unconscious minds. Consciously, we can learn to become more relaxed through a number of the exercises already discussed. We can also use our unconscious minds (i.e., our thoughts and feelings that are outside of our awareness) to learn to identify personal stressors and become more relaxed. Using self-hypnosis you can enter a trancelike state, a state of heightened relaxation, through one of several techniques. Therapists who teach self-hypnosis will initially guide you through a series of suggestions including hyper focusing on some bodily function (such as your breathing). Under hypnosis you will be guided through various relaxing scenes and be asked to generate those of your own. The therapist may make some suggestions to you about possible ways to approach your problems. As you consider these suggestions, you will continue to hear the therapist talking to you, but you will only pay attention to her or him some of the time. When the hypnosis session concludes, you may feel that you have had a journey of some kind. After hypnosis, many people spontaneously have new insights about what has been upsetting them in their lives. Sometimes these insights are not new, but were under-appreciated by the individual. The hypnosis experience helps women to relax both by the change in their tension level while in a trance-like state and by the insights gained regarding what they need to do to feel emotionally better in their lives. You will not lose any ability to control yourself during hypnosis. In fact, you have full control and can stop practicing with this strategy at any point in time.

Typically, your therapist will guide you through hypnosis the first time and then you can practice it on your own at home. It is best to find a comfortable chair or bed for self-hypnosis. The feeling you may experience during hypnosis may be similar to how you have felt in the past when watching a very engrossing movie or listening to a favorite song.

Tapering Off of Sleeping Pills

A final component of cognitive behavioral therapy is for the patient to stop using sleeping pills. Many people prefer to sleep without medication, but some feel they can't. Whether you take medication or not is a matter of personal preference. However, many people worry that they are developing a psychological dependence on sleeping medications (and sometimes a physical dependence as well). For example, one woman going through behavioral treatment for a sleep problem said that she liked to have her sleeping medication on hand just in case she needed it. She felt quite apprehensive and anxious on those occasions when she was unable to take it. Taking a pill for sleep tends to encourage the idea that you can't sleep on your own. In addition, sleep medication is costly. For these reasons, therapists work with patients to taper off the sleeping medication once they have learned other skills to manage their insomnia.

If a woman has been taking a sleeping pill regularly for several years, it could be dangerous to stop taking the pills cold turkey. Thus, the medication is stopped slowly, or tapered. Tapering usually involves reducing your medication to its lowest dose and taking it as often as you would normally. After you have adjusted to taking only a small dose of medication, the next step is to begin scheduling times when you will not take a sleeping pill, no matter what. It is best to set aside at least two nights for this. Many people try it on a weekend or at a time when they do not have many responsibilities. Most find that they feel anxious and have difficulty sleeping the first night without sleeping pills, but by the second night, most people are quite tired and sleep quite well unassisted. It typically takes several weeks to completely discontinue the sleeping pills and there can be lapses and difficult times during this period. Many people report feeling a sense of intense pride and a feeling of accomplishment upon completing this very liberating step. A study published in late 2003 reported that the combination of cognitive behavioral therapy plus tapering was much more effective than tapering alone in helping people stop using sleeping pills. After one year, 70 percent of those who received combined treatment were not using sleeping pills, compared to 24 percent in the group treated with tapering alone.

Back to the Woman with the Embarrassing Sleep Problem

It turned out that my twenty-five-year old patient had a lifelong history of sleepwalking and sleep terrors. While she slept, she would sometimes get up and walk around, and other times she would yell and scream and frighten everybody in the house. When she awakened the next morning, she never had any memory of these episodes, but other people would tell her about them, which would embarrass her. She had developed a fear of falling asleep that was closely linked to her fear of embarrassment. Unfortunately, this created a vicious circle in which her fear caused sleep deprivation, which in turn made her episodes of sleepwalking and sleep terrors even more common. I referred her to a psychologist for cognitive behavioral treatment. Several months later, I received a letter from her psychologist, reporting that the patient had significantly improved. She no longer had any fear of falling asleep, which contributed to better sleep and fewer episodes of sleepwalking and sleep terrors.

However promising, this therapy-based approach to treating insomnia won't work for every woman, especially if, as described elsewhere in the book, the insomnia is caused by an underlying condition that requires specific treatment. The next chapter covers patients who require drug treatment for their sleep problem.

20

Medications That Treat
Sleep Disorders

The Executive with Lifelong Insomnia

The patient was seeing me because she had insomnia. She was a thirty-five-year-old lawyer working as an executive for a financial company. Her work performance had recently deteriorated and she was concerned about making mistakes. Her insomnia had begun when she was a child, and her mother had told her she had always been a poor sleeper. She learned to cope with the poor sleep as a child and later as a student, and actually did quite well in school and in college.

Suddenly, about six months before seeing me, her insomnia had worsened to the point where she'd gone to her doctor for sleeping pills. She had always resisted using sleeping pills because she thought they were addictive. In desperation, she eventually began to take sleeping pills. If anything, the insomnia was worse than it had ever been, in spite of taking the pills. Her husband had started to complain that her sleeplessness and restlessness were causing him to lose sleep. Their bed was a complete mess each morning, with bedclothes everywhere.

A doctor's most powerful tool is the question. I was pretty sure I would be able to solve her problem with just a few.

What People Take to Fall Asleep

Many people depend on medications to help them fall asleep. Nothing else has worked for them and they see their lives and health to be better on medication than off. There are many products being marketed to help people sleep. Several are effective and safe, and medications with few side effects have been introduced.

Sleeping Pills

A very large number of products help people sleep. These can be categorized into four types.

1. Prescription drugs called hypnotics are drugs that have been tested and released for use specifically to treat insomnia.
2. Medications that have been tested and released for treating a specific disease, but have sleepiness as a side effect, are sometimes prescribed as medication to help people sleep.
3. Over-the-counter medications that you can buy in retail outlets such as drug stores are effective in some cases.
4. "Natural" products that are available in drug or health food stores.

Prescription Drugs or Hypnotics

Most people who take a sleeping pill believe that they take it and like magic it puts them to sleep. If only it were so easy. What actually happens is that you take a pill, it has to dissolve in your intestinal tract, get absorbed, pass through and get broken down by the liver, make its way into the blood, then to the brain, where it attaches to receptors. Throughout this process, the body tries to rid itself of the chemical. People are surprised to learn that a sleeping pill will not put them to sleep the moment after they have swallowed it. Here are some basic principles.

1. Different drugs have different onset periods. That means that the length of time it takes for the drug to go from the stomach into the body and finally into the brain varies by the drug and by the individual.

2. A medication only puts you to sleep when molecules of the drug have activated a certain number of sleep receptors in the brain.
3. The drug will continue to keep you asleep as long as the right number of sleep receptors continues to be activated.
4. Drugs vary in terms of how they are broken down by the body so that they have different durations of efficacy. Scientists measure how long the effects of a drug last by finding out how long it takes for half of the chemical to disappear from the body (the half-life). Thus, if a drug has a half-life of two hours, its level will have dropped by one-half in two hours, to one-fourth in four hours, and to one-eighth in six hours.

The types of chemicals used in prescription sleeping pills that affect sleep receptors have changed in the past few decades. Older drugs, including medications called barbiturates, were used to affect other receptors in the body and sometimes an overdose could cause death. These drugs are rarely used anymore as sleeping pills, but every once in a while I am surprised to meet a person who still uses them. Barbiturates were replaced by benzodiazepine medications, a large number of which are currently on the market. These medications attach more specifically to sleep receptors, but they have other effects as well. Lethal overdoses of benzodiazepine medications are rare, but they can occur in combination with other drugs or alcohol. The most recently introduced hypnotics activate the same sleep receptors, but are much more specific and are called non-benzodiazepines. Overdoses of these drugs are rarely lethal. The table on the next page lists the medications that act on the sleep receptors.

All prescription medications have two names, a chemical name and a brand name. Most chemical names of the benzodiazepines end in the letters *-pam*. The longer the half-life (the longer the drug takes to be eliminated from the body) the more likely the person is to have some residual sleepiness or drowsiness the following morning. Research suggests that among the benzodiazepines, the shorter the half-life, the more likely there will be side effects when the person stops using the medication. Generally, both the benzodiazepines and non-benzodiazepines are considered fairly safe because they do not depress breathing if taken in the normal doses that are suggested on the label. However, if you have a breathing problem, you should consult your doctor before using any sleeping medication.

Table 20-1 Drugs That Might Be Used for Insomnia in the U.S.

Chemical name	Brand name(s)	Peak level (hours)	Half life (hours)	Used for*
BENZODIAZEPINES				
Alprazolam	Xanax, Alprazolam Intensol	1 to 2	6 to 27	STAP
Chlordiazepoxide	Librium	unknown	24 to 48	STA
Clonazepam	Klonopin	1 to 4	30 to 40	SP
Clorazepate	Tranxene	Quickly	40 to 50	SA
Diazepam	Valium, Diastat, Diazepam Intensol, Dizac	1 to 2	30 to 100	SMTAP
Estazolam	ProSom	2	10-24	SI
Flurazepam	Dalmane	.5 to 1	47 to 100	SI
Halazepam	Paxipam	1 to 3	14	SA
Lorazepam	Ativan, Lorazepam, Intensol	2	12	SMTAP
Oxazepam	Serax	3	5 to 10	SAI
Quazepam	Doral	2	47 to 100	SI
Temazepam	Restoril	1.2 to 1.6	3.5 to 18.4	SI
Triazolam	Halcion	1 to 2	1.5 to 5.5	SI
NON-BENZODIAZEPINES				
Zaleplon	Sonata	1	1	I
Zolpidem	Ambien	1.6	2.5	I
Eszopiclone	Estorra	1	5 to 7	I

Compiled from several sources including, US National Library of Medicine and NIH, medical articles, and product inserts. Brand name information includes the original name, followed by names used by generic manufacturers for the same product. Some companies may no longer be marketing some of the products.

*Used for: S=sleep and as a tranquilizer; M=relax muscles; A=anxiety; P=panic; T=tremors (muscle shaking); I= indication by USA FDA for insomnia. The grayed rows are the drugs whose main use is as a sleeping pill. Your doctor may choose to use medications for conditions other than their main use.

Your doctor may choose to treat your insomnia with medications that are normally used for other conditions. Some antidepressants have sleepiness as a side effect. Thus, they have been used to treat sleep problems in some patients, especially those who also have symptoms of depression. This dual efficacy may help to explain why so many women are on antidepressants. The most widely used are trazodone (Desyrel), and some of the older antidepressants (examples include amitriptyline, imipramine, doxepin) that have sleepiness as a side effect.

Over-the-Counter Products

Most of the sleep aids or medications found on drugstore or grocery store shelves to treat insomnia have an antihistamine as their main ingredient. Many of these products were originally introduced to treat allergy problems, and their main side effect was sedation. Most women aren't aware that the newer antihistamines do not have this side effect. Women expecting the new antihistamines to help them sleep will find themselves disappointed. However, if they can't sleep because allergies are giving them a stuffy nose and an itchy throat, relief of these symptoms will help them sleep. The over-the-counter sleep aids that contain the older antihistamines have not been extensively or rigorously tested as sleeping pills. They are probably safe for short-term or occasional use. The main side effect of these medications is, you guessed it, sedation. People often feel dopey or groggy the day after having used these medications. This is because the medication may not have completely cleared from the body, or the type of sleep achieved may not have been optimal. Use of these medications for weeks, months, or longer is not advised because they affect the histamine system in the body, which can cause unwanted effects including nervousness, nausea, and more. People using these drugs should read the fine print on the package. As a general rule, I do not recommend sleep remedies that are manufactured for other therapeutic purposes. My caution is based on the fact that most of these drugs have not been adequately tested for any but their stated purpose.

Some women self-medicate with over-the-counter sleeping pills so they can sleep through their husband's snoring. For better ways to deal with a snoring bed partner, see Chapter 12.

"Natural" Products

Three products that are sometimes used to treat sleeplessness are available in health food and other retail outlets. They are melatonin, valerian root, and kava. These products were not tested as rigorously as the hypnotic medications that have been approved by the government and are prescribed by a doctor. The long-term effect of these medications and the ways in which they interact with other medications are generally not known. Also, women considering these natural products should be aware that there is actually much less scientific information about these products than the prescription sleep medications. As mentioned elsewhere in the book, just because a product is natural does not mean it is safe. We simply do not know whether taking such medications over extended periods is safe or effective. Many people complain that the natural remedies they've tried do not work for them, although there are many others who take these products and are satisfied with the results. The most important issue I want to emphasize here and throughout this book is that if you have a serious problem falling or staying asleep that lasts more than a few weeks, it is extremely important that you be assessed by a medical practitioner to make sure that the insomnia is not a symptom of another disorder. Sleeping pills do not cure any medical condition. Women should be very careful about using any medication to treat insomnia, particularly if they have used them every night for more than a few months.

Melatonin

Melatonin is a hormone produced by the human brain in the pineal gland. It has been called the hormone of darkness because sunlight brings a drop in the level of this hormone. Most people take melatonin to fall asleep because they have either insomnia or a problem with the body clock (see Chapter 8), usually as a result of jet lag or crossing time zones. In the United States it is widely available in health food stores, drug stores, and other retail outlets there. This drug is not legally available for retail sale in Canada.

Melatonin is one of only two hormones available without a prescription in the United States. The other hormone that does not require a prescription is DHEA, a product with male hormone properties that is frequently used by athletes to bulk up their muscles. Although people argue that melatonin is merely a chemical the brain naturally produces, the dosage usually taken is many times greater than that produced by even the most high-functioning pineal gland.

While most prescription drugs undergo rigorous testing to make sure they are effective and safe, melatonin has not been studied to find out whether it is safe when used over the long term by the general population. Additionally, there just haven't been the rigorous studies to determine whether melatonin is actually effective in the treatment of insomnia, what the optimal dose should be, and whether it is safe. Therefore, the effective dose to use has not really been determined. Information about side effects is usually not listed on the packaging (people might actually feel dopey and tired the day after using it).

Though there have been some studies as to melatonin's effectiveness in alleviating both jet lag and delayed sleep phase syndrome (see Chapter 8), the studies so far do not involve a large number of subjects. The fact that it is a natural substance does not mean that it is safe to use. One would never allow the widespread use of either insulin or thyroid hormone, both natural substances, because we know that taking too much of these hormones can cause severe medical problems. Also, unlike those who produce prescription drugs, manufacturers and importers of melatonin are not closely regulated by the FDA to ensure that the manufacturing process is safe and that the ingredients are accurately stated on the label or product insert. Melatonin is not classified as a drug in the United States; it is marketed as a dietary supplement as are vitamins and similar products. Melatonin is available because of a technicality in the U.S. drug laws and it really needs to be studied, in my opinion, as any other drug. Currently, research is being done on a synthetic version of melatonin that affects the body clock cells but not other parts of the body.

Valerian and Kava

Two other products available over the counter, especially in health food stores, are valerian and kava.

There have been very few medical studies published as to whether kava is effective for treating insomnia. What is known is that kava can, in rare cases, cause liver failure. This product has been removed from the market in Canada because it was not shown to be effective and it could pose a dangerous risk. In the United Sates, the FDA has issued an alert warning the public about this serious side effect. Valerian has been studied a bit more, but again the sampling of people studied using modern methods has in most cases been quite small (fifteen to thirty people), and the results are inconsistent. Some studies showed sleep-promoting benefits while others showed little or modest improvement.

The largest scientific review of all the articles about valerian concluded that the results were inconclusive. Medicine has learned the hard way that side effects of drugs, even those that happen only rarely, can be dangerous. These effects shouldn't be ignored or dismissed. For example, some side effects might only occur in one of every thousand (or perhaps ten thousand) people. Such findings would simply not be possible without studying large numbers of people. How can one recommend a treatment for millions of people when a study has examined only a small number of subjects?

Drugs People Use to Stay Awake

Sleepiness is a common consequence of our lifestyle, our world, and many sleep disorders. Many sleep-deprived people cannot function without their morning coffee and at the office, the coffee maker has become as ubiquitous as the computer.

Stimulants

These drugs increase the function of several organ systems including the brain and the cardiovascular system. At low doses only one organ—for example, the brain—might be stimulated and cause the person to be more alert. At higher doses several systems might be stimulated resulting in unwanted side effects.

Caffeine

Caffeine is probably the most commonly used stimulant drug in the world. It has been estimated that at least 80 percent of North Americans are exposed to caffeine during the course of a day. Caffeine is found in soft drinks, food products, and of course coffee and tea, as well as some medications. In an appendix at the end of the book, there is a table that lists the many products that contain caffeine.

After a woman has coffee (it doesn't really matter how much), it takes her liver three to four hours to reduce the caffeine blood level by half. That means it may take nine to twelve hours for the caffeine to clear her system. Birth control pills can slow down the body's elimination of caffeine even further.

Many women use caffeine to become more alert first thing in the morning and they may have two or three additional cups during the day. Trouble sleeping may develop if people ingest more than 200 milligrams of caffeine per day, especially if it is taken in the afternoon or evening.

Menopausal Women Take Note

Recent medical studies suggest that more than 300 milligrams of caffeine per day (eighteen ounces of brewed coffee) speeds up bone loss and may increase the risk of osteoporosis.

In excess amounts, caffeine also contributes to symptoms of anxiety. It's amazing how much caffeine children can be exposed to without realizing it, particularly in soft drinks. Some of the most popular soft drinks contain very high levels of caffeine. A study published in 2003 reported that caffeine intake was significant in seventh-, eighth-, and ninth-graders; 70 percent of them used caffeine daily, and almost 20 percent were using more than 100 milligrams a day. One eighth-grader used 380 milligrams a day!

During pregnancy the body breaks caffeine down more slowly. Pregnant women have many reasons to feel sleepy (see Chapter 4) and might believe that they could combat the sleepiness by drinking more coffee. Research from Sweden published in 2000 showed that women who consumed 300 to 499 milligrams of caffeine per day increased their risk of miscarriage by 40 percent, while those who consumed 500 milligrams or more per day increased their risk by 120 percent. Another study from Denmark in 2003 reported a 120 percent risk in miscarriage when caffeine use exceeded 375 milligrams per day. How much coffee is safe in pregnancy? Probably about one cup per day.

Prescribed Stimulant Medications

These drugs are used to treat sleepiness in patients with sleep disorders such as narcolepsy (see Chapter 13) and are also used to treat attention deficit hyperactivity disorder. Stimulant medications work by affecting cells in the central nervous system. Some stimulant medications—including amphetamine, dextroamphetamine, methamphetamine, cocaine, and methylphenidate—have become street drugs. They affect the sympathetic nervous system so they can cause changes in heart rate and rhythm and may increase blood pressure and cause jitteriness. These drugs increase the levels of the chemical dopamine in the brain and elsewhere, which can excite nerve cells including those that control heart rate and blood pressure.

Methylphenidate (Ritalin) is very widely used to treat children with attention deficit hyperactivity disorder (ADHD). It is also used for patients with narcolepsy (see Chapter 13). This drug can have effects on heart rate and blood pressure because of its effect on the sympathetic nervous system. It is normally used to combat sleepiness in narcoleptics, but seems to have the opposite effect in ADHD.

The amphetamines include amphetamine, dextroamphetamine (Dexedrine, DextroStat), and methamphetamine (Desoxyn). Adderall and Biphenatamine are combination drugs that contain both amphetamine and dextroamphetamine. Years ago, doctors prescribed these drugs widely as appetite suppressants; many women took them hoping to lose weight. One doctor told me that her mother had taken amphetamine around 1950 to lose weight while she was pregnant with her. The long-acting versions of these drugs are sometimes used to treat ADHD. These drugs are more difficult to prescribe than other types of medications because of the rigid controls on prescription drugs that have abuse potential. Pemoline (Cylert) is a stimulant medication that is still used in the United States but is no longer available in Canada because of concerns about side effects, especially liver problems. Mazindol (Mazanor and Sanorex), which is used to decrease appetite, is also sometimes prescribed as a stimulant.

Side Effects of the Stimulants

Ironically, the main effect and reason why a stimulant is used, alertness, is also its major negative side effect. The person's alertness might continue long into the night making it very difficult for her to fall and stay asleep. Over the years I have seen many patients, including children, with insomnia caused by excessive caffeine. Some people even become addicted to caffeine, drinking fifteen to thirty cups per day. Cutting back is difficult for them and they might develop symptoms such as headaches and nervousness when they try to reduce their intake. The best way for caffeine addicts to reduce their dependence is slowly over one or two weeks.

Alertness-Promoting Drugs

Modafinil (Alertec in Canada, Provigil in the United States) was introduced in North America in recent years to treat sleepiness in those suffering from narcolepsy (see Chapter 13). Modafinil works differently than the stimulants mentioned earlier because it does not stimulate several organ systems but instead seems to act on the centers of the brain that are involved in keeping the person awake. It is beginning to be used for many other conditions in which the person may be sleepy or tired, including multiple sclerosis, depression, Parkinson's disease, and cancer. It has been approved in the United States for use in treating people with sleepiness caused by shiftwork disorders and in treating sleep apnea patients who are using CPAP but have residual sleepiness. It is also undergoing research in the treatment of attention deficit hyperactivity disorder in children, as well as in disorders normally treated with stimulants. This is a medication that seems to wake people up without the sympathetic nervous system activation that is observed in those who take amphetamines. The medication is usually taken twice a day. The first dose is taken first thing in the morning and the second dose is taken at lunchtime. If patients take the medication later in the day, they may have trouble sleeping that night. This is a new type of compound that so far has not been shown to be addictive and has few side effects.

Back to the Executive with Lifelong Insomnia

The question that started us down the right path was, "What sleeping pill were you prescribed?" She named the medication. It was not a sleeping pill at all, but an antidepressant that she was taking at bedtime. She did not know that the drug she was taking was an antidepressant. Some doctors prescribe low-dose antidepressants for sleep because a side effect of these drugs is sleepiness, and they figure these drugs must be safer than "sleeping pills." Another side effect of the pills she was taking was that they actually made her more fidgety at bedtime; in fact, she had developed restless legs syndrome, which was what kept her husband awake at night. Before she began taking the sleeping pills she used to calmly lie in bed waiting for sleep. She now tossed and turned all night. She continued to take the pills assuming that her insomnia was getting worse, and she had not made the connection between taking the pills and her symptoms becoming worse.

In fact, the patient was experiencing primary insomnia (see Chapter 10), which she'd had most of her life. We discussed treatment options for her. She felt she had to use sleeping pills some nights in order to function at work the next day. We picked one of the new short-acting sleeping pills. A few weeks later she called me to tell me that her restlessness had vanished a couple of days after she stopped taking the antidepressant. She was having excellent sleep on the new sleeping pill, and there were absolutely no side effects. She was taking the pills three or four nights a week and was satisfied.

In this chapter you learned that pills used to treat sleep problems can improve symptoms. Medications can only be used safely when the doctor and the patient know what the problem is and have discussed treatment options. In some patients medication is the most acceptable option. The next chapter reviews much of what you have learned about sleep and how best to approach your own sleep problem.

21

Time for Bed

I f you are reading this book in bed, I hope you'll be able to close it at the end of this chapter and feel reassured that the solution to your sleep disorder will soon be within your grasp.

Sleep disorders and lack of sleep seriously affect many women's lives. These women are sleepy throughout the day, don't have the energy to get things done, and are at risk of health consequences. They can't or don't sleep properly at night so they can't stay awake during the day. As you've read, many aspects of a busy woman's life can negatively affect her sleep. These range from the effect of her hormones; pregnancies; menopause; taking care of family members, infants, and the elderly; her work schedule; her prescriptions; and the stresses of everyday life.

Females are different from males in all aspects of life, and sleep is no exception. For women of childbearing age, each month brings hormonal changes that can cause not only premenstrual syndrome, but also sleep disturbances. A common problem in hormone secretion, polycystic ovarian syndrome, can lead to a dangerous problem, sleep apnea. And when a woman becomes pregnant, a dramatic change occurs in her physiology and anatomy to prepare for the miracle of birth. The mother pays a price for this miracle. About 80 percent of pregnant women have disturbed sleep and some develop sleep apnea and movement disorders. Making sure that the mother-to-be does not become deficient in folic acid and iron might improve the mother's sleep and protect the developing baby from a permanent neurological condition.

Another big change in hormone levels occurs during menopause, which affects a woman in many ways. The reduction in the normal levels in female hormones increases a woman's risk of developing sleep-breathing problems and heart disease, and also causes severe menopausal symptoms, such as hot flashes, which can seriously disrupt sleep. More than half of menopausal and postmenopausal women have insomnia. Though there are treatments, the best way to treat sleep problems during menopause remains unclear. Some studies have shown that hormone replacement therapy may increase the risk of some diseases in some women. I hope you have learned to seek the knowledge and new research you need. I've provided a list of websites in the Resources section on page 299 that may prove helpful in this regard.

The modern woman wears many hats. She works at home and at the job. She often does shift work and is subject to the pressures of the modern world. In addition, it is usually the woman who suffers when children have sleep problems or her spouse has a sleep disorder such as sleep apnea. Sleeping next to someone with sleep apnea can be torture. At least 30 percent of all North American males snore—so there are many sleep-deprived women out there! The good news is that most sleep disorders can be treated.

The case of the farmer's fourteen-year-old daughter whose life was almost ruined by her big tonsils illustrated that sleep apnea can affect almost anyone, and sometimes the cure is simple. We now know that sleep apnea affects roughly 2 percent of all adult women. Furthermore, women's sleep apnea symptoms sometimes differ from those of men; consequently, women suffering from sleep apnea are often misdiagnosed and treated for depression. You have learned that sleep apnea is considered by many doctors and the general population to be a disorder of overweight men; however, many women have sleep apnea and they are not necessarily obese. One recently described form of sleep apnea, called the upper airway resistance syndrome, is more common in women than men, and many of these patients are not overweight. After reading this book, I hope that you will be able to recognize when you or a family member should seek professional help and what treatments have been proven to work.

The amount of sleep your body needs is as unique to you as your hair color, but you should now have a better understanding about how much sleep is normal, how sleep and dreaming are controlled by your brain, and how a clock in the brain controls sleepiness and alertness. This body clock helps to control many of your body functions. When your clock is different from that of the general population, you may either have trouble staying asleep all night if the clock runs early, or be unable to fall asleep if the clock runs late. Travel can seriously confuse this clock resulting in jet lag. You learned what can go wrong with the clock and what to do about it.

The case of the artist whose creativity was stifled illustrated how a heart problem can cause insomnia and have great impact on a woman's life. The most common sleep problem in women is insomnia. In fact, another truth about women's sleep is that insomnia is much more common in women than it is in men. The information on insomnia hopefully helped you realize that insomnia is not a disease; it is a symptom of something else going on in the body—a medical, psychological, or psychiatric condition or a reaction to stress. Medical diseases ranging from heart failure to diabetes, acid reflux, ulcer disease, arthritis, and many other painful conditions including cancer, can lead to severe insomnia. You learned how these conditions can cause insomnia and how your family doctor can help the insomnia, not with sleeping pills, but with specific treatment of the medical condition. I hope the clues to finding out what might be causing insomnia are now more easily identifiable.

The case of the doctor's wife who suffered needlessly from RLS for more than thirty years following her last pregnancy illustrated how restless legs syndrome and movement disorders can cause misery when the person is trying to fall asleep. These conditions may affect as much as 15 percent of the adult population; women are particularly at risk. Iron deficiency is an underlying cause of RLS. Women are much more likely to become iron deficient in their lifetime than men are because of menstrual cycles; and RLS frequently starts during pregnancy. You learned to recognize this condition in yourself and family members, and you became aware of simple treatments that can often cure this miserable disorder.

You have read much in this book about how the brain and nervous system wield great power over the quality and quantity of your sleep. Nearly all psychiatric disorders have disturbed sleep as a characteristic feature. The most common of these disorders is depression, which affects about 5 to 10 percent of adults. Women are more likely than men to be treated for depression, are therefore more likely to have sleep problems related to depression, and are more likely to be on antidepressant medications, many of which can cause disturbed sleep. Along with antidepressants, the effect of drugs on sleep can be good, bad, or ugly. Many sleep remedies, such as prescription drugs, over-the-counter medications, and those obtained in health food stores, have potentially negative effects on sleep. Many medications both prescribed and not prescribed, can worsen an already existing sleep problem and can even cause sleep problems. Because women statistically take almost twice as many drugs as men they are more likely to suffer from these unwanted effects.

Other brain-controlled sleep problems can disturb a woman's sleep and may result in a fear of going to sleep. These sleep problems include sleep-walking, sleep talking, sleep paralysis, hallucinations, and even violent behavior. In one disorder, the sleeper reacts to dream content and may defend himself and injure his bed partner. Though this disorder is much more common in males, it is the female bed partner who sometimes suffers the consequences. Thankfully, this problem can usually be treated quite easily.

Finally, the case of the medical student who discovered she had narcolepsy revealed that although this is a serious condition, it can be treated and people who have it can be quite successful. Although narcolepsy has been the butt of movie jokes, it is a serious disorder. It is a relatively rare neurological condition affecting the brain in which dreaming occurs at the wrong time— it can even happen while the person is awake! You learned that because it usually starts in the teenage years, it is devastating and can ruin a person's life if it goes untreated. It can masquerade as several other medical problems. The average female patient receives the correct diagnosis fifteen years after the onset of symptoms. You learned how to recognize this disorder in yourself or family members and help them live with this lifelong condition. Although this disorder sounds devastating, there is hope. When treated correctly, people with narcolepsy can lead successful lives.

From the extreme of narcolepsy to something as simple as drinking too much coffee, I've tried to catalog the many problems that can disrupt your sleep. If after reading this book you realize you have a sleep problem, the good news is that there is help available. There are clinics with doctors devoted to people with sleep problems all over the world.

Now that you've read this book, you are much more likely to recognize a sleep disorder in yourself or a family member. You have learned when you can help yourself and when it is time to discuss the sleep problem with your doctor. Armed with knowledge and your exact symptoms, you will be able to help your doctor help you.

The goal of this book was to give you the information and the tools that would help you to awaken every morning feeling rested, wide awake, and ready to tackle the world. In the meanwhile, I wish you sweet dreams.

Appendix A

The National Sleep Foundation Sleep Diary

National Sleep Foundation Sleep Diary

	COMPLETE IN MORNING							COMPLETE AT END OF DAY				
	I went to bed last night at:	I got out of bed this morning at:	Last night, I fell asleep in:	I woke up during the night: (Record number of times)	When I woke up for the day, I felt: (Check one)	Last night I slept a total of: (Record number of hours)	My sleep was disturbed by: (List any mental, emotional, physical or environmental factors that affected your sleep; e.g. stress, snoring, physical discomfort, temperature)	I consumed caffeinated drinks in the:	I exercised at least 20 minutes in the:	Approximately 2-3 hours before going to bed, I consumed:	Medication(s) I took during the day: [List name of medication/drug(s)]	About 1 hour before going to sleep, I did the following activity: (List activity; e.g. watch TV, work, read)
DAY 1 DAY ____ DATE ____	____ PM/AM	____ PM/AM	____ Minutes	____ Times	☐ Refreshed ☐ Somewhat refreshed ☐ Fatigued	____ Hours		☐ Morning ☐ Afternoon ☐ Within several hours before going to bed ☐ Not applicable	☐ Morning ☐ Afternoon ☐ Within several hours before going to bed ☐ Not applicable	☐ Alcohol ☐ A heavy meal ☐ Not applicable		
DAY 2 DAY ____ DATE ____	____ PM/AM	____ PM/AM	____ Minutes	____ Times	☐ Refreshed ☐ Somewhat refreshed ☐ Fatigued	____ Hours		☐ Morning ☐ Afternoon ☐ Within several hours before going to bed ☐ Not applicable	☐ Morning ☐ Afternoon ☐ Within several hours going to bed ☐ Not applicable	☐ Alcohol ☐ A heavy meal ☐ Not applicable		
DAY 3 DAY ____ DATE ____	____ PM/AM	____ PM/AM	____ Minutes	____ Times	☐ Refreshed ☐ Somewhat refreshed ☐ Fatigued	____ Hours		☐ Morning ☐ Afternoon ☐ Within several hours before going to bed ☐ Not applicable	☐ Morning ☐ Afternoon ☐ Within several hours going to bed ☐ Not applicable	☐ Alcohol ☐ A heavy meal ☐ Not applicable		

DAY 4

DAY_____

DATE_____

_____ PM/AM   _____ PM/AM   _____ Minutes   _____ Times

- ☐ Refreshed
- ☐ Somewhat refreshed
- ☐ Fatigued

_____ Hours

☐ Morning	☐ Morning
☐ Afternoon	☐ Afternoon
☐ Within several hours before going to bed	☐ Within several hours before going to bed
☐ Not applicable	☐ Not applicable

- ☐ Alcohol
- ☐ A heavy meal
- ☐ Not applicable

DAY 5

DAY_____

DATE_____

_____ PM/AM   _____ PM/AM   _____ Minutes   _____ Times

- ☐ Refreshed
- ☐ Somewhat refreshed
- ☐ Fatigued

_____ Hours

☐ Morning	☐ Morning
☐ Afternoon	☐ Afternoon
☐ Within several hours before going to bed	☐ Within several hours before going to bed
☐ Not applicable	☐ Not applicable

- ☐ Alcohol
- ☐ A heavy meal
- ☐ Not applicable

DAY 6

DAY_____

DATE_____

_____ PM/AM   _____ PM/AM   _____ Minutes   _____ Times

- ☐ Refreshed
- ☐ Somewhat refreshed
- ☐ Fatigued

_____ Hours

☐ Morning	☐ Morning
☐ Afternoon	☐ Afternoon
☐ Within several hours before going to bed	☐ Within several hours before going to bed
☐ Not applicable	☐ Not applicable

- ☐ Alcohol
- ☐ A heavy meal
- ☐ Not applicable

DAY 7

DAY_____

DATE_____

_____ PM/AM   _____ PM/AM   _____ Minutes   _____ Times

- ☐ Refreshed
- ☐ Somewhat refreshed
- ☐ Fatigued

_____ Hours

☐ Morning	☐ Morning
☐ Afternoon	☐ Afternoon
☐ Within several hours before going to bed	☐ Within several hours before going to bed
☐ Not applicable	☐ Not applicable

- ☐ Alcohol
- ☐ A heavy meal
- ☐ Not applicable

Appendix B

Caffeine Content of Common Products

Note that some formulations for products may vary in different countries. Read the label.

Products	Serving Size	Caffeine Content (mg)
Soft Drinks		
7-UP	8 oz.	0
Barq's Diet Root Beer	8 oz.	15
Barq's Root Beer	8 oz.	15
Caffeine-free Coca-Cola	8 oz.	0
Caffeine-free Diet Coke	8 oz.	0
Coca-Cola	8 oz.	23
Diet Coke	8 oz.	31
Diet Dr. Pepper	8 oz.	28
Diet Mountain Dew	8 oz.	37
Diet Pepsi	8 oz.	4
Diet RC Cola	8 oz.	36
Diet 7-UP	8 oz.	0
Diet Sprite	8 oz.	0
Diet Sun Drop	8 oz.	46
Diet Wild Cherry Pepsi	8 oz.	24
Dr. Pepper	8 oz.	28
Jolt	8 oz.	48
Mello Yello	8 oz.	34

Products	Serving Size	Caffeine Content (mg)
Soft Drinks (continued)		
Minute Maid Orange Soda	8 oz.	0
Mountain Dew	8 oz.	37
Mr. Pibb	8 oz.	40
Mug Root Beer	8 oz.	0
Pepsi	8 oz.	25
Pepsi ONE	8 oz.	37
RC Cola	8 oz.	36
Shasta Cola	8 oz.	45
Sprite	8 oz.	0
Sun Drop	8 oz.	42
Sunkist Orange Soda	8 oz.	28
Surge	8 oz.	35
Tab	8 oz.	47
Wild Cherry Pepsi	8 oz.	25
Energy Drinks		
Black Stallion	250 mL	80
Lift Plus	250 mL	36
Liptorian	250 mL	50
Red Bull	250 mL	80
Red Eye Gold	250 mL	48
Red Eye Power	250 mL	50
V	250 mL	50
Coffees		
Arizona Blue Luna Iced Coffees	8 oz.	40–50
Arizona Iced Coffees	8 oz.	40–50
Brewed, drip method	8 oz.	85
Cafe Vienna	8 oz.	90
Caffe Americano, grande	16 oz.	105
Caffe Americano, short	8 oz.	35
Caffe Americano, tall	12 oz.	70
Caffe Latte	6 oz.	90
Caffe Mocha	6 oz.	90
Cappuccino	6 oz.	90

Products	Serving Size	Caffeine Content (mg)
Coffees (continued)		
Cappuccino, Amaretto	8 oz.	90
Cappuccino, decaf	8 oz.	4
Cappuccino, French vanilla or Irish cream	8 oz.	45–50
Cappuccino, mocha	8 oz.	60–65
Cappuccino, orange	8 oz.	102
Coffee	8 oz.	110
Coffee, decaf	8 oz.	5
Coffee, grande	16 oz.	550
Coffee, short	8 oz.	250
Coffee, tall	12 oz.	375
Espresso	1 oz.	90
Espresso, decaf	1 oz.	10
Instant	8 oz.	75
Swiss Mocha	8 oz.	55
Viennese chocolate Café	8 oz.	26
Teas		
Arizona Iced Tea, Black Tea	8 oz.	16
Arizona Iced Tea, Green Tea	8 oz.	7.5
Arizona Iced Tea, Rx Power and Energy	8 oz.	30
Brewed, imported brands	8 oz.	60
Brewed, major U.S. brands	8 oz.	40
Iced	8 oz.	25
Instant	8 oz.	28
Lipton Brisk Iced Tea	8 oz.	6
Mistic Teas	8 oz.	17 (avg.)
Snapple Iced Tea, all kinds	8 oz.	21
Water Products		
Aqua Blast	8 oz.	40
Aqua Java	8 oz.	25–30
Java Water	8 oz.	60
Krank 20	8 oz.	45

Products	Serving Size	Caffeine Content (mg)
Water Products (continued)		
Nitro Water	8 oz.	28
Water Joe	8 oz.	35
Chocolate Products		
Baker's chocolate	1 oz.	26
Chocolate milk beverage	8 oz.	5
Chocolate-flavored syrup	1 oz.	4
Cocoa beverage	8 oz.	6
Dark chocolate, semi-sweet	1 oz.	20
Milk chocolate	1 oz.	6
Milk chocolate bar w/cappuccino filling	1 oz.	20
Frozen Desserts		
Cappuccino chocolate chunk or cappuccino mocha fudge ice cream	8 oz.	8
Coffee frozen yogurt, fat-free	8 oz.	40
Coffee fudge ice cream, low fat	8 oz.	30
Coffee ice cream	8 oz.	58
Coffee ice cream, assorted flavors	8 oz.	40–60
Frappuccino bar	2.5 oz (one bar)	15
No-fat coffee fudge frozen yogurt	8 oz	85
Pills and Medications		
Anacin	2 tablets	26
Aqua Ban	1 tablets	100
Cafergot	1 tablets	100
Caffedrine	2 capsules	200
Coryban-D	1 tablets	30
Darvon Compound	1 tablet	32
Dexatrim	1 tablet	200
Dristan	1 tablet	30
Excedrin, maximum strength	2 tablets	130
Fiorinal	1 tablet	40

Products	Serving Size	Caffeine Content (mg)
Pills and Medications (continued)		
Midol	1 tablet	32
Migralam	1 tablet	100
Neo-Synephrine	1 tablet	15
NoDoz, maximum strength	1 tablet	200
NoDoz, regular strength	1 tablet	100
Percodan	1 tablet	32
Permathene Water Off	1 tablet	100
Pre-Mens Forte	1 tablet	50
Prolamine	1 tablet	140
Triaminicin	1 tablet	30
Vanquish	1 tablet	33
Vivarin	1 tablet	200

Used with permission of the National Sleep Foundation. To use the Caffeine Calculator, visit www.sleepfoundation.org/caffeine.html.

Resources

A ll of the websites mentioned in this section were valid as of January 2004.

Three Vital Information Sources

A key part of the National Sleep Foundation's mission is to improve public health and safety by educating the public about sleep and its disorders. From the organization's website, you can link to patient support groups, professional sites, sites for students, and many other useful organizations.

National Sleep Foundation
1522 K Street, NW, Suite 500
Washington, DC 20005
Phone: (202) 347-3471
Fax: (202) 347-3472
E-mail: nsf@sleepfoundation.org
Website: www.sleepfoundation.org

The American Academy of Sleep Medicine (AASM) is an organization for sleep medicine professionals. An important part of its mission is to ensure that patients receive quality care. From the AASM website you can get a listing of member centers that have been accredited by the AASM. You can contact the organization via e-mail for additional information about centers including accredited nonmember centers.

The American Academy of Sleep Medicine
One Westbrook Corporate Center, Suite 920
Westchester, IL 60154
Phone: (708) 492-0930
Fax: (708) 492-0943
Website: www.aasmnet.org

The National Institutes of Health have two resources of great interest to the public: Medline Plus, which has excellent information about health topics and drugs and has an online medical encyclopedia, and the Garfield Star Sleeper website, which has information about sleep disorders for children, parents, teachers, and pediatricians.

Medline Plus: www.nlm.nih.gov/medlineplus
Garfield Star Sleeper www.nhlbi.nih.gov/health/public/sleep/starslp

About Sleep Medicine Services

Sleep medicine services are covered by most U.S. health insurance plans including Medicare. The resources available to Americans vary considerably depending on where you live, what coverage you have, and other factors. Medicare covers most services needed by patients with sleep disorders.

Military Personnel

U.S. Army

The following information was supplied by Dr. David Kristo, Lieutenant Colonel Medical Corps, Director Sleep Disorders Center, Walter Reed Army Medical Center, Washington, D.C.

Initial complaints are assessed at the primary-care level. The Army has sleep centers at: Landstuhl Regional Medical Center, Germany (Pulmonary Service); Walter Reed Army Medical Center, Washington, D.C. (Pulmonary Service); and Madigan Army Medical Center, Tacoma, Washington (Neurology Service). Personnel with access to these sites are referred to the respective sleep disorders center. Those assigned elsewhere are referred to civilian services.

Patients are given CPAP under the Army insurance coverage, Tricare. A diagnosis of sleep apnea sometimes requires therapy other than CPAP, one that is applicable to field duty (surgery, oral appliance). Walter Reed has a dental service offering oral appliance treatment to active-duty personnel. Elsewhere the patients are required to obtain a referral for civilian services to access oral appliance therapy. Military ear, nose, and throat surgical services are available in most sites for cases of required corrective surgery. If there is no therapy available besides CPAP after one year from diagnosis, the soldier is required to undergo medical board evaluation to determine if he or she is fit to remain on active duty.

Similarly, narcolepsy patients undergo medical board examination, preferably after treatment is optimized. Patients must generally undergo wakefulness testing to assess the efficacy of medications. Following medical separation, personnel are awarded a percentage disability that equates with pay. Those with 30 percent or more disability may continue to access military hospitals, those with less than 30 percent disability are referred to the Veterans Administration hospitals.

Other Branches of the Military

The other military services have similar approaches. The Navy has sleep disorders centers in Bethesda, Maryland, and Portsmouth, Virginia. The Air Force has a large center at the Wilford Hall AFB in San Antonio, Texas.

Seeing a Sleep Specialist

Some American doctors have taken the American Board of Sleep Medicine Fellowship examination. To take this exam a doctor generally has to complete all medical training (medical school, internship), then usually must complete additional postgraduate training in a specialty (for example, internal medicine, pulmonary medicine, neurology, or psychiatry) and then have additional specialized training (usually a year) in sleep medicine. Many doctors have taken all the training but have chosen not to take the examination. The website that lists U.S. doctors that have passed this examination is www.absm.org/Diplomates/listing.htm. In this listing *Internal Medicine* refers to a doctor who specializes in medical diseases in adults. *Pulmonology* refers to a doctor who has received certification in respiratory disorders.

Online Resources Related to Chapter Contents

Chapter 1: *What Is Sleep?*

National Sleep Foundation
1522 K Street, NW, Suite 500
Washington, DC 20005
Phone: (202) 347-3471
Website: www.sleepfoundation.org

This is the major foundation dealing with all aspects of sleep and its disorders.

National Heart, Lung, and Blood Institute
National Center on Sleep Disorders Research
Two Rockledge Center, Suite 10038
6701 Rockledge Drive, MSC 7920
Bethesda, MD 20892-7920
Phone: (301) 435-0199
Website: www.nhlbi.nih.gov/about/ncsdr/index.htm

This is the major U.S. government agency that provides information about sleep and its disorders.

General Information About Sleep in Women
www.sleepfoundation.org/publications/women.html
www.sleepfoundation.org/PressArchives/womensleep.html
www.sleepfoundation.org/publications/1998womenpoll.html

Syllabus About Sleep for University Students
www.sleephomepages.org/sleepsyllabus

Chapter 2: Sleep Through the Stages of Life

Sleep in Infants and Toddlers
www.sleepfoundation.org/publications/J&Jbrochure.pdf
www.nhlbi.nih.gov/health/public/sleep/starslp

Chapter 3: How the Menstrual Cycle Affects Sleep

www.fwhc.org/health/moon.htm
www.postgradmed.com/issues/2000/05_00/frye.htm
www.sleepfoundation.org/publications/women.html#2

Chapter 4: How Pregnancy Affects Sleep

General Information About Pregnancy
www.babycentre.co.uk/pregnancy

Websites About Sleep in Pregnancy
www.babycentre.co.uk/refcap/547469.html
www.sleepfoundation.org/publications/women.html#4

Chapter 5: How Menopause Affects Sleep

Latest Data and Recommendations
http://medlineplus.gov

General Information
http://womenshealth.about.com/library/blmenoindex.htm
http://www.nlm.gov/medlineplus/tutorials/menopause.html

Hormone Therapy
http://www.4woman.gov/menopause/index2.htm

Alternative Treatments
    http://nccam.nih.gov/health/alerts/menopause
    www.acog.org/from_home/publications/misc/pbo28.htm
    www.ncbi.nlm.nih.gov/entrez/query.fcgi?cmd=Retrieve&db=
        PubMed&list_uids=12435217&dopt=Abstract

Chapter 7: My Family's Sleep Problems Are Keeping Me Awake

America's Families from the 2000 Census
    www.census.gov/prod/2001pubs/p20-537.pdf

Canada's Families from the 2001 Census
    www.canada.com/national/features/special

SIDS
    www.nlm.nih.gov/medlineplus/suddeninfantdeathsyndrome.html

Alzheimer's Disease
    Alzheimer's Disease and Related Disorders Association
    919 North Michigan Avenue, Suite 1000
    Chicago, IL 60601
    Phone: (800) 272-3900 or (312) 335-8700
    Website: www.alz.org

    Alzheimer's Disease Education and Referral Center
    P.O. Box 8250
    Silver Springs, MD 20907-8250
    Phone: (800) 438-4380 or (301) 495-3334
    Website: www.alzheimers.org

NIH Websites About Alzheimer's
    www.nlm.nih.gov/medlineplus/ency/article/000760.htm
    www.nlm.nih.gov/medlineplus/alzheimersdisease.html

Clinical Trials of Alzheimer's
    http://clinicaltrials.gov/ct/gui/action/FindCondition?ui=
        D012893&recruiting=true

Chapter 9: Sleeping in a World That Never Sleeps

Shift Work
   www.sleepfoundation.org/publications/shiftworker.html

Facts About Driving and Drowsiness
   www.sleepfoundation.org/activities/daaafacts.html
   www.aaafoundation.org/pdf/wakeup.pdf
   www.drowsydriving.org

Chapter 10: Insomnia

National Sleep Foundation
   www.sleepfoundation.org/publications/sleepaids.html
National Heart Lung and Blood Institute
   www.nhlbi.nih.gov/health/public/sleep/insomnia.pdf
American Insomnia Association
   www.americaninsomniaassociation.org

Chapter 11: Restless Legs Syndrome

Restless Legs Syndrome Foundation
819 Second Street, SW
Rochester, MN 55902-2985
Phone: (507) 287-6465
Website: www.rls.org

National Institute of Neurological Disorders and Stroke
P.O. Box 5801
Bethesda, MD 20824
Phone: (800) 352-9424
Website: www.ninds.nih.gov/health_and_medical/disorders/
   restless_doc.htm

Worldwide Education & Awareness for Movement Disorders
   (WE MOVE)
204 W. 84th Street
New York, NY 10024
Phone: (800) 437-MOV2 (x6682) or (212) 875-8312
Website: www.wemove.org

Chapter 12: Sleep-Breathing Disorders: Snoring and Sleep Apnea

Information About Sleep Apnea from the Canadian Lung Association
   www.lung.ca/sleepapnea

Excellent Online Handbook for Newly Diagnosed Sleep Apnea Patients
   www.lung.ca/sleepapnea/handbook/Sleep_Apnea_Action_
   Handbook.pdf

American Sleep Apnea Association
1424 K Street NW, Suite 302
Washington, DC 20005
Phone: (202) 293-3650
Fax: (202) 293-3656
Website: www.sleepapnea.org

National Institute of Health Fact Sheet on Sleep Apnea
   www.nhlbi.nih.gov/health/public/sleep/sleepapn.pdf

Tutorial from the National Library of Medicine
   www.nlm.nih.gov/medlineplus/tutorials/sleepdisorders.html

Chapter 13: Narcolepsy

Narcolepsy Network National
10921 Reed Hartman Highway
Cincinnati, OH 45242
Website: www.narcolepsynetwork.org

Stanford University: Medications Used in Narcolepsy
www.med.stanford.edu/school/Psychiatry/narcolepsy/
medications.html

Chapter 15: Medical Conditions

This chapter reviewed many medical conditions. An excellent place to learn
more about many of these medical problems is a site at the National Library
of Medicine, which has tutorials on many chronic diseases: www.nlm.nih.gov/
medlineplus/tutorials.html.

Migraine
Migraine: Tutorial from National Library of Medicine
www.nlm.nih.gov/medlineplus/tutorials/headacheandmigraine.html
Medical Information About Migraine
www.neurologychannel.com/migraine

Cluster Headache
American Academy of Family Physicians
http://www.familydoctor.org/handouts/035.html
Support Group with Extensive Information
www.clusterheadaches.com

Parkinson's Disease
Tutorial from National Library of Medicine
www.nlm.nih.gov/medlineplus/tutorials/parkinsonsdisease.html
Sleep Problems in Parkinson's Disease
www.parkinson.org/SleepDisturbances.htm

Gastroesophageal Reflux
Tutorial from National Library of Medicine
www.nlm.nih.gov/medlineplus/tutorials/gerd.html
Heartburn and Pregnancy
www.babycentre.co.uk/refcap/547412.html
Peptic Ulcer Disease
www.niddk.nih.gov/health/digest/pubs/pepticulcers/pepticulcers.htm

Diabetes
Tutorial from National Library of Medicine
www.nlm.nih.gov/medlineplus/tutorials/diabetes.html

Chapter 16: Psychiatric Disorders

National Alliance for the Mentally Ill (NAMI)
Colonial Place Three
2107 Wilson Blvd., Suite 300
Arlington, VA 22201-3042
Phone: (800) 950-NAMI (x6264) or (703) 524-7600
Website: www.nami.org

National Mental Health Association (NMHA)
1021 Prince Street
Alexandria, VA 22314-2971
Phone: (800) 969-6642 or (703) 684-7722
Website: www.nmha.org

National Mental Health Consumers' Self-Help Clearinghouse
1211 Chestnut Street, Suite 1000
Philadelphia, PA 19107
Phone: (800) 553-4KEY (x4539) or (215) 751-1810
Website: www.mhselfhelp.org/index2.html

Depression and Bipolar Support Alliance (DBSA)
730 N. Franklin Street, Suite #501
Chicago, IL 60610-7204
Phone: (312) 988-1150
Fax: (312) 642-7243
Website: www.DBSAlliance.org

National Foundation for Depressive Illness, Inc.
P.O. Box 2257
New York, NY 10116
Phone: (800) 239-1265 or (212) 268-4260
Website: www.depression.org

National Alliance for Research on Schizophrenia and Depression
(NARSAD)
60 Cutter Mill Road, Suite 404
Great Neck, NY 11021
Phone: (516) 829-0091
Website: www.narsad.org

From the National Institutes of Health
National Institute of Mental Health
Information Resources and Inquiries Branch
6001 Executive Boulevard
Room 8184, MSC 9663
Bethesda, MD 20892-9663
Phone: (301) 443-4513
Fax: (301) 443-4279
nimhinfo@nih.gov

General Information on All Psychiatric Disorders
www.nimh.nih.gov
www.nimh.nih.gov/depression
General Review of Mental Illnesses in Women
www.nimh.nih.gov/publicat/womensoms.cfm
Information on Depression (800) 421-4211
www.nimh.nih.gov/publicat/depressionmenu.cfm
Information on Anxiety (888) 8-ANXIETY
www.nimh.nih.gov/anxiety/anxietymenu.cfm
Information on Schizophrenia
www.nimh.nih.gov/publicat/schizoph.cfm

Chapter 17: Drugs and Products That Contribute to Sleep Disorders

Useful Websites
www.nlm.nih.gov/medlineplus/druginformation.html
This is an excellent site that allows you to check on the drugs that you are taking including what they are supposed to be used for and any known side effects.

www.fda.gov/cder/consumerinfo/druginteractions.htm
This site provides information about drug interactions and side effects among drugs you might be using.

www.sleepfoundation.org/caffeine.html
This site reviews caffeine and lets you calculate how much caffeine you are taking in each day.

http://kidshealth.org/teen/food_fitness/nutrition/caffeine.html
This site provides kids with information about caffeine.

www.drugabuse.gov/drugpages/Clubdrugs.html
www.drugabuse.gov/drugpages/mdma/ecstasy.html
www.whitehousedrugpolicy.gov/drugfact/club/index.html
These sites have valuable information on the various types of street drugs that are being used in clubs—important reading for parents.

Index